Practical Symbolic Interactions in the Shrine of the South

Practical Symbolic Interactions in the Shrine of the South

Conversations with a Damn Yankee

John F. Cataldi

LEXINGTON BOOKS
Lanham • Boulder • New York • London

Rowman & Littlefield
Bloomsbury Publishing Inc, 1359 Broadway, New York, NY 10018, USA
Bloomsbury Publishing Plc, 50 Bedford Square, London, WC1B 3DP, UK
Bloomsbury Publishing Ireland, 29 Earlsfort Terrace, Dublin 2, D02 AY28, Ireland
www.bloomsbury.com

Published by Lexington Books
An imprint of The Rowman & Littlefield Publishing Group, Inc.
4501 Forbes Boulevard, Suite 200, Lanham, Maryland 20706
www.rowman.com
86-90 Paul Street, London EC2A 4NE
Copyright © 2023 by The Rowman & Littlefield Publishing Group, Inc.

British Library Cataloguing in Publication Information available

Library of Congress Cataloging-in-Publication Data
ISBN 978-1-66692-369-8 (cloth: alk. paper)
ISBN 978-1-66692-370-4 (electronic)

To T. My best friend. My better half and an outstanding proofreader.

Contents

List of Tables and Figures

Preface

In 2011, the Lexington city council, in Rockbridge County, Virginia, decided to ban public display of the Confederate Battle Flag on their city light poles for the annual Lee-Jackson Day celebrations. Southern symbols such as the Confederate Battle Flag evoke powerful reactions in many communities as well as throughout the nation. One of the contributing factors toward Lexington community tensions surrounding the public display of the Battle Flag is that Lee-Jackson Day is celebrated in the same weekend as Martin Luther King (MLK) Day. This is not by nefarious design. In what could be viewed as a bit of warped cosmic humor, the birthdays of all three men fall within the same week in January (King-15th, Lee-19th, and Jackson-21st). For many not from the South, the display of the Confederate Battle Flag and the celebration of the birthdays of Robert E. Lee and Stonewall Jackson are not only insignificant but are not easily comprehensible as they are relegated to a part of our imperfect American history. However, the significance of these symbols for some Southerners and the social interactions resonating within a community with a deep Confederate history provide an opportunity to observe powerful lessons of tolerance and intolerance that very well may resonate on a larger scale.

After retiring from government and military service, I decided to go back to graduate school and pursue a PhD in Sociology. I hoped to synthesize my practical experiences as a sailor, soldier, and law enforcement officer with an intense study of sociological theory and the research findings of academic experts. Ultimately, I hoped to build a metaphorical bridge between the academic world and the world of practice as I attempted to reconcile disturbing questions that resonated throughout my years of service. Along my journey in graduate education, I was dubbed an *unconventional student*, which I later learned was code for "old, military, and cop." This was a dubious moniker in the academic milieu, but it allowed me to express unique perspectives in seminar discussions which were not always graciously received by peers or professors. Still, the experience was worthy and one that I would characterize along with others that I have had as a *character-building exercise*.

I was intrigued by the Lexington Confederate Battle Flag scenario and decided to conduct a cultural study of symbolic interaction for my dissertation. I passed through Lexington many times throughout my official travels, and I found it to be a lovely town. It is home to the universities of Washington & Lee University (W&L) and Virginia Military Institute (VMI) which are deeply steeped in Confederate history. Although Lexington is located at the approximate intersection of Interstates 81 and 64, it remains stoically nestled in the Blue Ridge Mountains and is still considered by many as the *Shrine of the South* because it is the burial place for both Lee and Jackson. My experiences as an FBI investigator and Special Forces operator naturally led me to utilize a micro-sociological perspective via ethnography. Initially, I sought to examine the roots of Southern cultural significance that I suspected were racially divided and which held a Durkheimian religious appeal and repellency for various community members. I thoroughly embedded with indigenous folks to authentically unravel the mystery of Confederate symbols and their significance to various community members in the Lexington, Virginia, area. I joined the community as a new member and participant observer. I attended social functions and celebrations to include the 2020 MLK Day parade and the Lee-Jackson Day parade that were held on the same weekend. I volunteered at the food pantry at a local Black church and at Habitat for Humanity. I also engaged with community members and neighbors as I assisted them with daily chores and joint activities. I fully disclosed that I was conducting doctoral research with every intent of presenting a book. Most folks were eager to engage. I interviewed, worked with, and spent quality time for over a year with hundreds of community members of various demographics as they shared their intense feelings with me as a fellow community member, but still a *Simmilian stranger* or "Damn Yankee." Throughout my research I encouraged folks to simply express themselves about Southern symbols as I tried to answer the following research questions:

1. Why are some Southern symbols still so significant to some people?
2. In a Southern milieu, how are community members divided concerning sentiments of Southern symbols like the Confederate Battle Flag?
3. How do those with diverse sentiments toward Southern symbols socially interact when engaging with other community members on a daily basis?

As my investigation progressed, I found nuanced, varied voices and sensibilities that do not neatly fit into conventional sociological paradigms. Further analysis of data revealed unique trends, and some of my findings were unanticipated. Nonetheless, they were evidentiary of the attitudes of the cohort interviewed and that sampling is arguably, imperfectly representative, and somewhat randomized of the local population. My study does not make the claim that it is absolute or definitive in its findings as unequivocally representative of the local population. My study only claims that there are many folks in this community, black and white, who do not subscribe to the conventional narrative as represented in the media or by many in the sociological academy. I suggest that their sentiments represent a larger segment of the greater forbearing society than we are given to believe.

Community members can be organized into three clusters regarding their sentiments concerning the Confederate Battle Flag and other prominent symbols of the Confederacy. The first cluster is Reformers, those who find the Flag a repugnant symbol of racism and who deploy mechanisms of *Southern guilt* as a strategic tool to challenge the sanctity of the Confederate symbols and the moral authority of Retentionists. Retentionists, who make up the second cluster, hold Confederate symbols to be something like Durkheimian sacred totems; they weave sentimental threads of *hearth and home* into a *nostalgic fabric* to support their *Cherished Southern identity*. The third cluster are Forbearers (as in those who exhibit forbearance) who find the Confederate Battle Flag neither sacred nor necessarily offensive, but instead ordinary or mundane. They recognize and accept the various symbolic interpretations of the Flag. Reformers and Retentionists are seen by community members as unyielding factions of virtucrats that are directly opposed to each other. Both opposing clusters are in the numerical minority, and their mutual intolerance is based predominantly on assessments by ideological association rather than on personal interaction. Forbearers exhibit greater tolerance toward others and represent the numerical majority of black and white community members in this study. They are relatively ambivalent and prefer to avoid discord in matters concerning contentious Southern symbols. Forbearers may or may not view Confederate symbolism with suspicion, but they are also wary of Reformer ideological rigidity. Forbearers base their assessments of the individual on situational context and personal social interactions during their daily exchanges rather than on association by ideological cluster alone. The data demonstrate that even during pivotal times of change, most respondent community members navigate a social balance between the extremes of conservation and progress as a way to productively coexist and unify as a community rather than maintain an insular posture or cause division based solely on symbolic ideology. This suggests that contention over Southern symbols is intensified by the few who are clustered at the ideological extremes, but the controversy may be overrepresented as being a social problem for the many in the middle. Additionally, in an environment of multiple interpretations of symbols, well-intentioned Reformers may appear as intolerant to many members of the community. This loss of moral high ground can result in a reduction of strategic gains for reform.

This book is important because it productively challenges conventional paradigms and broadens the discussion of what tolerance and situational context mean for a large spectrum of community members who live in the milieu of Confederate symbols every day. This work advances academic knowledge and general knowledge by deeply investigating a Southern microcosm for those who live with the ghosts of the Confederacy. Yet the generalizability of this research is profound as the findings offer significant exceptions to perceived racial rules of alignment concerning such symbols. Tensions surrounding contentious icons like the Confederate Battle Flag are only important to the ideologically polarized, vociferous few, who categorically view it as either a symbol of *heritage* or *hate*. Most community members interviewed, both black and white, were tolerant of the Confederate Battle Flag and Robert E Lee, recognizing their potentials for both heritage and hate, but not categorically. These folks found it unnecessary to ideologically condemn those who publicly display the Flag or revere Lee and sought ways to find common ground through pleasant and productive interaction and communication, as a way to live in communal harmony. They were trying to be and were assessing others simply by the standards of what constitutes "good people" in their actions and interactions, regardless of ideologies.

I am grateful to all the "good people" of the Lexington-Rockbridge community. Thank you for taking the time to interact with this "Damn Yankee." I am indebted to some of the fine professors at Northwestern University and the University of Chicago for guiding this "unconventional student" through the gauntlet of academic wickets. My special thanks to Wendy Griswold, Gary Fine, Laura-Beth Nielsen, David Nirenberg, Dain Borges, Elina I. Hartikainen, and Sharon Hicks-Bartlett for their time and efforts on my behalf. I also extend my gratitude to Courtney Morales, Emma Ebert, and Linda Kessler of Lexington Books and all those folks who were part of the review and publication process.

Most importantly, my deepest love and gratitude to my wife, T, for all her support and encouragement in this project and all the other adventures we have embarked upon together.

During these challenging times, I salute all those folks who actively seek to expand their consciousness through forbearance and unity; *Sine ira et studio.*

Introduction

Prior to this project I held a visceral dislike for the Confederate Battle Flag. I saw it as a strong indicator of racism and sedition. As a young soldier I was stationed at Fort Belvoir-Virginia, Fort Bragg-North Carolina, and Fort Benning-Georgia. I was perturbed that these military installations were named after either Southern plantation owners or Confederate generals. As a leader, I did not tolerate Confederate Battle Flag display in Army quarters. For me, displaying the flag of a defeated army or cause was treasonous. Yet many fine soldiers I served with were from the South and they exhibited no overt signs of racial prejudice or national subversion, but they still adored the Confederate Battle Flag. It was at this point I became intrigued by the significance of the Flag for many Southerners. After retiring from thirty-two years of government service, I decided to go back to graduate school in furtherance of beginning a second career in academia. In order to conduct this research and reach greater objectivity, I emptied my proverbial *cup* of preconceived notions, in the Zen tradition. As a researcher, *stranger*, and a new member of the community, I wanted to represent the multifarious perceptions of the local population while reserving proscriptive rebukes. Through this investigation I have learned that there is a spectrum of interpretations of assorted Southern symbols that local community members hold and that there is not necessarily a racial divide in these interpretations. The Confederate Battle Flag holds no significance for me other than representing a cause that was lost. However, this study is not about my sentiments as a sociologist, soldier, or law enforcement officer; it is about the symbols, sentiments, and interactions of community members of the Lexington-Rockbridge area.

This book is an exploration of the significance of contentious symbols such as the Confederate Battle Flag to various community members, in the Lexington-Rockbridge area, as they frame cultural boundaries and bonds within their social world. Although the topic of race is an underlying part of this study, the reader should be aware that this book is not focused on a normative assessment of whether community members can be categorized in the spectrum of sociological taxonomy of *racist*. Rather, it is a study of how community members view each other and whether they exhibit ideological tolerance or intolerance as a social strategy in their daily interactions based on their various interpretations of cultural objects. American sentiments appear to be sharply divided on the topic of contentious signification, particularly the public display of Southern symbols like the Confederate Battle Flag. By investigating contentious Southern symbols in the city of Lexington and the surrounding area of Rockbridge County, Virginia, I reveal intricate and significant social factors of importance within this community. I have found that there are intense, polarized ideological convictions held by uncompromising clusters which create situational tensions and result in a mutually antagonistic *disunity* within the community. However, there is a larger, more discrete cluster that exhibits forbearance, tact, and a yielding mind as they rely on individual interactions, rather than ideological associations, in their daily social negotiations within the comm-*unity*. The findings of this work provide a venue to understand combative symbols not only at the local level of a small Southern town but suggest the potential to generalize the social significance and relevance of such sentiments in a larger context concerning other contentious topics and corresponding polarized ideologies, such as gun control, abortion, and policing. In contentious times that seem to divide society, this book offers a hopeful prospective of unification that is *practiced* by most forbearing community members in the Lexington-Rockbridge area in their interactive search to bond with "good people."

In 2019 I began this sociological study of Southern symbols in the rural milieu of Rockbridge County, Virginia, where the town[1] of Lexington is the county seat. Lexington is often referred to as the *Shrine of the South* (Mills and Simpson 2003) as it is home to the burial grounds of Confederate Generals Robert E. Lee and Stonewall Jackson. It is also home to the universities of Washington & Lee University (W&L) and Virginia Military Institute (VMI) which have histories imbued in Confederate tradition. This research centers on Southern symbols and their various interpretations by community members in their varied perceptions of their surrounding social world and their reactions to it (Bourdieu 1996). As a mechanism to distinguish various "worlds" or clusters, I use the Confederate Battle Flag as the initial "cultural object" of focus for respondents (Blumer 1969; Griswold 2013). I introduce other symbols such as Southern identity, Confederate monuments, utilization of the Lee name on buildings and institutions, and the song "Dixie" to understand community social tension and tolerance and to illustrate an ever emerging "cultural system" (Geertz 1973). Applying elements of "grounded theory" to provide inductive conclusions (Glaser and Strauss 1967), this research attempts to explore how these relationships affect the larger social context (and vice versa), and how individuals and groups affect changes within the local, regional, and national environment in managing disagreements about contentious symbols.

I started with three primary research questions:

1. Why are some Southern symbols still so significant to some people?
2. In a Southern milieu, how are community members divided concerning sentiments of Southern symbols like the Confederate Battle Flag?
3. How do those with diverse sentiments toward Southern symbols socially interact when engaging with other community members on a daily basis?

I gathered the perspectives of community members concerning Southern symbols using three initial respondent categories for orderly data collection: (1) non-displaying white[2] community members, (2) Black community members,[3] and (3) members of the Sons of Confederate Veterans, United Daughters of the Confederacy, and ardent Confederate Battle Flag supporters. I analyzed the data and identified three main clusters based on "the activities of the collectivity as being formed through a process of designation and interpretation" (Blumer 1969). The Confederate Battle Flag is used as the single defining element in distinguishing clusters. Thus, clusters are operationalized based on their "racist" interpretation toward the display of Confederate Battle Flag; this is similar to *sometimes*, *always*, *never* responses. The first cluster is Reformers. They *always* find Confederate Battle Flag display repugnant and a symbol of racism, hate, and white supremacy. For Reformers there is no credible argument for the public display of the Flag outside of a museum. The second cluster is Retentionists. They hold the display of the Flag and other Confederate symbols as sacred and as part of their *Cherished Southern identity*. They generally belong to the Sons of Confederate Veterans or the Daughters of the Confederacy, but not always. Retentionists emphatically state that for them, their display of the Flag *never* represents hatred or racism. They do not demonstrate or espouse an overt posture of white supremacy. Retentionists recognize the potential of racist signification in the Confederate Battle Flag, but they actively distance themselves from traditional white supremist groups such as the Ku Klux Klan, Nazis, and Aryan Brotherhood. The third cluster is Forbearers. They make up the majority of community members that view the Confederate Battle Flag as having the symbolic potential for both racial hate and Southern heritage. Forbearers may personally support, oppose, or be ambivalent toward the Flag but they believe it only *sometimes* represents racial hate. Having identified the clusters, the concept of *Practical Symbolic Interactionism* is used to frame how community members interpret cultural objects like the Confederate Battle Flag and how they view each other as they apply strategies of tolerance or intolerance in their social interactions.

PRACTICAL SYMBOLIC INTERACTIONISM

The term "symbolic interactionism" is a mouthful, but it can be better understood from some of its constituent elements of *I, others, interactions,* and *symbols*. Cooley regards "I" as the instinctive emotion of "self-feeling" (Cooley 2018, 76). The "I" is oriented in social function and significance through the body when self-comparing to others and also in deeds or inanimate objects that we feel represent us. "In precisely the same way we may call any inanimate object 'I' with which we are identifying our will and purpose. This is notable in games, like golf or croquet, where the ball is the embodiment of the player's fortunes. You will hear the man say, 'I am in the long grass down by the third tee'" (Cooley 1998, 81). Cooley refers to the social self as the "looking-glass self" which is composed of three elements of "imagined" perception: (1) imagined appearance of the "I" to the other person, (2) imagined judgment by the other person of that appearance, and (3) adjusted "self-feeling" such as pride or shame (Cooley 2018, 82). This process illustrates the social nature of the "I" in the interaction with the *other* and the resulting self-reflections as a product from imagined interpretations of the other's sentiments beyond mere lone self-reflection. Cooley refers to *sympathy* as a "requisite to social power" (Cooley 1998, 94–95). In this context sympathy is not the emotion of compassion but rather the ability to "share a mental state" with others using social imagination (Cooley 1998, 96).

In his analysis of human behavior, Mead's objective was to address the "gap between impulse and rationality" in man's social conduct (Mead 1934, xxiv). These impulses seek expression in a social dimension and are not predominantly contemplated or individually calculated. At birth we are physiological organisms that have limited instincts and are conscious of our senses, but we are not *self-conscious*. The self does not exist at birth but "arises in the process of social experience and activity" (Mead 1934, 135). The transformation from biological individual to the self-conscious self is accomplished through the symbolic communication with others and is ultimately culminated in language. The *symbol* is stimulus whose response is given in advance (Mead 1934, 181). For the individual to interact, communication with others begins with response to symbols and accompanying signs through the *conversation of gestures* (Mead 1934, 140). The conversation of gestures is an instinctive posturing and role-playing to determine position within the social interaction. At its most basic form the gesturing can be seen when dogs initially interact and determine threat and positional hierarchy for that situation. "A symbol does tend to call out in the individual a group of reactions such as it calls out in the other, but there is something further that is involved in its being a significant symbol: the response within oneself . . . is one which is a stimulus to the individuals as well as a response" (Mead 1934, 71). Human beings exist in "worlds . . . their groups are composed of objects and these objects are the product of symbolic interaction" (Blumer 1969, 10). As such people may live in the same community and live in different worlds. The worlds are created "only on the objects that given human beings recognize and know . . . their meaning must be seen as social creations . . . being formed . . . out of the process of definition and interpretation" (Blumer 1969, 11). From this vantage point, symbolic interaction views social life as a "process in which objects are being created, affirmed, transformed, and cast aside" (Blumer 1969, 12). Collins provides, in his model of *Interaction Rituals*, a way to "unravel symbols" and offers insight as to why a thorough analysis of everyday symbols is important:

> We operate through an emotional magnetism toward and repulsion from particular thoughts and situations in the flow of everyday life; we are seldom reflective about this and are grossly inaccurate in our assessment when we are reflective. Social action has a very large unconscious component. It is unconscious precisely because by focusing our attention upon a collective object of action, or upon symbols derived from it, our attention is defocused from the social process in which we are entrained while doing so. (Collins 2005, 97)

Cognitive sociology provides a useful multilevel approach to understanding who we are as individuals, humans, and social beings. Zerubavel refers to perception as *social optics* that are not purely sensory but are based on preexistent schematic mental structures of expectations of understanding and courtesy (Zerubavel, 1997). As social creatures we interact with each other in a continuous cautionary mode of discerning and categorizing "friend or foe" (Omi and Winant 2015, 105) or in the military vernacular IFF (Identify: Friend or Foe). For soldiers on patrol or aviators in the air, this is a vital and hasty assessment of an interaction with a party whose intentions are unknown. In the combat theater, this is critical for survival; but for most social interactions, such categorizing is not of the same dire importance. However, IFF assists actors in making sense of interactions and their lives by positioning themselves in existing social hierarchies (Zerubavel, 1997). The Confederate Battle Flag provides a "social optic" to scrutinize boundaries and bonds as each cluster attempts to identify friend, foe, and neutral parties. Through IFF and the "social division of the world," agents classify and organize environment into mental compartments as social beings (Zerubavel 1997, 67). It is through perception and organization that agents understand themselves, others, and the group they wish to be a part of and the *others* they wish to distance themselves from. This is particularly evident under perceived threat conditions of loss.

When illustrating the problems of group membership, Simmel describes the social psychology of the *stranger* and presents the concept of *social distance* (Levine, Carter, and Gorman 1976, 829; Simmel 1971). The stranger "is an element of the group" that exists "both far and near . . . an element whose membership within the group involves both being outside it and confronting it" (Simmel 1971, 144). Simmel provided an abstract framework of social distance that requires "factors of repulsion and distance work to create a form of being together, a form of union based on interaction" (Levine, Carter, and Gorman 1976, 835; Simmel 1971, 144). Building on Simmel's outline, the *Bogardus Social Distance Scale* attempted to operationalize the concept of social distance via the "*sympathetic understanding* which respondents had to members of other groups" (Levine, Carter, and Gorman 1976, 836). The scaling technique measured social distance between "ethnic relations, social classes and social values generally . . . to judge their social standing . . . from exclusion from the country to close kinship by marriage" (Scott and Marshall 2015). The interviewer can use the tool to quantify tendencies of intimacy/indifference or civility/hostility in daily social interactions.

Social distancing and reactions to perceptions of threat through social optics and subsequent social divisions are not only cognitive but multifaceted in nature. The emotional dynamics focus on sentiments of affiliation in alliances. There is a profound importance of "emotional self-interest" as expressed by the cluster (Hochschild, 2016, 228). It is through the perception of the particularized encounter that individuals make reference to the generalized as they seek common outlook of self-interest within the immediate present community and attempt to create or sustain a common emotional energy (Collins 1981). I submit that reactions to threats to Cherished Southern identity and the Confederate Battle Flag for some groups are not only cognitive and emotional in nature but also religious-like in the Durkheimian sense. When beliefs are shared by a definite group who professes them followed by corresponding rites, the cluster is united by their imagery of the sacred world.

When introducing the concept of symbolic interactionism, Blumer provides for three core premises. First, people react toward symbols based on the meanings certain cultural objects hold for them. Second, meanings or interpretations of the symbol are derived from social interactions. Third, these meanings are *handled* and *modified* through an interpretive process of reflective self-interaction to guide continuing interactive conduct in human society (Blumer 1969). In *practice*, conclusions are then drawn based on the handling and modification of symbolic meanings which are interpreted as acceptable, not acceptable, or somewhere in between. For some people at the extremes, these conclusions become reified and dogmatic as they then apply their interpretive meaning of the symbol and categorize *others* who may or may not share their analyses. Practical symbolic interactionism is, thus, the tool used in deciding social interactive conduct, after conclusions are made concerning the symbol, to identify potential friends or foes.

Uniforms and badges and the subsequent social interactions are clear examples of practical symbolic interactionism at several levels within the military. A specific uniform worn in accordance with established protocols indicates to all who wear the uniform an identification of the *generalized friend*. Those who wear the uniform of an opposing force are recognized as the *generalized enemy*. Specific badges, hats, unit designator, and accoutrements, such as service ribbons, medals, and specialized accomplishments, provide practical symbolic recognition of *specialized friend* based not only on the generalized uniform but also on shared specialized experience. For those in uniform, individuals who are not in uniform, that provide no practical symbolic indicators, are neither friend nor foe until additional intelligence is gathered. Interestingly, hybrid forms of specialized friend or intense *specialized foe* designation can also be determined by practical symbolic interaction. Aviators from opposing forces often identify as specialized friend and view each other with a mutual respect even though their uniforms indicate generalized foe. Conversely, paratroopers often mock non-Airborne soldiers in their unit as "legs" in a form of derision for their lack of specialization. Lastly, a submariner or a bomber pilot that is captured by an opposing force, is often practically identified as a specialized foe regardless of their involvement in any direct action such as the recent sinking of navy surface ships or strategic carpet bombing. Their combat specialty can earn them especially brutal treatment in captivity.

Lexington and the surrounding county of Rockbridge are set in the Blue Ridge Mountains and Shenandoah Valley of Virginia. Southern symbols are unavoidable here because of the area's substantial Confederate history and institutional legacies. I search for the various meanings that cultural objects have and the interpretive process used by community members that arise out of their everyday social interactions (Blumer 1969). In this study, I gather perceptions and insights of various community members concerning controversial Southern symbols such as the Confederate Battle Flag, monuments, and military personalities who are enshrined here. Using the Confederate Battle Flag as a *collective object of action*, I explore the social process for the cluster and the individual as producers and receivers of social meaning within their social world. Goffman illustrates that the social individual engages in "performances" and that the performer "can be fully taken in by his own act; he can be sincerely convinced that the impression of reality which he stages is the real reality" (Goffman 1959, 17). I investigate collective *reality* through "unity and discord" for various members in various clusters in an effort to illustrate "the ultimate wholeness of that group" (Simmel 1971, 73). In doing so I probe the individual "self" as it is "organized about the social individual" (Mead 1934, 171). Some folks are resolute in their practical application of the symbol toward others, while other folks are less staunch. Practical symbolic interactionism is utilized in this study as a perspective and a method to view and assess community conduct based on their interpretations of significant cultural objects and their practical application of these interpretations in categorizing others. I use contentious southern symbols like the Confederate Battle Flag, the name Robert E. Lee, Southern monuments, and the song "Dixie" as the local cultural objects that define local social interactions. These symbols hold some positive, negative, or neutral value to folks in the Lexington, Virginia, area. This is a story that presents the perspectives not only of the vociferous few but also the views of those many community members who are much more reticent, but when specifically asked, they too wish to be heard.

This is a cultural study of community interactions where contentious symbols still resonate. Along with *culture*, *race* plays a part in the story, as well as *collective identity* and *class*. To present the clearest picture from the "stranger's" perspective, I analyze group boundaries and bonds that create social divisions while looking for recurring themes and organize them into clusters of like-mindedness. I scrutinize the constituent elements of these clusters and how they interact with each other ideologically and socially during times of contentious zenith as well as during their everyday interactions. In doing so, I ultimately illustrate how the various clusters in this community manage significant disagreement concerning highly provocative symbols. In Lexington, aka the Shrine of the South, daily interactions are conducted among various community members based on adopted divergent social protocols that for polarized groups, focus on either actions (*acta*) or ideology (*verba*).

SYMBOLIC INTERPRETATIONS AND OUR CONCLUSIONS: OUR MULLIGAN STEW

Practical symbolic interactionism is a paradigm to view the panoply of perspectives that various community members have toward contentious Southern symbols. Conclusions are drawn about significant symbols on an individual basis as they are interpreted as being acceptable, not acceptable, or somewhere in between. The interpretations become *practical* when they are implemented to define interactions (or the lack of) with others. Interpretations are individually formed based on various influences over the course of the agent's lifespan. These influences, both those intentionally sought and those inadvertently acquired, can be thought of as ingredients in a recipe that create our *Mulligan Stew*. The Mulligan Stew that is concocted suits the agent's specific social and psychological taste based on available ingredients. That is, it provides a reasoning, an understanding, and a comfortable position for the individual to launch social interactions or exclude others. Sociological topics such as age, gender, and health are examples of ingredients for individually devised Mulligan Stews depending on the symbol of interpretation. For this study, the common key ingredients that I present in the Mulligan Stew for the Lexington-Rockbridge community are culture, race, collective identity, and class. It is imperative to discuss the piquant and pervasive ingredients of the Mulligan Stew as they offer insights to the voices in the community of study that follow in later chapters. I present these ingredients from a variety of perspectives so that the reader can blend and modify their own Mulligan Stew.

Culture

Culture is a set of shared repertoires "that structure people's ability to think and share ideas" (Eliasoph and Lichterman 2003, 735). Culture can also be described as the result of two related processes: (1) a stable, predictable component of collectively constructed knowledge and (2) pragmatic usage through ongoing individual and interpersonal actions (Patterson 2015, 26). The concept of culture is essentially a semiotic one "that man is an animal suspended in webs of significance that he himself has spun" (Geertz 1973, 5). As a symbol, the Confederate Battle Flag is a polysemous "collective representation" that can "take on different meanings in different contexts" as it exerts powerful social forces in a community (Alexander 2004; Eliasoph and Lichterman 2003; Swidler 1986; Vaisey 2009). The Confederate Battle Flag was originally the battle standard for Robert E. Lee's Northern Army of Virginia and is commonly and incorrectly labeled the "Confederate flag" (Wright and Esses 2017). For my analysis, the original producing agent of the Confederate Battle Flag was Lee, the commander of the Northern Virginia Army. His "probable intentionality" was based on the character of the producing agent as a warrior leader and the dire circumstance surrounding the Civil War (Griswold 1987). Lee's "charge,"[4] or situational prompt for action, was to be victorious in battle and to defend his native state of Virginia from Federal oppression based on the *states' rights* argument (Coski 2005; Nesbett and Cohen 1996; Poole 2004). However, after the Civil War, "Lee distanced himself from divisive symbols" and per his request no flags, Federal or Confederate Battle Flag, were flown at his funeral (Brumfield 2015). The original producing agent's intention should not be "confused with consequences" (Griswold 2013). Other re-producing clusters and agents, both currently and throughout the history of the South, must be considered when accurately analyzing Southern symbols and the Confederate Battle Flag. Today, sentiments concerning the Flag are distilled down to those of *hate* and *heritage*. The message of hate is easily discerned when the Confederate Battle Flag is used by traditional white supremacist groups like the Ku Klux Klan. However, Retentionists vocally distance themselves from these groups and I suggest that they hold the Flag as a sacred totem of their civil religion of Cherished Southern identity.

In sociology, religion is composed of *beliefs* that are operationalized by *rites* that are individually accepted by members of the group and unify the cluster through the mechanism of a common *faith* (Durkheim 1912, 34, 41). Beliefs and rites confront and mutually confirm each other by making the collective "ethos" intellectually reasonable and their "worldview" emotionally reasonable (Geertz 1957, 623). Religious beliefs classify what is real or ideal into two opposing genera, the *sacred* and the *profane* (Durkheim 1912, 34). Durkheim focused on the "absolute . . . profoundly differentiated . . . two worlds with nothing in common . . . not only separate but also as hostile and jealous rivals" (Durkheim 1912, 36–37). The sacred and profane are juxtaposed in reference to the totem as a *collective representation*, a symbol, emblem, or *flag* which is "the archetype of sacred things" (Durkheim 1912, 118, 228). Southern symbols, like the Confederate Battle Flag, are cultural objects and sacred for Retentionists as part of their cultural identity (Durkheim 1912; Griswold 2013). Retentionists embrace, with a *religious* fervor, the totem of the Flag to unify and excite. As a symbol, totems can be multivocal in that they can express many themes simultaneously depending on receiving actors (Swidler 1986; Turner 1973). As cultural objects, symbols can be considered implements that are conveniently drawn from "tool kits" by cluster members (Swidler 1986). Cluster members learn how to use these tools based on their collective past and how to best utilize them for their prospective future (Fine 2021).

The Confederate Battle Flag is certainly polysemous both locally and nationally. For Retentionists, the totem stands foremost in the ranks of sacred things as it "constitutes an organizational center which gravitates a set of beliefs and rites, a cult of its own" (Durkheim 1912, 8). The totem is the sacred symbol that provides a receptacle for meanings to be stored (Geertz 1957). It is the "store of information, both for actors and investigators" (Turner 1973, 1103). The sacredness of the totem is based on "the material representation of the clan" of Retentionists and that it stirs religious feelings (Durkheim 1912, 124, 127). Symbols, representing a national sentiment, such as the Confederacy, provide arguably the strongest, clearest statement of identity (Cerulo 1993, 244; Nesbett and Cohen 1996, 38). Beyond the collective aspect of the sacredness of the totem is the very personal sacredness of experiencing unification of the individual and the totem of the clan in a sense of oneness, that he is participating in something extraordinary, something transcendental (Durkheim 1912, 133, 222). The totem is emblematic as it arouses feelings based on the complexity of what is sacred, and these emotions are transferred to the "symbol that is loved, feared and respected" and what is processed and simplified into impressions (Durkheim 1912, 220). The "peculiar power" of sacred symbols is based on their "presumed ability to identify fact with value at the most fundamental level" (Geertz 1957, 623). Durkheim directly correlates totems and flags in a way that serves my research well:

> The totem is the flag of the clan. . . . It is the symbol that one sacrifices oneself. The soldier who dies for his flag dies for his country, but the idea of the flag is actually in the foreground of his consciousness . . . the flag is only a symbol that has no value in itself but only brings to mind the reality it represents. The flag itself is treated as if it was that reality . . . the totemic emblem is . . . the visible body of the god. (Durkheim 1912, 222)

Bellah provides that *civil religion* is the religious dimension of a people "through which it interprets its historical experience in the light of transcendent reality" (Bellah and Tipton 2006). For this study I use Herberg's definition of civil religion as simply a "common religion emerging out of the life of folk" which centers on identity as a cultural question (Wilson 1980). It is this identity, and the attachment to the sacred through *hearth and home*, that Retentionists and many others feel is under attack and results in a pending sense of doom and loss. One of the purposes of this book is to describe the cultural significance of the Confederate Battle Flag at a micro-sociological level "aimed at revealing the significance of events by relating them to a larger cultural pattern" (Wuthnow 1987, 349). As a collective representation the Flag provides meaning in everyday life and how people perceive each other. Through culture in interaction, groups "make these meanings in relation to each other as they perceive each other" through "shared ground for interaction" or "group style" (Eliasoph and Lichterman 2003, 736). Group style can be studied via three dimensions: (1) group boundaries, (2) group bonds, and (3) speech norms (Eliasoph and Lichterman 2003, 739). Boundaries establish who is in and who is out in an effort to define the group relationship in greater society. Bonds define commonalities, like-mindedness, and rules of membership within the group. Speech norms illustrate acceptable rhetoric and the rationalization for the specific group. Understanding group style and the various dimensions provides a mechanism to operationalize clusters.

In this community, contentious Southern symbols and totems such as the Confederate Battle Flag invoke pride for Retentionists and invoke humiliation and anger for Reformers (Brewer 1993). Forbearers hold no firm or fixed ideological stance concerning the Flag. They may be for, against, or ambivalent toward the polysemous symbol but they are not zealously invested in it as a defining mechanism for social interaction. Reformers and Retentionists do not "accept the validity of one another's intention" (Alexander 2004, 528). Reformers do not see the Flag as sacred or even profane. Their sentiments transcend mere ambivalence toward this sacred object for Retentionists. They signify it as an *anti-totem, anti-sacred,* and *offensive.* They use it as a symbolic means of identifying and othering Retentionists as anti-reformist and racist. Retentionists view Reformers as the aggressors who are illiberal, when it comes to viewpoints other than their own, and hypocritical in that they do not represent the views of the majority, black or white, in the community. Reformers and Retentionists are polarized ideological clusters that maintain firm virtucratic stances. They hold religious-like commitments to their ideas and engage in a strategy of *othering* opposing opinions. They engage in mutual antagonisms and condemnations based on "open-ended conflict" and "intractable" differences. Conversely, Forbearers use tolerance, tact, and negotiation as tools and a method for "building flexible but durable relations" based on community and unity (Fine 2021). They embrace an "us" strategy of coexistence without condemnation.

Race

This book focuses on symbols as cultural objects and how various community members perceive them. However, *race* is an important aspect of this study concerning symbolic interpretation and the practical application of these interpretations toward others. Southern symbols and the public display of the Confederate Battle Flag can evoke racially perceived divergent reactions. Retentionist factions see these symbols as history and tradition as well as expressions of freedom. Reformer elements see the dire need to banish these symbols of hate, racism, and white supremacy. For many sociologists, race, ethnicity, and whiteness are ways of perceiving the social world (Brubaker 2006, 17). Race can be normatively conceived as a term of "social geography," a way to identify people geo-morphically by phenotypes, implied geographic origin, and cultural characteristics (Goldberg 2009, 7). It is considered a historically contingent social system that attaches meanings to morphology and ancestry (Haney Lopez 2006). Race is theorized to be a social construct along with class that results in a social reality that produces "real effects" on actors (Bonilla-Silva 2018). Furthermore, race "signifies and symbolizes social conflicts and interests" relative to perceptions of difference in human bodies (Omi and Winant 2015, 110). However, the concept of race is very complex and thoroughly peppered with inconsistencies. "While race is a dynamic phenomenon rooted in political struggle, it is commonly observed as a fixed characteristic of human populations; while it does not exist in terms of human biology, people routinely look to the human body for evidence about racial identity; while it is a biological fiction, it is nonetheless a social fact" (James 2008, 32).

What is the difference between race prejudice, discrimination, bias, and racism? *Race prejudice* is relative to "group position" and the constituent "feelings which members of one racial group have toward members of another racial group" (Blumer 1958, 3). Consequently, "race prejudice is pre-judgement about others based on racial constructs. . . . *Discrimination* is action taken based on such prejudice" (Diangelo 2018, 18–19). Race prejudice can be understood through the process by which groups identify themselves and others as a "basic human disposition to form group-based social hierarchies" (Sidanius and Pratto 1999, 38). There are four basic types of feeling that are always displayed by the dominant group in race prejudice: (1) superiority, (2) difference, (3) entitlement, and (4) fear of loss (Bashi-Treitler 2013, 63; Blumer 1958, 4). The classification and defining of people are not restricted to distinctions based on race alone (Blau and Duncan 2014, 506). Gender, class, sexuality, race, age, religion, and many other categories of distinction "are frequently evoked to justify structures of inequality, differential treatment, and subordinate status" (Grusky 2014, 8; Omi and Winant 2015, 215). *Bias* is a form of prejudice that can be expressed individually and structurally. For psychologists, *cognitive bias* is recognized as an individualized thought process based on a "predictable pattern of mental errors that result in us misperceiving reality" (Tsipursky 2020). *Unconscious* or *implicit bias* is a specific structural perception between different groups for the society and the group we are a part of (Tsipursky 2020). Implicit bias is internalized as part of group culture and not necessarily a flaw of the individual who might not consciously endorse the bias to distinguish others.

Racism is the belief in a social hierarchy that places people of color at the bottom and "the tendency of whites to judge their own worth by distance from that bottom" (Hochschild 2016, 147). In this social hierarchy, "the purpose of race is to assign differential value to human lives" (Bashi-Treitler 2013, 11). Racism also creates or reinforces dominating structures based on "racial significations and identities" (Omi and Winant 2015, 128). Racism occurs organizationally when race prejudices and biases lead to systemic discrimination and a structuralized imbalance of power. It is "a network of social relations at social, political, economic, and ideological levels that shapes the life chances of the various races" (Bonilla-Silva 2018, 8, 18, 78).

Various forms of racism can be distinguished from prejudice and discrimination as being structural and systemic. When a "collective prejudice" produces discrimination and is reinforced by legal and institutional structural authority, it becomes racism (Diangelo 2018, 19–21). *Racial hierarchy* became economically entrenched in American society during European settler colonization. It can be described as an economic tool to rationalize the acquisition of land via conquest and the tending of these lands through chattel slavery (McGhee 2021). As such the American economy "depended on systems of exploitation" that robbed "racialized others" of their land and freedom as it created a "zero-sum competition" model (McGhee 2021, 7). That is, in order to profit, wealthy white colonizers robbed the assets of others, leaving no room for any rewards for those racially oppressed. The rationale for this model resonates today as many people today feel that the inverse is true, "progress for people of color means a loss for white people" (McGhee 2021, 255). Accordingly, white Americans engage in a "possessive investment in whiteness" as it provides for monetary compensation through advantages and profits made through discriminatory markets, unequal educational opportunities, and especially "intergenerational transfers of inherited wealth that pass on the spoils of discrimination to succeeding generations" (Lipsitz 2018, v).

Racism is commonly associated with a "good/bad binary" where racists are categorized as "bad, ignorant, bigoted, prejudiced, mean spirited, old and Southern" as typically associated with traditional racists (Diangelo 2018, 72). However, this binary "obscures the structural nature of racism." "The focus on the individual incidences masks the personal, interpersonal, cultural, historical, and structural analysis that is necessary to challenge this larger system" (Diangelo 2018, 73). More subtle forms of racism, such as *colorblind racism*, have been identified by race scholars. Colorblindness has "dominated national thinking and discussion about race" and as a broad ideology it states emphatically that "problems of racism and segregation . . . have been solved" (Burke 2012, 58). From this vantage point, colorblind racism is a method used to maintain or justify white privilege.

When discussing the topic of race, it is important to analyze the terms anti-racism and anti-racialism. *Anti-racism* is a firm and explicit stance of agency where one refuses to be subjugated or one refuses to dominate based on racial differentiation (Goldberg 2009, 10). *Anti-racialism* implies a weak stance against racism that requires no action (Goldberg 2009, 10). Anti-racism requires a commitment to remembering and accounting for historical conditions of racial degradation whereas anti-racialism suggests "forgetting, getting over, and moving on" (Goldberg 2009, 21). Anti-racialism is closely associated with colorblind racism and laissez-faire racism that maintains the racial status quo of white dominance under the veil of equality for all (Bonilla-Silva 2018, 17; Haney Lopez 2006, 162; Lavelle 2015, 7). Anti-racialism handily utilizes a collective memory that is selective in interpreting the past as a mechanism for white identity maintenance (Lavelle 2015, 181).

Whiteness is part of the racial hierarchy and is a form of elevated social status distinction that differentiates whites from non-white others via a benefit or "wage" for being white (Du Bois 1975; Lipsitz 2018; Metzl 2020). Whiteness coexists with other social identities such as culture, gender, class, religion, and ethnicity (Haney Lopez 2006). This *compensation* serves a dual structural purpose of maintaining the status quo by placating working-class whites with elevated social status and by discouraging them from "forming a common cause" with working-class blacks (Metzl 2020, 17). Whiteness is subject to continuous social modification and is viewed as a "complexly constructed product of local, regional, national and global relations, past and present" (Frankenberg 1993, 236). Race scholars characterize a prime condition of whiteness as a type of obliviousness or *white invisibility* to being white. As such, whites experience a "lower degree of self-awareness about race and their own racial identity than do members of other racial groups (Hughey 2012, 6; Frankenberg 1993). This white invisibility is a regularizing state of racial thoughtlessness within the social order where racial difference is identified from a white reference point:

> The invisibility of whiteness in white (which is to say dominant) discourse is of a piece of its ubiquity. . . . Whites are everywhere in representation. Yet precisely because of this and their placing as a norm they seem not to be represented to themselves as whites but as people who are variously gendered, classed, sexualized, and abled. At the level of racial representation, in other words, whites are not of a certain race, they are just the human race. (Dyer 2017, 3)

Closely associated with white invisibility is the concept of *white fragility*. White fragility illuminates the range of defensive responses that some white people have when reacting to the stress of being informed of their white privilege. Though white fragility is triggered by discomfort and anxiety, it is born of superiority and entitlement. "White fragility is no weakness per se. In fact, it is a powerful means of white racial control and the protection of white advantage" (Diangelo 2018, 2). Scholars further argue that whites do not exist as a natural group but only as a legal creation that enjoys white privilege and structural white supremacy. *White privilege* is described as an "invisible weightless knapsack of special provisions, maps, passports, codebooks, visas, clothes, tools and blank checks" that provide for "unearned assets" which can be "counted on (for) cashing in each day" of which the beneficiary is meant to remain oblivious to his privilege (McIntosh 1989, 10). Privilege in this sense relates to the advantage in structural position rather than economic status:

It is important to note that whites are privileged relatively to non-whites not merely through the direct benefits of whiteness, but also through its functions as a category of structural power and control. Regardless of the personal difficulties that an individual white person might experience, he or she is, ultimately, the beneficiary of his or her group's dominant status. Access to resources and opportunities is substantially greater for members of the dominant group even if specific individuals are unable to take advantage of it. (McDermott 2020, 5)

Structural white supremacy can be defined as a "sociopolitical economic system of domination" based on race that "privileges, centralizes and elevates white people as a group" (Diangelo 2018, 30). As such, the "law constructs" race and citizenship, and white identity is the remainder set of two binary sets after identifying and categorizing "others" as non-white (Guglielmo 2003; Haney Lopez 2006, 14). White supremacy is an institutionalized system of material benefit for people socially defined as white through the use of racial domination of non-whites (C. W. Mills 1999). Whiteness may be more accurately conceived as an experience with "highly variegated nuances across the range of social axes and individual lives" (Haney Lopez 2006, xxi). As such, ethnicity, race, and whiteness are ways of perceiving the social world (Brubaker 2006, 17). According to race scholars, although whiteness is a created identity, "it has real consequences for the distribution of wealth, prestige, and opportunity" (Molina 2014, 47). These scholars clearly illustrate whiteness as related to dominance with expectations of entitlements and privilege.

Several scholars have investigated race and whiteness from distinctive perspectives. Hughey conducted a comparative analysis of two antithetical white organizations, a white nationalist group and a white antiracist group. He discovered that although these organizations are ideologically opposed, they may share practical platforms for their messages and that they both assert racial distinctions via *hegemonic whiteness* as an ideal white self. "Through practices of inter- and intra-racial 'othering' to define and pursue different situational dimensions of an ideal white self, these actors well demonstrate how white nationalism and white antiracism may be insidiously related, knotted, and crocheted" (Hughey 2012, 185,187). Metzl conducted a longitudinal study on political policies in Missouri, Tennessee, and Kansas and the mortal health risk factors for their citizens. He found that ideological policies that failed to support generalized social safety to include health care and economic safety net programs but were permissive of gun proliferation led to "illness and death patterns" that mirrored other "man-made pathogens, such as water pollution, secondhand smoke or not wearing seat belts in cars" (Metzl 2020, 16). Finally, Zuberi and Bonilla-Silva demonstrate that the physical and social sciences, to include sociology, are not immune to scrutiny concerning structural racism and whiteness in their collection of works by various scholars, *White Logic, White Methods*. White logic refers to the supremacy and domination of elite white scholars in defining "techniques and processes of reasoning about social facts" (Zuberi and Bonilla-Silva 2008, 17). "White methods are the practical tools" to gather and analyze evidence "to support the racial stratification in society" (Zuberi and Bonilla-Silva 2008, 18).

As a counterpoint to some of the points previously provided on the topic of race, some conservative scholars feel that in their efforts to study and elucidate racism many liberal race scholars lean on a black narrative based on victimization. "The conflict of this story is first slavery, then segregation and legal disenfranchisement. The meaning of the story is group victimization, and every black person is the story's protagonist" (Johnson 2008, 34). The "centuries of indisputable injustice" (Steele 2006, 24) of racism that black Americans have suffered is not denied or diminished. However, there is a group of black scholars that does not accept the "blanket application of the term *racism* as a causal explanation—as distinguished from simply an epithet" (Sowell 2005, 61). These authors find that cultural differences provide for major economic and social impact and that black Americans today are "complex and multifaceted people who defy easy categorization" (Johnson 2008, 37; Sowell 2005). These scholars see "that heterogeneity of class and culture are as much as a feature of black America as they are of the rest of America" (Robinson 2010, 24). The concept of a singular authentic as black narrative became an "identity fetish" which has been "perpetuated by white and black intellectuals" in their efforts to generalize racial conflict (Sowell 2005, 58–59). "The ghetto black was the authentic black" and "more successful blacks were increasingly depicted as either irrelevant non-members of the black community or even as traitors to it" (Sowell 2005, 59). For Sowell the concept of a singular, authentic black American narrative represents a form of "post-1960s black identity intolerance" that creates an "intellectual blockade against ideas differing from those prevailing" (Sowell 2005, 59). Steele, another conservative black scholar provides insights on *white guilt*. For Steele, white guilt has two pillars: (1) "the vacuum of moral authority that comes from knowing that one's race is associated with racism," and 2) "white guilt is quite literally the same as black power" (Steele 2006, 24). White guilt provided a platform of political and cultural liberalism of *dissociation* from America's racist past in an attempt to garner moral authority (Steele 2006, 150). Those that fail to actively disassociate are entitled to no "moral authority" and are vulnerable to ad hominem attacks and stigmatized as racists (Steele 2006, 144, 151). When considering the categories of whiteness, McDermott's group of *transcendent* is closely associated with white guilt. "Socially progressive whites can feel regret at being a part of a group that has continuously oppressed people of color for centuries while at the same time gaining privileges from this oppression. Such an attitude is sometimes referred to as 'white guilt.' As a result of it, some of these whites seek actively to distance themselves from a polluted white identity" (McDermott 2020, 75).

McWhorter identifies many current forms of liberal antiracism agendas as intolerant and frames the zealous movement as the "Third Wave Antiracism" religion. "Third Wave Antiracism exploits modern American's fear of being thought a racist to promulgate not just antiracism, but an obsessive, self-involved, totalitarian, and utterly unnecessary cultural reprograming" (McWhorter 2021, 14, 23, 47). Congregants of the religion could be labeled as "Inquisitors . . . social justice warriors . . . or woke mob" but McWhorter most prefers the term *"the Elect."* "They do think of themselves as bearers of wisdom . . . while implying a certain smugness" (McWhorter 2021, 18–19). This religion is evangelical and one replete with clergy, "Catechism of Contradictions," "committees of anti-heresy," apocalyptic prognostications, and "original sin" of "white privilege" (McWhorter 2021, 8, 28–47). To be appropriately converted, whites must engage in a cleansing of "self-mortification" and "embrace a self-flagellational guilt for things you did not do" (McWhorter 2021, 20, 33, 68). Those that are "insufficiently aware of this sense of *existing while white*" are damned to "eternal culpability" and "require bitter condemnation and ostracization" (McWhorter 2021, 5). "In 1500 it was about not being Christian. In 2020 it's about not being sufficiently antiracist, with adherents supposing that this is a more intellectually and morally advanced cause than antipathy to someone for being Catholic, Jewish, or Muslim. They do not see that they, too, are persecuting people for not adhering to their religion" (McWhorter 2021, 20).

Collective Identity

Collective identity, memory, and commemoration are closely related and intertwined with each other. *Collective identity* is "an individual's cognitive, moral and emotional connection with a broader community" which embraces a "perception of shared status or relation" (Polletta and Jasper 2001, 285). Collective identity can be distinguished from personal, social, and ideological identities. Personal identities are "self-designations and self-attributions regarded as distinctive" (Snow and Corrigall-Brown 2015, 174). Social identities or role identities are attributions "grounded in established social roles, such as 'teacher' and 'mother'" (Snow and Corrigall-Brown 2015, 174). Collective identity provides for a sense of *we* through positive sentiments of those like *us* while differentiating from others which distinguishes it from ideological identity that does not require positive feelings for members of the group (Polletta and Jasper 2001; Snow and Corrigall-Brown 2015). In the construction of shared status through the recognition of "bonds, interests and boundaries," individuals collectively segment their social world as a way to make sense of it (Snow and Corrigall-Brown 2015, 285, 298). In her study of rural Wisconsin, Cramer found that "rural consciousness" was a powerful sense of identity for rural folk and that it "structures the way people understand politics" and that the "core of that identity is rooted in place and class" (Cramer 2016, 12, 89). Cramer found three facets of perception to rural consciousness that centered on distributive injustice and formed their "politics of resentment": (1) distinct culture and lifestyle from urban and suburban folk and that their way of life is not respected, (2) rural areas are not well represented in the decision-making process, and thus (3) rural areas do not receive a fair share of public resources (Cramer 2016, 23). These findings directly relate to those similar sentiments found in the Lexington-Rockbridge area where there was significant divide in the identity of those who hailed from Rockbridge County and those from the town of Lexington.

Collective identity is a particular form of culture and is expressed in cultural objects such as the Confederate Battle Flag (Polletta and Jasper 2001, 285). Thus, collective identity is not static in its construction. It can be multidimensional and multilayered in cognitive, emotional, and moral constitution (Snow and Corrigall-Brown 2015, 179). Through this multiplicity members who share a larger collective identity may utilize features to react differently to perceived threats to unpopular aspects of that identity. Organizational identity scholars present three identity concepts: (1) identity threats, (2) split identification, and (3) identity recalibration. *Identity threats* are "experiences appraised as indicating potential harm to the value, meanings, or enactment of an identity" (Petriglieri 2011, 644). Such identity threats are perceived by groups like Reformers and Retentionists. Under perceived threat conditions some members of the community utilize *split identification* which "allows members to retain their identification with normative aspects" of a group, while disassociating with other unacceptable aspects (Gutierrez, Howard-Grenville, and Scully 2010, 674). This is experienced by Reformers who still identify as Southerners but actively distance themselves from symbols like the Confederate Battle Flag in an effort to retain some acceptable aspects of their Cherished Southern identity. *Identity recalibration* or "identity refocusing" is an adaptive mechanism, used by Forbearers, to dismantle and recalibrate boundaries for productive purposes rather than protecting and reifying such boundaries (Lifshitz-Assaf 2017, 26). It is the individual cognitive, moral, and emotional interactions while recalibrating or reifying within a broader community that provide a bridge to the perspective of practical symbolic interactionism.

Collective memory is recollection of a shared past that are retained by members of a group (Schuman and Scott 1989, 361–62). It is the building block for collective identity which in turn fosters in-group loyalty, sometimes to the detriment of the out-group (Brubaker 2006; Whitlinger 2020). Collective memory is group-based, socially constructed, and historically rooted but subject to adjustment based on perspective and cultural needs. "Collective memory specifies the temporal parameters of past and future, where we came from and where we are going, and also why we are here" (Eyerman 2001, 6, 10). Halbwachs provides that collective memory is a type of "illusion" that requires effort by a group to "immobilize time" and "keep the memory alive" and is fundamental in forming a collective identity:

> Every group . . . immobilizes time in its own way and imposes on its members the illusion that, in a given duration of a constantly changing world certain zones have acquired a relative stability and balance in which nothing essential is altered. . . . It is current of continuous thought whose continuity is not at all artificial, for it retains from the past only what still lives or is capable of living in the consciousness of the groups keeping the memory alive. (Halbwachs 2011, 143, 149)

Accordingly, there can be multiple collective memories, some opposing each other, concerning the same time period (Halbwachs 2011, 143). This is clearly demonstrated with divergent perspectives on the Civil War. Lost Cause sentimentality that is embraced by some white Southerners is in direct conflict with the collective memory or "cultural trauma" associated with slavery that affects black Americans:

> Cultural trauma refers to a dramatic loss of identity and meaning, a tear in the social fabric affecting a group of people that has achieved some degree of cohesion. In this sense, the trauma need not necessarily be felt by everyone in a community or experienced directly by any or all. . . . The notion of cultural trauma implies that direct experience of an event is not a necessary condition for its inclusion in the trauma process. It is through time-delayed and negotiated recollection that cultural trauma is experienced, a process which places representation in a key role. (Eyerman 2001, 2, 12)

In this study, Retentionist collective memory of *good ole days* of valor and glory is juxtaposed with the Reformer collective memory of Confederate strategies to maintain chattel slavery. Thus, collective memory is a perspective based on "historical and unhistorical," that is selective in remembering and selective in forgetting (Nietzsche 2011, 75). Both are *true* and *real* based on selected perspective of each group. In a community of competing collective memories, "control of history" and contentious symbols are disputed and "reputational politics is an arena in which forces compete to control memory" (Fine 1996, 1159, 1161). Here institutionally well-placed "reputational entrepreneurs" utilize group ideology and politics to advance agendas and strategies to further personal and group interests based on the perceived plausibility and credibility of their perspective (Fine 1996, 1186). They are found in the vocal leadership elements of both Reformer and Retentionist clusters.

The Civil War is a traumatic event in the history of the United States, and a particularly sensitive one for white Southerners and black Americans. The memory of slavery denotes differences in social and historical understanding. "While some whites might have condemned slavery as an evil institution and bemoaned its effects on the body politic of American society, blacks viewed slavery as a social condition, a lived experience, producing a distinctive way of life, a culture, a community, and thus an identity, which affected not only the past and the present, but also future possibilities" (Eyerman 2001, 17). Most commemorations to the Civil War, for the North and the South, are in the form of monuments to soldiers and battlefields. Issues of slavery and oppression were not the primary concern but rather Christian bravery and deeds of heroism. As such, an unusual form of "commemoration and reconciliation" occurred for newly re-united white Americans but only at the cost of neglecting the newly liberated black population. "This was also the context in which 'whiteness' and 'blackness' were constructed as overarching categories, transcending regional differences. With slavery out of the picture, there could be reconciliation between opposing sides, each being allowed to mark their own heroes, thus sweeping aside one of the main contentions of the war" (Eyerman 2001, 18). Commemorations, such as memorials, flags, and events, are the reflections of collective memories. Recent and continuing conflicts concerning Confederate iconography demonstrate that commemorations stemming from various and divergent collective identities and memories can have multiple meanings, promoting positive values for Retentionists and negative values for Reformers (Whitlinger 2020, 5). Commemorations, like a parade on Lee-Jackson Day or a parade on Martin Luther King Day, are the demonstration of something deemed worthy of remembrance based on the collective identity of the initiating group. "In this way, commemoration is a product of social construction: families, neighborhoods, organizations, nations and other collectivities identify the people and events deserving of distinct recognition, a process that can become self-reinforcing once commemorative activities are institutionalized" (Whitlinger 2020, 4). This ritualized remembrance reinforces group membership and collective belonging (Durkheim 1912; Halbwachs 2011). *Memory movements* are "sustained efforts to change or preserve particular representations of the past," and their objectives can be cultural and political as *memory activists* draw upon historic symbols to "negotiate meanings about the past in the context of present institutional constraints and often in competition with other agents of memory" (Whitlinger 2020, 7–8). Interestingly, some commemorations may attempt to represent virtue, justice, recognition, or harmony but conflicting interpretations may also "intensify group-based division, foster conflict, and inhibit peace" by creating *memory battles* when interpreting the meaning of "difficult pasts." "Those who construct official public memory advance their agendas by flooding public space with their version of the past, often at the expense of countermemories—a phenomenon well documented by historians of the American South who have demonstrated . . . the resilience of the 'Lost Cause' narrative to the detriment of other explanations for the American Civil War" (Whitlinger 2020, 6, 38–39, 174). As such, memory "movements produce commemorations and commemorations produce movements" (Whitlinger 2020, 175). Commemorations can foster inclusivity, exclusivity, or a combination of both depending on perspectives and temporal passions.

Collective identity, collective memory, and commemoration can be closely associated with race. When discussing racial temporality in France, Fleming describes a tendency in racist agendas for "collective forgetting, denial, or marginalizing of the racial past and its connections to the present" (Fleming 2017, 16). This collective overlooking is a strategy of convenience and/or ignorance often deployed in constructs of collective memory to rationalize stratified cluster position in furtherance of a palatable "historical imagination" for the in-group (Fleming 2017, 217). Interpretive and biased collective memory of racist past shapes and legitimizes the "established racial structure of today's society" (Feagin 2013, 17). Nostalgic reflection of whites upon the *good ole days*, can be sociologically perceived as "a hallmark of white supremacy" (Diangelo 2018, 59). Conducting interviews in Greensboro, North Carolina, of white Southerners who were born in the first half of the twentieth century, of the Jim Crow era, Lavelle asked the general research question: *How is memory linked to identity maintenance?* Specifically: How do elder white residents of Greensboro engage in constructing "good" white moral identity that distances itself from past and present racial oppression (Lavelle 2015)? It is here we see an example of *collective overlooking* used to create a historical imagination for memory entrepreneurs in construction of "mnemonic fragmentation" (Fleming 2017, 216). Lavelle found that nostalgia can have revisionist tendencies by denying fundamental realities of the past while constructing positive identity traits. Her interviews found a theme of "white-protectionism" that maintained a nostalgia for the Jim Crow era as they fabricated a past-self that was enlightened or innocent in racial interactions while trivializing the Civil Rights Movement in general (Lavelle 2015, 185). These researchers have found that a variety of white agents feel that their collective white identity is important to them (Hartmann, Gerteis, and Croll 2009; McDermott 2020, 41).

In her study of "African Americans who matriculated through the 'colored school' system of Harlan County, Kentucky" as Jim Crow laws were being abolished, Brown utilized a "cultural trauma framework" to analyze the complicated aspects of collective identity and memory of "children of integration" (Brown 2016, 196). Her study found that some of the "hidden injuries" of desegregation included (1) a loss or "negation of their cultural identity," (2) a loss of personal attention and care given by black teachers to black students resulting in (3) an invisibility of the black student in the integrated but predominantly white school system. Brown illustrates that the "act of integration" did not generate the negative feelings but rather "the procedure in which the process was carried out." "For them, it was not integration, but a habeas corpus in which their black bodies were called upon to move from a place where they had constructed a social world to one where they had no familiarity or advocacy. . . . Overall, almost all participants responded that they are glad that school desegregation happened, some just wish that it had not happened to them personally" (Brown 2016, 212, 216).

When considering collective memory from the perspective of those oppressed, Steele refers to a powerful type of collective memory related to the Old South called "enemy-memory":

> This memory is a weight because it pulls the oppressions forward, out of history and into the present, so that the former victim may see his world as much through the memory of his oppression as through this experience in the present. What makes this a weight is that the rememberer will gird himself against a larger and more formidable enemy than the one he is actually encountering. . . . None of this is to say that the real enemy has entirely disappeared. Nor is it to suggest that we should forget our oppression, assuming this was even possible. It is only to say that our oppression has left us with a dangerously powerful memory of itself that can pull us into warlike defensiveness. (Steele 1991, 150–51)

Steele refers to the literary term "objective correlative" and provides that "enemy-memory works by such correlation, by connecting events in the present to powerful memories of the enemy" (Steele 1991, 153). Visual iconography that falls into the category of *objective correlatives* are "Confederate flags, and pickup trucks with gun racks" (Steele 1991, 154). A Southern accent can be a correlative to racial emotions by virtue of audio association. Steele indicates that blacks in America are surrounded by these unpleasant associations and that whites can be insensitive to this collective pain. "Tragically, the most relentless visual correlative may be white skin itself, especially for blacks with little experience in the larger society. . . . White insensitivity in this area is a form of power, an unearned and unfair power that feels to blacks like another manifestation of their victimization" (Steele 1991, 154). However, Steele warns that enemy-memory is "to look backward rather than forward" and can "skew the vision" by providing an "exaggerated sense of the enemy" (Steele 1991, 152).

Class

For many scholars, class along with race is socially constructed and cannot be rigidly defined (Kruse 2005; McDermott 2006). Within the constructs of race, ethnicity, and class, there are "a hundred shades of white" that are situationally differentiated (Hartigan 1999, 83). As with whiteness, the topic of class, as it is intertwined with race and ethnicity, is complicated. *Class* can be a viewed as a "a composite of occupation, residential location and family history" (Hartigan 1999, 8). Many ethnographic scholars use a method of self-identification by their research subjects to provide for their collective self-understanding (Hartigan 1999; Lamont 2000; McDermott 2006). Many Forbearers and most Retentionists in this study self-identified as "working for a living," "working man," or working-class. The working-class can be positioned at the lower end of the larger middle-class taxonomy, as the sub-class that is between the poor and the upper middle-class and they can be described as blue-collar and lower white-collar workers that are consistently employed and have high school but generally no college degrees (Lamont 2000, 10). Working-class respondents in this study, generally differentiated themselves from upper middle-class academia and lower class "red-necks" in orienting themselves in the local class stratification system. According to 2015 Census data, working-class whites comprise approximately 43 percent of the total US population which is the largest single group in America (Ehrenfreund and Guo 2016).

Previous research illustrates that the rudiments of work setting, the neighborhood and the home set the stage for the working-class. These elements are cultural objects that provide shared significance of collective norms and values for a specific group. A key, self-expressed, moral component for many American white workers was an emphasis on providing for and protecting their family (Kefalas 2003). Providing entailed the minimum of food on the table and a roof overhead. Protection was an equal priority as many white working-class felt they were on the edge of constant neighborhood threat or conflict (Kefalas 2003; McDermott 2006). An extension of their protective mantra and normative masculinity, white workers saw themselves proudly as Americans and defenders of moral order (Kefalas 2003; Lamont 2000). They tended to be great defenders of nationalist ideologies and American international dominance as part of maintaining the greater world order that they valued and espoused through overt demonstrations of patriotism (Kefalas 2003; Lamont 2000).

At the nucleus of their collective identity, white workers proudly identified themselves as engaged in a constant moral struggle. White workers emphasized the moral qualities of honesty, responsibility, integrity, and work ethic which they embraced and believed that others did not (Hochschild 2016; Lamont 2000). They ascribed traits such as dishonesty, irresponsibility, and laziness as negative attributes of others (Bonilla-Silva 2018; Kefalas 2003; Lamont 2000). Morality was the standard workers used to define us and others in what Lamont refers to as "boundary work" (Lamont 2000, 3). These standards served as an alternate to economic measures of success in providing distinctiveness through superior self-worth to "locate themselves above others" (Lamont 2000, 19). White workers utilized a variety of self-constructed, self-validating measures to construct a sense of personal dignity. It was through the creation and preservation of dignity that workers expressed individual identity and competence (Lamont 2000). Most Retentionists and many Forbearers share these collective sentiments.

In their research scholars determined that working-class whites found solidarity at work, home, and in the neighborhood, reinforced through cultural glue and the exclusion of others. A perceived loss of any of these rudimentary elements threatened their self-identity and their very culture. The cultural repertoires that the white working-class drew from consisted of elements of Protestant work ethic, their understanding of the republican social contract of unified effort, and masculinity (Lamont 2000, 26). Deploying these cultural repertoires, white workers drew upon a variety of "tool kits of symbols, stories, rituals and world-views" as a means of making sense of "settled culture" in times that appeared unsettling to them (Swidler 1986, 274, 282). For white workers, their version of morality was of critical importance and defined a sense of collective worth (Lamont 2000, 53; Lavelle 2015, 185). The elements of change to work, home, and neighborhood challenged these repertoires and directly threatened the sense of worth for white workers (Hochschild 2016). These factors demonstrate a perceived threat to group worth and to collective morality that are clearly reflected in the sentiments of Retentionists.

By studying situational micro-encounters, "contours of situations which shape the emotions and acts of individuals who step inside them" can be observed (Collins 2008, 1). Privileges of whiteness are nuanced as demonstrated by the research of Hartigan and McDermott. Their work focusing on neighborhood through situational micro-encounters, identified non-privileged aspects of whiteness particularized by the intersectionality of class and economic status. McDermott conducted an embedded study as a store cashier in two predominately white working-class urban neighborhoods that bordered black neighborhoods in Atlanta and in Boston (McDermott 2006). In her study she focused on interracial interactions in public settings as "not merely situated but situational" (McDermott 2006, 15). This study provides that white working-class identity in two different areas with similar demographics have divergent understandings of whiteness (McDermott 2006, 49). Simply stated, in racially mixed working-class milieus, whiteness may be a burden or *stigma*, instead of a privilege as with living in a trailer park (McDermott 2020, 53). In the Atlanta study, working-class whites felt "aware of other's perceptions of them as individual failures" as they were not successful and coexisted in the same neighborhoods as black citizens (McDermott 2006, 149). Here, whiteness became a "badge of inferiority" that was expressed by blacks and whites through generalizations that whites in this neighborhood were "alcoholic, addicted to drugs or mentally ill" (McDermott 2006, 40–41). However, in the Boston area, whiteness was classically demonstrated as relative privilege and pride in the working-class identity and the close association with the ethnic aspect of their neighborhood (McDermott 2006, 55). Here, high levels of unionization and strong ethnic bonds provided a protective attitude of neighborhood and a superior attitude to blacks and, especially, Haitians (McDermott 2006, 27). Ultimately, McDermott surmised that whites express their white identity in three ways: (1) stigma, when they fail economically to live up to expectations to themselves or others, (2) defensive, when they feel they are under attack by non-whites, and (3) transcendent, when they are "hyperaware of their white identity and try to escape it" (McDermott 2020, 42).

Embedded in neighborhoods of Detroit, Hartigan continues the micro-sociological tradition of study as he analyzes three predominately white Detroit neighborhoods with diverse socio-economic patterns (Hartigan 1999). This study provides insight into those white workers who did not engage in white flight but chose to stay, in a changing urban environment that left them as a city-wide minority. He finds that each neighborhood has "marked identities that can be assigned to whites" (Hartigan 1999, 18). He focuses his attention on the disparate and unstable interpretations of race as part of each neighborhood's daily social interaction with attention to the specific local settings and situations where racial identities are expressed, affirmed, and contested (Hartigan 1999, 14). Hartigan specifically identifies gaps within defined whiteness based on a "web of assumptions of normativity maintaining the social privileges and powers linked to white skin" (Hartigan 1999, 6). He identifies neighborhood objectifications of whiteness through labels such as *hillbilly, gentrifier*, and *racist* as not only descriptors of historical residency but also as a part of an embroiled class stratum of each neighborhood collective (Hartigan 1999, 280). It is important to review sentiments concerning *hillbillies* as they are closely related in stratified social positionality to *rednecks.* Respondents in my study of the Lexington-Rockbridge indicated that the term *redneck* can have negative and positive connotations, but it generally refers to country Southerners that are in the poor or lower end of the middle-class socio-economic scale and who are less formally educated.

In his study of the Briggs neighborhood, Hartigan illustrates that *hillbilly* was a term ascribed to white domestic migrants from the South that arrived in Detroit from 1940–1960s. The term *hillbilly* analyzed here was scorned by native white Detroiters and stigmatized as lacking refinement and sophistication and generalized as a "disgrace to the white race" for their failure to assimilate into middle-class whiteness (Hartigan 1999). Hillbillies undermined the easy assertion of whiteness as they shared many regional characteristics with Southern blacks that migrated to Detroit at the same time. Hartigan illustrates a 1950s survey that was conducted by Wayne State University. One of the questions asked was, "What people in Detroit are undesirable?" Criminals, gangsters, and so forth were listed first, as the most undesirable. *Hillbillies* were identified as the second most undesirable group. Non-self-supporting, transients, drifters, and so forth were listed third, and fourth were "Negros" (Hartigan 1999, 31).

In his 1990's study, Hartigan found that whiteness was not hegemonic in Detroit and that "blackness is locally dominant" (Hartigan 1999, 16, 17). He did not find whites uniformly treated "blackness as an *other*" but rather, they "invoked mobile class distinctions between themselves and their neighbors" (Hartigan 1999, 17). Hillbillies in Briggs proudly self-identified as hillbillies, but not necessarily as part of conventional middle-class whiteness, but rather as somewhere in-between as part of the "hundred shades of white" (Hartigan 1999, 115). Factors such as these intensely shaped how whites racially identified their position and socially interacted with others outside their class but within their neighborhood. Each class-category had distinctive local silhouettes that provide greater detail and clarity to the importance of local history on micro-interactions when considering the macro-applications of defined whiteness. It appeared that people were provisional in their racial assessments. These were the result of complex "competing interpretive repertoires" that were "textured by class distinctions" (Hartigan 1999, 15). Contrary to many researchers, Hartigan concludes, "Instead of drawing generalized assertions and summary judgments about race, I suggest that the economy of racial explanation and analysis needs to be reoriented toward a greater dependence on retention of the particular situations and settings where race is at work" (Hartigan 1999, 282). Both Hartigan and McDermott demonstrate whiteness is not always a prevailing privilege for all working-class whites. They demonstrated that the topic is complicated and depends greatly on micro-situational contexts.

The complex topics of *culture*, *race*, *collective identity*, and *class* are key ingredients in the Mulligan Stew for the Lexington-Rockbridge community.

Each ingredient has its unique flavor and depending on the individual recipe, it may have a place of dominance or subordinance in each person's stew. However, as with all culinary creations, the ingredients become blended and difficult to distinguish in the brew. Each cluster shares variations of these ingredients in their stew, but the constitutive portions and uses of these elements vary greatly. Agents in the community ingest their Mulligan Stew to make practical conclusions of others based on the symbol in question. Rigid clusters of Reformers and Retentionists consume their blend of Mulligan Stew as they firmly hold to their recipe and proportions of favorite ingredients, based on their ideology. This results in practical and ideological exclusion and thus limits their social interactions with others as they seek distinction. The more flexible cluster of Forbearers incorporate all the main ingredients for their interpretations and conclusions, but they often vary the blending of these ingredients, depending on their daily individual social interactions. This strategy results in a unifying effect within the comm-*unity* as they pursue commonality.

A DAMN YANKEE IN THE SHRINE OF THE SOUTH

Field research began in the Lexington-Rockbridge area in July 2019. My wife and I sold our home in Illinois and moved into temporary quarters just outside the city of Lexington. We initiated our search for more permanent residence while conducting area study and engaging in participant observation by attending local festivals and social gatherings. My past experience with government and military transfers taught me that there is a reluctance of indigenous community members to sincerely engage with those they deem to be temporary residents or transients. Developing rapport would take time. I utilized Blumer's symbolic interactionism as a perspective as well as a strategic methodology. I sought answers to questions based on the "obdurate and elusive character" of my "empirical social world under study" (Blumer 1969, 23). As such, collective life in the Lexington-Rockbridge area consists of what folks experience and do, individually and collectively, as they earn a living and socially interact (Blumer 1969, 35). In order for me to develop firsthand experience with the daily life under study, I embraced Blumer's principal suggestions. I did a lot of free exploration of the Lexington-Rockbridge area as I got close to the people in the community. I directly observed a variety of situations when folks socially interacted, noting the surrounding tensions and the various methods of dealing with those tensions. To complement my symbolic interactionist posture, I also embraced Geertz's "thick description" as an ethnographer to seize on various interpretations of symbols and follow the social interplay with other symbols as a local cultural system emerged (Geertz 1973, ix, 27).

Multiple tactical methods were used to study the Lexington-Rockbridge community. As a starting point I conducted a thorough *area reconnaissance* in an effort to learn the lay of the land and plot the density of Confederate Battle Flag display to get a feel for prevalence compared to other flags. I focused on town and rural areas within the radius of 35 kilometers extending from the center of the city of Lexington into Rockbridge County. This included the two incorporated cities of Lexington and Buena Vista, and the small county towns of Fairfield, Goshen, Raphine, and Natural Bridge as well as the rural farmlands in-between. From there, I integrated into the community through *participant observation* as I intermingled in county and city community activities as well as volunteer work to meet residents and build rapport. As relationships developed, people granted *informal* and *formal interviews*. Most respondents did not request anonymity, but for this book all community members have been given pseudonyms. I also listened and *engaged with speakers* over Lee-Jackson/MLK weekend. Lastly, *archival* data was gathered in digital and written form specifically related to Retentionists.

Although I embedded in the community, I was relatively detached from any "emotional or ideological engagement" on the subject of contentious symbols and the Confederate Battle Flag (Coski 2005, x). This was a preferred stance for me to conduct objective research of all community perspectives and one that was thrust upon me as a "damn Yankee." My position in the community and the "specific form of interaction" I embraced is most closely associated with Simmil's "social type . . . *the stranger*" (Simmel 1971, 143). My place in the community was found based on "factors of repulsion and distance . . . to create a form of being together, a form of union based on interaction" (Simmel 1971, 144). These interactions provided a blend of "remoteness and nearness, indifference and involvement" and a "distinctly *objective* attitude . . . not confined by custom, piety, or precedent" (Simmel 1971, 145, 146). In Army Special Forces parlance, there was little concern that I was going to go "indige" (indigenous). Through natural interactions, I strove to become closer to the community by extending "similarities of nationality or social position, of occupation or general human nature" (Simmel 1971, 147). Through this positioning in the community, I was able to receive "most surprising revelations and confidences, at times reminiscent of a confessional, about matters which are kept carefully hidden from everybody with whom one is close" (Simmel 1971, 145).

Flags can be cultural objects and symbols of shared significance. From the same cloth they can be capricious and relatively insignificant in nature like simple garden flags, or they can be powerful in sentiment like the black POW/MIA flag. Flags like the Confederate Battle Flag can be forms of expression that can represent indices of nostalgic fabric and identity. Many community members in the Lexington-Rockbridge area create various accoutrements to facilitate their Cherished Southern identity. A range of significant flags was commonly exhibited in the Lexington-Rockbridge area with the American Flag being by far the most common and revered. Hundreds of American Flags were seen displayed in the community. The Virginia State Flag, local school flags, and a variety of armed forces military flags (Army, Marine Corps., etc.) were the second most commonly demonstrated. Interestingly, the Virginia State Flag is emblematic of its historical abhorrence to domination. This flag depicts *Virtus*, the Roman deity of virtue, resting on a spear in her right hand, and holding a parazonium in her left hand, pointing upward. Her left foot is on the form of *Tyranny* represented by the prostrate body of a man, his fallen crown nearby with the words *sic semper tyrannis* (ERD 2020).

Confederate Battle Flag display was the third most publicly displayed flag to be revealed in the area. Since WWII more people have displayed the Flag in a variety of venues such as at football games, stock car races, on T-shirts and hats, in their yards, and at functions than "fought under them during the Civil War" (Coski 2005, 97). In the Lexington-Rockbridge area an imperfect empirical count provided for sixty-six public displays of the Confederate Battle Flag at residences. This did not include the massive presentations in cemeteries or displays on Lee-Jackson Day 2020. Along with the conventional Confederate Battle Flags recorded, over a dozen blended flags were viewed to include the Flag overwritten with "Heritage Not Hate." An equally observed flag is the Gadsden Flag which is characterized by *Don't Tread on Me.* It is yellow in background and depicts a coiled rattlesnake ready to strike.

A rough survey of Confederate Battle Flag display was conducted within a 35-kilometer radius of the city of Lexington, but it did not include the entire county. Of the total of sixty-six public displays of the Confederate Battle Flag that were recorded, fifty-five displays were observed in the county. Within 2 kilometers of the center of Lexington, five private displays of the Flag were found, and within 2 kilometers of the center of Buena Vista six were recorded. This does not include the many displayed in various cemeteries to include the Lexington Cemetery formerly named Stonewall Jackson Cemetery or the relics in museums. This cemetery is home to at least 144 Confederate States of America (CSA) markers and the Stonewall Jackson memorial. As demonstrated, the liberal posture ascribed to Lexington does not make it immune to Confederate Battle Flag displays within the city.

By September 2019, productive rapport was burgeoning with the community. My wife and I began volunteer work at Habitat for Humanity working most Thursday afternoon shifts. It is here where we met a valuable source, George. We also volunteered at the food pantry at the Church of God twice a month as needed, for bulk offloading of pantry items to help the church deacons, Arthur and Carla. I spent over 200 hours engaged in these and other volunteer activities. Ultimately, most of these endeavors were not only extremely productive in garnering interviews but also in observing unusual scenarios such as the interaction between the black, Church of God, and the older white resident, Richard, who lived directly across the street and proudly displayed multiple variations of the Confederate Battle Flag.

As rapport was developed and my research progressed to the interview stage, I found that academic "strangers" were especially suspect in the Lexington-Rockbridge area. Community members were generally polite, but many still held me at a noticeable arm's length. This was certainly not unusual when dealing with newcomers. I generally maintained a position of listen only as I tested the waters and hoped that future interactions would illuminate any stumbling blocks. As the interviews gathered momentum and I became a more familiar "stranger," I found that *the waters were testing me.* People politely scrutinized my agenda, and I was getting direct feedback that there was concern that my research was going to be an academic expose of "gotcha." Many community members wanted assurances that I was not a pedagogical dilettante who was going to ferret out dirty secrets and belittle community members as I depart for the ivory towers back North and callously present the ignorant ways of the aboriginal Southerner. At the end of a formal interview, the mayor of Lexington, Gene, breathed a noticeable sigh of relief. "I was waiting for the *gotcha.* . . . You need to convince community members there is *no gotcha.*" I heeded his advice and adjusted interactions to directly address this concern by overtly stating to future respondents that there is "no gotcha." Thomas, a local independent produce vender, provided other important words of advice: "Don't ever talk about nobody here . . . you never know who is kin to who . . . a lot of people are kin to each other around here . . . you have to watch what you say. . . . That is one thing about being in a small area . . . like this . . . people know each other." From these bits of wisdom received, I presented my intentions to respondents that I would report objectively, and, in the process, I hoped to develop positive relationships as neighbors and, if possible, even friends. This protocol of "the trader as a middleman . . . objective . . . a stranger" appeared to be well received but it was just the beginning (Simmel 1971, 144).

The overt *no gotcha* approach was valuable to state but not enough on its own merit to gather valuable information for this study. As part of presenting "similarities . . . of social position . . . or of general human nature" (Simmel 1971, 147), my background and experience were critical in establishing community credibility. Veteran status was respected in and of itself especially in Virginia and the South. Being a graduate from a federal military academy provided greater access to VMI employees, and as an Army Green Beret an even greater level of authenticity and appreciation particularly with the

Sons of Confederate Veterans and the United Daughters of the Confederacy. Disclosure as a retired law enforcement and FBI allowed critical access and *nearness* to Lexington Police Department, Rockbridge County Sheriff's Office, Virginia Department of Conservation & Recreation, and the Virginia State Police as it raised the eyebrows and a sense of *remoteness* with the Sons of Confederate Veterans and so forth. My research credentials provided a comfort zone with employees associated with W&L and VMI. Lastly, as a researcher who wanted to represent rural voice, many enjoyed the prospect of being in a book either anonymously or overtly. Interviews began slowly as "targets of opportunity" presented themselves. Most were formal in nature, and most respondents preferred to remain identifiable. Interviews lasted anywhere from forty-five minutes to over three hours. Most respondents found the experience pleasant and productive and recommended other community members to speak with me as many considered it a "form of therapy."

As previously stated, although the focus of this book is on contentious symbols and community interactions, race is an underlying topic of interest. As part of the formal interview process, social distance questions reminiscent of the *Bogardus Social Distance Scale* and Reed's research (Reed 2008, 95) were used to penetrate a veneer of racial tolerance in an effort to uncover racial prejudice (Levine, Carter, and Gorman 1976, 836). The following *Objectives of the Interview*, from my Interview Guide, were read to each respondent during formal interviews:

> This is a cultural study of Lexington and Rockbridge County. Institutions, cemeteries, memorials, songs, symbols, and war heroes are used as discussion points. This is not a judgmental study. This study seeks to identify what is important to the people of Rockbridge County and why. All perspectives are valid, and none are wrong.

Data was collected concerning the general topics of (1) demographics, (2) social groups and organizational membership, (3) regional consciousness, (4) personal identity, image, and values, (5) politics, policy, and programs, (6) symbols, songs, and monuments, (7) social distance, and (8) community movements and organization reflection. Within these general topics specific questions were scattered throughout the interview process about familial and social diversity and social distancing of *unlike others*. These others included those who were differentiated outside respondent normal social network by race, citizenship, creed, lifestyle, and politics. The strategy of the interview guide was to build a crescendo of passionate responses, with rhythms of ebbs and flows, so as not to appear antagonistic or have the respondent feel *gotcha*. Most interviews allowed the respondents to express themselves freely while trying to probe and guide the interview to collect data. Not all questions were addressed in all the interviews. A second method used to penetrate any veneer of racial tolerance was my attendance of significant functions that tended to exhibit greater cluster collective effervescence such as SCV monthly meetings and Lee-Jackson Day functions.

As part of the "stranger" methodology, I engaged the community with a balance of subtlety, candor, and humor. Very early in the interactions I was politely reminded that I was a damn Yankee. What exactly is a damn Yankee? Oliver grew up in the town of Lexington and lived in the vicinity of one of the town's traditional Southern matrons, Mrs. Dade, who would tell tales of the Lost Cause. Mrs. Dade's father was reputed to be one of the surgeons who removed Stonewall Jackson's arm. She provided the local children, like Oliver, with many "romanticized version(s) of the Civil War." She spun "tales of heroics" of Southern gallantry and warned the young of the dastardly ways of the "damn Yankees." Jesse, a former member of the Sons of Confederate Veterans and a gay man, identifies strongly with the South and provided a riddle for me at the beginning of our interview to test my fortitude. "You know what the difference between a Yankee and a damn Yankee is? [Chuckling and a pause] The damn Yankee never leaves!" Obviously being a damn Yankee is not a positive attribute for community members in the Lexington-Rockbridge area as it is a designation of "stranger" and a method of othering, distancing, detachment, and estrangement. Yet, I learned early on that the term was not necessarily presented as an insult as much as a test of character and a test of one's sense of humor. In an attempt to pleasantly disarm community members, I thought it best early on to self-identify as a "damn Yankee" who was born and raised in New York City but who also called New Orleans, Louisiana, his last home. This approach provided entrée via humility and humor. I introduced a *Southern* connection via New Orleans as another sacred land of the South as well as graciously accepting a self-imposed affront of being from up North. A commitment to staying in the area was established while also demonstrating a detached and objective posture as I claimed no Cherished Southern identity, no hearth and home sentiments, and no nostalgic fabric to influence my work. I merely claimed to be a new community member, the "stranger" who was willing to listen and not judge. It was at this stage of my research where I heard the term "good people" being used as a powerful compliment toward fellow community members and a desirable moniker to obtain: "Joe, he's okay. He's good people."

Along with all the efforts stated above to develop rapport, the greatest assurance to embeddedness for community members of both county and city was my purchase of land in the county. My early interviews began with questions of where I currently live. My initial renting in a reputed transient area provided for a general suspicious response of, "Oh." As a landed "stranger" of the Lexington-Rockbridge area, my credibility soared. Simmel describes the relationship of the stranger and the ownership of land. "The stranger is by his very nature no owner of land—land not only in the physical sense but also metaphorically as a vital substance which is fixed, if not in space, then at least in an ideal position with the social environment" (Simmel 1971, 144). However, my land ownership still provided me a status of Simmelian "supernumerary" as I interacted with the community but did not truly affect the "economic positions already occupied" (Simmel 1971, 144). Most landowners of over five acres have beef or dairy cows and grow corn and triticale for feed. I am converting former farmland in an afforestation project and have planted thousands of trees in an effort to create wildlife habitats. As such, I tend the land, utilize farm equipment, mend the fences, repair my home, and help the neighbors. These country activities of land-labor have endeared me with the local county folk as a credible worker, but I pose no economic threat to them. I productively engaged with realtors, lawyers, city and county employees, farmers, farm equipment salesmen, butchers, produce growers, seamstresses, hunters, poachers, church administrators, and a panoply of other neighborhood actors as a fellow community member. Interviews presented themselves and snowballed into more interviews via natural interactions with respondent categories of diverse racial, economic, and class backgrounds.

In summation, my commitment to embeddedness as a *stranger* in the community and respecting "social, religious, and cultural norms of the target population and (to) adopt an empathetic approach towards the respondent and his/her milieu" was paramount for interview integrity and data collection (Cohen and Arieli 2011, 432). My position as veteran, retired law enforcement, engineer, and current landowner intrigued many community members and allowed me entrée into various social circles to include those of the Retentionists. Productive skill sets were continuously tested through integrity checks by community members. Passing these tests provided me with *country cred.* The ability to tend your own land and home and make repairs independent of others is a valued commodity that distinguishes a "damn Yankee" carpet bagger from a community newcomer. Examples of such social credibility checks consist of knowing chainsaw nomenclature, engaging in tractor repair, and the demonstrated productive use (as opposed to dilettante use) of implements to tend the land. This *country cred* gave me a productive venue to break the ice with people in the community in spite of being a stranger. This was especially true with reluctant respondents such as the Retentionists and many Forbearers. Reformers, however, needed little encouragement and appeared to be the most eager to speak with me.

NOTES

1. Lexington is technically a city by incorporation.

2. Non-displaying whites is a categorical name to differentiate from the Sons of Confederate Veterans, United Daughters of the Confederacy, and other ardent displayers of the Confederate Battle Flag.

3. Black community members are those who self-identified as black.

4. Double entendre intended.

Chapter 1

Observing and Reporting in the Shrine of the South

Until 2020 Lee-Jackson Day was a Virginia state holiday. It was established over a 100 years ago and was observed on the Friday preceding the third Monday in January (Stewart 2020). This effectively made it the Friday before Martin Luther King Day which became a federal holiday in 1986. For the past twenty years the Sons of Confederate Veterans and the Daughters of the Confederacy held commemorative functions to celebrate Lee's and Jackson's birthdays over Lee-Jackson Weekend to include a parade on Saturday in the town of Lexington. Customarily this included a request to display the Confederate Battle Flag on city light posts for twenty-four to forty-eight hours. Requests such as these were common as university flags were displayed for school functions throughout the year for both Washington & Lee University (W&L) and Virginia Military Institute (VMI). In 2011, Lexington's City Council denied the routine request of the Sons of Confederate Veterans and banned the display of the Confederate Battle Flag from its street poles for that year's Lee-Jackson Weekend based on the offensive potential of the Flag to black community members. CBS reported the event as "Va. City Bans Public Confederate Flag Displays" (AP 2011). The opening statement of this article provided: "Lexington, Va. - Officials in the rural Virginia city where Robert E. Lee and Thomas 'Stonewall' Jackson are buried voted late Thursday to prohibit the flying of the Confederate flag on city-owned poles."

In 2015, W&L removed the Confederate Battle Flags from its campus. That year the *Richmond Times-Dispatch* featured an article titled, "Lexington has Battled over Confederate Flag Issue for Years" (Oliver 2015). The opening lines provided:

Lexington—In 2011, Lexington's City Council banned Confederate flags from its street poles. Rather than resolving the debate, the historic city has become a stage for people who think the emblem should still be displayed prominently

37

across the South. "For some people, we're the shrine of the South," the city's mayor, Mimi Elrod, said this week. "I think even though Richmond was the capital of the Confederacy, Lexington has taken on a very strong meaning for them."

In 2020, the *New York Times* featured an article, "A Liberal Town Built Around Confederate Generals Rethinks Its Identity" (R. J. Epstein 2020). The preface provided: "In Lexington, VA., where Robert E. Lee and Stonewall Jackson are buried, people are reassessing the town's ties to a legacy that symbolizes slavery and oppression."

Sentiments are polarized for some in the community. Liberal-reformer community members celebrate the Confederate Battle Flag ban and the progressive movement as a way to deny racist signification and deter gestures of white supremacy. Conservative-retentionist elements such as members of the Sons of Confederate Veterans and United Daughters of the Confederacy feel aggrieved that their ability to celebrate and conserve their traditions and their *Cherished Southern identity* are being denied to them. It is important to clarify that the request for the display of the Confederate Battle Flag by the Sons of Confederate Veterans was only for the Friday and Saturday of Lee-Jackson Weekend. Procedurally, the request for the display of any flag required the city of Lexington to install them for one week because of the manual efforts to raise and lower them by city laborers. Tucker, a ranking member of the Sons of Confederate Veterans, provided his perspective:

> Various groups including the colleges were allowed to post flags on the streets until we began doing so. They changed the law to specifically target us, but since they now allow nobody to do so, there isn't much we could do about it although we did pursue a federal court suit against the city. . . . Our request was for the week prior to and through the event. The city typically installs and removes banners, etc. on Mondays. We didn't care if they removed them on Sunday. The conflict was that the public works typical policy would have left them up on MLK Jr. Day. . . . It's a damn shame due to fate they share similar birthdays as if Lee and Jackson conspired 100 years earlier to be born on that day to infuriate Leftist reactionaries.

The proximity of birthdays of Lee and Jackson and King along with Lexington city installation/removal policies exacerbated the situation. Would community sentiments, and national sentiments, have been as powerful if the birthdays were months apart? Would the Confederate Battle Flag display in Lexington have been as visceral if it were up for one to two days rather than seven, the last being MLK Day? The juxtaposition of the proximity of the birthdays appears to have set the stage for contention. It is apparent that the 2011 Confederate Battle Flag ban did not have an ameliorative effect for the community. What was once only four Flags flown at the back of Lee Chapel on W&L campus has grown to dozens of Flags planted and flown on the sides of Virginia highways and private property (Oliver 2015). Confederate Battle Flag removal has led to differentiated emotions which have spread throughout the nation reminiscent of the sentiments concerning commemorative efforts for the Vietnam Veterans Memorial in the 1980s (Wagner-Pacifici and Schwartz 1991). Lexington-Rockbridge community members remain divided on what the provocative Southern symbols like the Confederate Battle Flag signify. Because of its history and the current controversy, Lexington continues to be a focal point for the Flag as a cultural symbol.

THE SOUTH AND CONTENTIOUS SYMBOLS

The South can be operationally defined as the eleven former Confederate states (Alabama, Arkansas, Florida, Georgia, Louisiana, Mississippi, North Carolina, South Carolina, Virginia, Tennessee, and Texas) plus Kentucky and Oklahoma, for a total of thirteen Southern states (Reed 1986, 14). Reed distinguishes the South into two entities, the Deep South and the Peripheral South. The Deep South comprises "South Carolina, Georgia, Alabama, Mississippi and Louisiana" (Reed 2018, 120). When considering the War Between the States, "Southerners justifiably believed that interference with slavery was a violation of a constitutional and customary understanding upon which the nation was founded" (Coski 2005, 17). Yet, to be Southern is not simply a membership group to the heritage of the Confederacy that lost the Civil War. It is a reference group that displays a "regional consciousness" and that this group may be thought of "as roughly coterminous with a Southern ethnic subsociety" (Reed 1986, 10; 2008, 27). Wilson refers to postbellum South, "the South's Kingdom was to be of culture . . . the attitude known as the *Lost Cause* . . . basis for the Southern religious-moral identity, and identity of a *chosen people*" (Wilson 1980, 1). In his research Reed found that Southern identification was generally not based on race as "racial ideology is no longer, if it ever was, a shibboleth for Southern affiliation" (Reed 2008, 22). However, in his self-reflective work on the South and his own family, Dew found that race plays a critical part in many affluent Southern families. "Once notions of white supremacy and black inferiority are in place in the American South, they are passed on from one generation to the next with all the certainty and inevitability of a genetic trait" (Dew 2016, 166).

Coski traces the origins and evolutions of the Confederate Battle Flag. He found that most Southern communities and many Northern ones have historical and contemporary stories to tell about the Flag (Coski 2005). He adopts a relativist, non-normative approach that attempts to explain from where

Confederate Battle Flag meanings originated and "why people believe them" (Coski 2005, viii). He identified the emotional, cognitive, and ideological motivations in Flag constructions. "What is at stake is not so much history as *heritage*. . . . Heritage is more akin to *religion* than history. It is a presentation of the past based not on critical evaluation of evidence but on *faith* and the acceptance of *dogma*" (Coski 2005, 291). "Heritage affirms the historical myths essential for national, cultural or subcultural identity" (Coski 2005, 291; Lowenthal 1996). Wilson argues that the "*Lost Cause* was a mythic construct that helped white Southerners define a cultural identity in the aftermath of Confederate defeat . . . white Southerners made a *religion* out of their history" (Wilson 1980, x). With the loss of the Civil War, "fearing that crushing defeat might eradicate the identity forged in war, Southerners reasserted that identity with a vengeance" (Wilson 1980, 7). The Lost Cause "provided the rationale for Southerner maintaining a culture separate from the nations" replacing a political dream of a separate Confederacy with a Southern cultural one (Wilson 1980, 161). Wilson focused on the religious history of the South and of the Lost Cause as part of a "Southern civil religion, which tied together Christian churches and Southern culture" from the end of the Civil War until the end of WWI (Wilson 1980, 1). As part of sacred Southern ceremonies, Wilson describes a significant ritual of the Lost Cause. On 26 October 1875, Richmond, Virginia, the Confederate "soldier's Mecca," was the site "of the dedication of the first statue in the South to Stonewall Jackson" (Wilson 1980, 18).

In his recent historical study of the rural South Carolina Upcountry, Poole found that after the Civil War local churches became "evangelical fellowships of faith" which "became centers of *Confederate religion*" (Poole 2004, 73). Poole found that conventional churches "played a crucial role in shaping a Confederate identity, conjoining this identity with the peculiar institution [slavery], southern honor, manhood, and evangelicalism . . . fashioning a Confederate religion" (Poole 2004, 38). Many "Confederate holy warriors became ministers" and their objectives were that of preservation. "Confederate virtue . . . duty, courage, and the high demands of honor. . . . The world they created would see itself at war with modernity, seeking to preserve the folk mores. . . . The construction of an aesthetic of the Lost Cause with Confederate religion as an organizing theme came to act as a standing critique of the work the Yankee made" (Poole 2004, 53).

When considering Southern identity, Reed chose to analyze the Southern ethnic group by comparing in-group/out-group differences or North-South differences by measuring prejudice, social distance and boundary maintenance (Reed 2008, 95–107). This work utilized national surveys and Reed identified three significant distinctions: (1) attachment to local community,

(2) attitudes toward the private use of force and violence, and (3) religious beliefs and practices (Reed 1986, 4). Reed found that Southerners are more likely to (1) be conventionally religious, (2) embrace the right of defense of body and home through the private use of force, and (3) be more anchored in their community (Reed 1986, 83). This results in the overall American perception that being Southern is to be more rural, less educated, and less middle class (Morland 1971, 39) while not being Southern is to "appear more urban, more educated and more white-collar than one is" (Reed 1986, 83). Reed concluded that some aspects of Southern culture and identity can be, at times, mechanisms for dealing with a "hostile outside" and that if their "collective interest or pride" is threatened, "the old back-to-the-wall imagery is resurrected" and the "tattered Confederate Battle Flag will be unfurled" (Leigh 2017; Reed 2008, 90). In his later work, Reed found the Confederate Battle Flag "has come to mean many different things, and neither the Sons of Confederate Veterans nor the NAACP has a monopoly on interpretation" (Reed 2018, 132). He provides two principle findings: (1) "Substantial dis-agreement" between black and white Southerners in the symbolic meaning of the Flag, and (2) "Blacks, young people, the better educated, and migrant to the South are more likely than others to see Confederate symbols as signify-ing racism" (Reed 2018, 132).

Kruse conducted a post–Civil War historical study on home and neighbor-hood in Atlanta, Georgia. He found that whites were abundantly concerned with homeowner's rights, community protection, and safe-productive neigh-borhood schools (Kruse 2005). It is in their home areas that Southern whites took the threat of neighborhood change personally (Kruse 2005). Perceived encroachment of black people and others "not like us" into these neighbor-hoods was not just an affront to their personal preference of homophily but also a monetary concern of property value and collective identity. In an effort to salvage the "southern way of life," Southern whites resisted desegrega-tion out of a fear of change in beneficiary of privilege that would alienate and oppress the white citizen instead of the black citizen (Kruse 2005, 54, 218). They were also fighting for the right to select their neighbors, their employees, their coworkers, their shopping, lodging, eating associates, their children's classmates, and the right to exercise their privilege to operate their business and private life as they saw fit with no forcible integration and no interference from the federal government (Kruse 2005, 227). From this vantage point the defense of segregation was a defense of white "right" for selective association (Kruse 2005, 163).

Southern symbols are highly antagonistic and divisive for Reformer and Retentionist clusters. Both groups exhibit virtucratic tendencies. As such, polarized cluster "views are not merely correct but deeply, morally righteous in the bargain" (J. Epstein 2003). Previous research on the Confederate Battle Flag debate has distilled the argument to either a *heritage* or *hate* position. I suggest that this reductionism fails to account for personal and contextual attachments that are more clearly seen at a micro-view utilizing the lens of practical symbolic interactionism. I demonstrate that some Southern symbols, like the Flag, are repulsive for Reformers and sacred for Retentionists, as well as a potential social obstacle to be negotiated by Forbearers when conducting everyday business. Investigating the cultural significance of contentious symbols of the South utilizing symbolic interactionism and a Durkheimian religious perspective is important in understanding local social tensions and the social interactive protocols utilized by the various clusters.

Coski provided that in exploring the history of the Confederate Battle Flag there are fundamental disagreements about America's past, which in turn affects the perceptions of the present and the future (Coski 2005). I have found that Retentionists hold Southern symbols like the Confederate Battle Flag as Durkheimian sacred totems within their religion of Cherished Southern identity. The nature of an object, like the Flag, "consists of the meaning that it has for the person for whom it is an *object*" (Blumer 1969). Understanding the powerful religious-like significance of the Confederate Battle Flag furthers our knowledge into the challenges of ceremonial remembrance and opposing collective memories. "The problem of commemoration is an important aspect of the sociology of culture because it bears on the way society conceives its past" (Wagner-Pacifici and Schwartz 1991). The conceptions and constructions of the Confederate Battle Flag are not about facts, "they are about meaning" (Thornton 1996). As part of Retentionist "collective representation" these religious meanings are interpretive, selective, "delusive" and do not "do without a certain delirium" (Durkheim 1912). Utilizing the perspectives and methods of symbolic interactionism and viewing cluster sentiments through a religious lens provides a way to focus and frame cultural boundaries within the community as a social world.

A 2015 CNN poll found that "57% of Americans see the flag more as a symbol of Southern pride than as a symbol of racism. . . . Opinions of the flag are sharply divided by race, and among whites, views are split by education" (Agiesta 2015). But in locations where context in the social world provides meaning, are the opinions of black and white community members sharply divided by race? Contrary to several studies, my research determines that in the Lexington-Rockbridge area sentiments on contentious Southern symbols are not necessarily based on a racial divide. The clusters of Reformers and Retentionists are engaged in their respective holy crusades directed against the other. Mutual intolerance is expressed by these clusters against each other based on opposing ideological membership espoused (*Verba*). Little room is left for individual interactions (*Acta*) to find common ground. As such, Reformers and Retentionists utilize a *Verba non Acta* (words not deeds) distancing assessment protocol to disassociate from each other based solely on ideological membership. Forbearers may or may not view Retentionist attachment to Confederate symbolism with suspicion, but they are generally wary of Reformer ideological rigidity. Forbearers focus on individual interactions (*Acta*) with community members and are less concerned with ideological cluster association (*Verba*). They demonstrate an *Acta non Verba* (deeds not words) assessment protocol and associate with other clusters to negotiate daily interactions as well as determine acceptable social boundaries regardless of collective membership.

There are two recent journal articles that focus on the Confederate Battle Flag and best frame my interests and concerns in Cherished Southern identity. Both articles question: *Is support for the Confederate Battle Flag Southern pride or is it simply a symbol of racism?* These articles used survey methods that encompass large regions in the South, but they resulted in dissimilar conclusions. Strother and colleagues find strong support that prejudice against black people bolsters white support for Southern symbols. However, Wright and Esses challenge the claim that all supporters of the Flag are generally being driven by negative racial attitudes toward black people. In the first article, "Pride or Prejudice? Racial Prejudice, Southern Heritage, and White Support for the Confederate Battle Flag" Strother, Piston, and Ogorzalek (2017) ask: What motivates some whites to support Southern symbols and others to oppose them? Their findings support the idea that exposure to the Flag activates negativity toward black community members because it is associated with racism and prejudice. "As such the Confederate flag is better understood as a polarizing symbol of white Southern heritage than as a non-racial symbol of some shared regional heritage" (Strother et al. 2017, 296). For these authors the *heritage* argument is distilled to the *Lost Cause* argument (Wilson 1980). Ultimately, they find that credence for the Southern heritage argument is mixed and that the survey data do little to "substantiate claims that white support for the Confederate Battle Flag stems from Southern pride" (Strother et al. 2017, 311). For these authors, symbols such as the Confederate Battle Flag "point to the essentially racist signification" historically and in modern usage (Strother et al. 2017, 302).

In the second article, "Support for the Confederate Battle Flag in the Southern United States: Racism or Southern Pride?" Wright and Esses (2017) approach the Confederate Battle Flag debate by trying to understand the motivations for Flag support. They focus on two primary perspectives in determining driving factors: (1) racial ideology: group-based dominance based on racism, and (2) Southern heritage: social identity based on Southern pride (Wright and Esses 2017, 225). Southern heritage is described here as a deep pride in Southern culture that is framed in social identity group as a way to "orient oneself to the rest of the United States." "We embed the importance of geography in the life space of individuals within our concept of Southern pride, which ultimately is defined by the cognitive act of being, the affective admiration for place and entity, and the geography of space and history" (Wright and Esses 2017, 226). In their research, Wright and Esses provided for three perspectives: (1) Southern heritage, (2) racial ideology, and (3) principled-conservatism (Wright and Esses 2017, 226–227). The vast majority of Confederate Battle Flag supporters show positive racial attitudes toward black people and are not motivated by blatant racism, demonstrating that support assumes intention of exhibiting racism may be incorrect (Wright and Esses 2017, 235). The authors conclude that Southern pride as expressed in support of the Flag is not linked to racial out-group animosity and can be considered a form of patriotism as "an entity devoid of dominance and ethnocentrism" (Wright and Esses 2017, 226). For Wright and Esses, the Confederate Battle Flag can be hermeneutically examined as a symbol of Southern self that embodies pride, both emotionally and cognitively. This aligns with Polletta and Jasper who provide that "collective identities are expressed in cultural materials" such as symbols (Polletta and Jasper 2001, 285).

LEXINGTON-ROCKBRIDGE AREA:
THE SHRINE OF THE SOUTH

The area of my study is broken down into two distinct entities, city and county. Table 1.1 shows the city of Lexington having a population of approximately 7,000 and Rockbridge County with a population close to 23,000. Buena Vista is the only other incorporated city in Rockbridge County, but it is considered part of the county for this study as it is outside and dissimilar from the city of Lexington. The distinction of an incorporated city is important to the identity of city-dwellers and county-dwellers. Once designated as a city, there is a relative emancipation from the judication of the county and autonomy of operation for dwellers. City councils can be formed, and police departments created. Unincorporated towns are subject to county regulations and enforcement.

Community members of the Lexington-Rockbridge area are predominately white at 82 percent in the city of Lexington and 92 percent in the county of Rockbridge. Lexington could be described as a type of "small town Whitopia" by Benjamin's definition,[1] as the town enjoys population growth and a certain "je ne sais quoi—an ineffable social charisma, a pleasant look and feel" (Benjamin 2009, 5, 12–13). Many community members hail from

Scots-Irish decent. In a humorous reference, one respondent provided that the Rockbridge County phone book was reputed to have the largest membership of *Mc-* in the country with its own tab in the alphabetic listing between *M* and *N*. My farm area is home to the extended clans of McClung, McCorkle, McDowell, McCormick, and McComas. The Scots-Irish have a long history and memory of "invasion, oppression, and resistance." "Again and again, they have found, or put themselves in the position of, well insurgents. This history of incessant conflict, together with the Scottish clan structure, the Protestant Reformation and rural isolation, has 'ingrained' certain attitudes and values in the Scots-Irish" (Reed 2018, 44).

Black community members are at 6.4 percent in the city and 3.4 percent in the county which is significantly less than the national percentage which is between 13–15 percent depending on the source. The county has a higher median house income of $54,804 compared to the city of $36,466 and a lower poverty percentage of 12 percent compared to that of Lexington at 21.6 percent. Rockbridge County identifies as approximately two-thirds Republican while Lexington identifies as two-thirds Democrat. The city of Lexington is home to VMI and W&L universities and to the gravesites of Robert E. Lee and Stonewall Jackson. Because Lexington is considered by many community members, in varying degrees and perspectives, as the *Shrine of the South*, it is the focal point of collective memories of "difficult pasts" (Whitlinger 2020).

Table 1.1: Lexington-Rockbridge Demographics (Author created: Drawn from US Census Bureau: QuickFacts and Politico.com)

2019	*Rockbridge County*	*Lexington City*
Population	22,752	7,136
Race %		
White	92%	82%
Black	3.4%	6.4%
Hispanic	2.1%	5.1%
Asian	.7%	3.7%
Mix	1.7%	3.2%
Foreign Born %	2.7%	4.4%
Computer Use %	78%	80%
Education %		
High School or>	87%	90%
Bachelor's or>	27%	40%
Median House Income	$54,804	$36,466
Poverty %	12%	21.6%
2016 Voting % (*Based on Politico.com)		
Democratic	33%	62%
Republican	63%	31%
Other	5%	7%

However, Lexington does not have a notorious history of racial violence or a "silenced past" like Philadelphia, Mississippi (Whitlinger 2020, 38). A search was conducted of the Equal Justice Initiative's, "Lynching in American: County Data Supplement" (EJI 2021). This supplement presents the numbers of documented African American victims of racial terror lynching killed in the United States between 1877 and 1950, per county/parish. Although Virginia reported 84 victims as a state, none of these atrocities occurred in Augusta-Rockbridge County. In comparison, the state of Mississippi reported 654 such murders. The last reported hanging in Lexington occurred in 1906 (Rife 2014), when a drunk white man killed his white next door neighbor for refusing to go hunting with him.[2]

"Americans are profoundly divided in political matters" (Skocpol and Tervo 2020, 317). The Lexington-Rockbridge area is no exception. Although once considered a "bastion of conservatism," many see Lexington as a "liberal college town" (R. J. Epstein 2020). Respondents, both city and county, observed, "It is an island of blue surrounded by a sea of red," referring to the city's position in the county. Gene, the mayor, joked, "The seven Republicans (in town) are kind nice people, and they go out in the light of day." Lexington, is "far more liberal than Rockbridge County." However not all in Lexington are liberal and "you just know they [some] are voting Republican." The tensions between progressive and conservative entities in the area community provide an opportunity to study various social dynamics and cultural boundaries. These tensions create a "conflict environment" where some community members "perceive their needs, goals or interests to be contradicted by the goals or interests of the other side" (Cohen and Arieli 2011, 424; Kreisberg 1998).

Almost all respondents attribute the liberal nature of the city of Lexington to the colleges of W&L and VMI. Unsurprisingly, the teaching faculty are considered the most liberalizing elements of both institutions. Equally unsurprising, W&L faculty are considered significantly more liberal than those at VMI. VMI, as the "West Point of the South," tends to cling to tradition and conservative values (Wilson 1980, 153). However, the liberal tendencies of W&L are a fairly recent phenomenon. Prior to the American Revolution, the institution was known as the Augusta Academy. In 1776 it was renamed Liberty Hall and then Washington College in "light of George Washington's financial contributions" (Wilson 1980, 152). After the Civil War, the institution was near financial ruin and the trustees recruited Lee as their new school president. It was at this time the college "earned the reputation as the home of the Lost Cause" and as the "University of the South" (Wilson 1980, 152). The religious and traditional values of Washington College "flowed from the influence of one man," Robert E. Lee (Wilson 1980, 154). Nevertheless, after the Civil War, Lee "reminded his countrymen of, in his words, 'the duty of everyone to unite in the restoration of the country and the reestablishment of peace and harmony'" (Reed 2018, 84). Upon Lee's death Washington College was renamed Washington & Lee. W&L is also home to Lee Chapel (renamed in 2021, as University Chapel) which houses the memorial, *Recumbent Statue of General Robert E. Lee*, by Edward Valentine and a family crypt in the lower level. The remains of Lee's beloved horse, Traveller, are still interred in a plot outside the museum entrance.

Although by 1920 W&L "reflected the movement towards reconciliation with the North," it also maintained "a sense of continuity with the past . . . preserving for the Southern young an awareness of their origins" as well as "discouraging a truly objective view of the past" (Wilson 1980, 159). As such the "postwar South was suspicious of intellectual speculation" and "heretics were not welcome in the Lost Cause South" (Wilson 1980, 160). W&L maintained its insular conservative posture well into the 1960s and 1970s, but the arrival of new professors and burgeoning student diversity began to change the complexion of the school. Oliver recalled that he started at W&L in the fall of 1970, which "was the first year there were more than three blacks in a class." According to Oliver, co-education was introduced at W&L in 1986, when they "started accepting women, and became more diverse." Oliver advised that people thought the school began to accept women as part of a "move of political correctness." However, he felt it was more about competition for national school rankings. "The applicant pool at W&L had just gotten horrible. . . . The only way . . . to bring that up was to admit women." Oliver felt that W&L certainly has greater diversity than it did 50 years ago. Though, there is still a strong influence of the "Southern Planter Class." "Some things do not change."

The year of 2007 was a pivotal one for W&L as the university received a $100 million gift from Rupert Johnson Jr.,[3] that became known as the "Johnson Scholarship." The purpose of the endowment was to recruit from a more diverse pool of student candidates and encourage new teaching staff so as to "move the University into a different competitive universe" (Hanna 2011). Oliver described the program, "So, they have this Johnson Scholarship Program. . . . Where they have a couple of hundred kids a year, for four years . . . they get every penny paid for. . . . It is not need-based. It is kind of competitive." Gene felt that until the Johnson Scholarship the W&L student body was much more conservative. "A W&L alumnus, Rupert Johnson, wanted to help the school be more competitive for a variety of students and have W&L become more like an Ivy League school. He donated $100 million with 85 million to underwrite 40 scholarships/year . . . and 15 million to supplement professor salaries. In one year, the applications for 400 slots at W&L rose from 3,200 to 6,500 because of the new program." Gene described the new students attracted to W&L as "just remarkable . . . many of them tend to be more academic and arguably more liberal than the, you know, 'What company does your daddy own.' . . . whether you graduate or not, you are going back to work in the family business." Gene felt that this new diversity was quite different from the "W&L [Southern] gentlemen of 1960s and 1970s."

Rockbridge County, or the County, has a distinct culture from Lexington. The generalized characteristic of living in the county is that of *country*. Alex, a man of color and mixed heritage, said, "Country folk are more pure, living off the land, simple, what you see is what you get, pull no punches . . . honest." There are immediate indicators that distinguish us from them. The first is linguistic tropes and accent. Mispronunciation of names like Kerrs Creek (*Cars crick*) and Staunton (*Stan-ton, like can-ton*) will cause community members to visibly blanch. Frank, a history professor at W&L, provided that during the Civil War Yankee spies were identified by their pronunciation of Staunton as "Stawnton." A second distinguishing characteristic of the county is the attachment and adoration of the land. The use of the land as well as the relative spacing provides greater privacy and an expectation of solitude. A third indicator is politics. Dan, a Virginia State Trooper, laconically described the separation. "Lexington is liberal, and the county is conservative." Francine, a former ranking city official, provided greater specificity. She sees the county as being "very, very different" from Lexington. There is a "division" between the city and the county. She felt that people in the county were "very conservative" and have property and while some are wealthy, "generally they are not that wealthy . . . and I think that they sort of, take some of that out on some other people."

Buena Vista (pronounced *Biew-na vista, like view-na sista*) is the only other city in Rockbridge County. Buena Vista is commonly referred to by community members as simply BV. It is considered by many in the area as blue-collar, conservative, and distressed. Those from BV take great pride in their proximity to the mountains and their simple way of life without pretense. Buena Vista is economically struggling as floods have taken its toll and many industries have closed in the past fifty years to include Blue Bird Bus construction and Mohawk carpet makers. It is home to Southern Virginia University (SVU) which is affiliated with the Mormon Church. Lexington is characterized as "looking down" on Buena Vista and the county, and, in turn, they snub Lexington as elitist snobs. It is in the pronunciation of Buena Vista and the rapid correction by many community members, that an immediate identification of an outsider, or stranger, is made.

CHERISHED SOUTHERN IDENTITY, NOSTALGIC
FABRIC, AND SOUTHERN GUILT

As previously noted, public display of the Confederate Battle Flag is controversial throughout the country, and much of the literature reduces the argument into two divided camps. The first is that the Confederate Battle Flag represents hate and racism as epitomized by white supremacists such as the Ku Klux Klan, Nazis, and Aryan Brotherhood (Strother, Piston, and Ogorzalek 2017). The second is that the Flag is an ethnic symbol representing Southern heritage (Wright and Esses 2017). However, the heritage argument, as it is presented by many researchers, reflects only the cognitive and affective attachment that Retentionists have for the Flag (Wright and Esses 2017, 226). When studying the Confederate Battle Flag as a cultural object for Retentionists in the Lexington-Rockbridge area, a more *religious* dynamic is revealed where the Flag is a sacred *totem* using the Durkheimian trope. Within this perspective, Confederate Battle Flag banning represents a threat to the Retentionist civil church of Cherished Southern identity and others who hold the Flag dear. Durkheim defines a *religion*: "A religion is a unified system of beliefs and practices relative to sacred things, that is to say things set apart and forbidden—beliefs and practices which unite into one single moral community called a Church, all those who adhere to them" (Durkheim 1912, 44).

When considering social interaction, "it is the social process in group life that creates and upholds the rules, not the rules that create and uphold group life" (Blumer 1969, 19). In the construction of shared status through the recognition of "bonds, interests and boundaries," individuals collectively segment their social world as a way to make sense of it (Polletta and Jasper 2001, 285, 298). French historian, Marc Bloch provided that memory, whether by cluster or individually, "does not preserve the past precisely; it is constantly reconstructing and reformulating in the light of the present" (Bloch 2011, 152). For Southerners, the reconstructed memory of Cherished Southern identity is constructed from *nostalgic fabric* and is woven and rewoven to construct sensible memories. Metaphorically, nostalgic fabric is used to create comfortable accoutrements, such as a blanket of reflection, that many in the community cling to when embracing their challenged identity. The Confederate Battle Flag and other Southern symbols are manifestations of nostalgic fabric.

What is the nostalgic fabric of Cherished Southern identity made from? Wilson's study is an excellent reference and superb starting point for my research. He conveniently locates Lexington-Rockbridge as a Confederate "shrine" and a place of "melancholy focus for the Lost Cause" with Valentine's white marble statue of Lee recumbent on a sarcophagus and Jackson's statue erected in 1891 (Wilson 1980, 156, 157). However, the preponderance of Wilson's study is the influence of conventional religion and religious leaders on the Lost Cause mentality to form a civil religion up until WWI. This provides me with a research gap to investigate the current civil religion of Cherished Southern identity for Retentionists in the Lexington-Rockbridge area. My investigation illustrates that the heritage argument, presented in earlier studies, is insufficient to adequately describe sentiments of Cherished Southern identity and support for the Confederate Battle Flag. The term *heritage* is a good starting point to view the zeal and dogma of Retentionists, but it is an inadequate term when trying to reveal the constituent threads of nostalgic fabric. I advance the *hearth and home* argument by individualizing the importance of specifics and context concerning the "geography in the life space of individuals" and the "affective admiration for place an entity, and the geography of space and history" (Wright and Esses 2017). The sacred quality of the nostalgic fabric for Retentionists is woven from threads of very personalized sentiments of hearth and home. As such, the threads of hearth and home are constructed from core fibers of three deeply held virtues: (1) kith and kin, (2) ancestral land, and (3) conservation of honor. Hearth and home provides greater cultural clarity, context, and positional understanding of the religious-like passion that is involved for Retentionists in substantiating their Cherished Southern identity.

For Steele *white guilt* is a "vacuum of moral authority" and is "the same as black power" because the white race is associated with racism (Steele 2006, 24). McDermott provides that white guilt is a form of embarrassment for progressive whites "by the presumed racist content of their white identities" (McDermott 2020, 75). I build upon the concept of white guilt and develop the term *Southern guilt*. Southern guilt can be a tool for Reformers to self-distance from "racist content" or an implement of othering to label Retentionists as a form of practical symbolic interactionism. Thus, it is a remedy used to gather moral authority for Reformers, or as means to deny any such moral authority to Retentionists. Although Reed does not specifically refer to Southern guilt, he does refer to "Lapsed Southerners" as those Southerners who see "Southernness as something one can accept or reject" or modify (Reed 2008, 21). Here he illustrates examples of people who distance or divest themselves of Southernness based on ideological or cultural differences, American patriotism (in opposition to Southern or Confederate patriotism), regional affiliation, or military service that provided a sense of unification beyond the South.

Southern guilt, as a self-distancing tool, can be viewed as a derivative of the "looking-glass self" (Cooley 2018). The "imagined" appearance, judgment, and consequential "self-feeling" vary by cluster and in degree. White Reformers *imagine* their appearance as Southerners to be judged by others as potential racists. Their consequential self-feeling is mortification, and they distance themselves or *reconstruct* away from Southern identification. This reconstruction is an effort to *disassociate* from the South's racist history and, in this renunciation, garner moral authority. Some white Forbearers, liberal and conservative, embrace degrees of Southern guilt as they adjust their *self-feeling* based on the imagined judgment of others. As a result, they generally reconstruct their Cherished Southern identity without complete disassociation. Many engage in various forms of "letting go of the past" as a courtesy to others. As with the other clusters, Retentionists imagine their appearance to others and the corresponding judgment of others. However, they do not adjust their self-feeling in consideration of racist potential, but rather insist on retaining their sense of tradition. Retentionists refuse to disassociate from the Confederate Battle Flag and cling fiercely to it while claiming moral authority through hearth and home sentiments.

Black and white community members that are Reformers self-identify as progressive and liberal. Southern guilt ideology coalesces most powerfully in this cluster not only as a distancing mechanism for white Reformers but also as an offensive tool of labeling used by all Reformers. This strategic tool of othering is used by Reformers to label Retentionists as racist based on the cluster logic, "If you display the Confederate Battle Flag, you are a racist!" Retentionists resent that Reformers use Southern guilt as an implement of racist othering and they feel that their civil religion of Cherished Southern identity is threatened by anti-Flag sentiments. They further feel that they are denied any social moral authority by Reformers for Retentionist failure to renounce the Flag and other Confederate symbols. Retentionists counter as a cluster, "Others who display the Confederate Battle Flag may be racists, however, we are not!" White Southern Forbearers embrace varying degrees of Southern guilt as a distancing tool of courtesy so as not to offend. They do not use it as an offensive tool of labeling. As a cluster Forbearers feel, "If you display the Confederate Battle Flag, you are not necessarily a racist. You might be. I need more evidence and I'll give you a chance to prove yourself either way."

The aforementioned studies do much to further the research on the significance of the Confederate Battle Flag. However, as with all research there are limitations and research gaps available for forward advancement. Wright and Esses explicitly state while some empirical work has been conducted on Confederate Battle Flag support, "it is minimal and that which has been done suffers from methodological flaws and fails to account for alternative theoretical perspectives" (Wright and Esses 2017, 227). As part of the self-identified limitations of the their study, Wright and Esses (2017, 237) ask two questions: (1) Why do some black people choose to support the Confederate Battle Flag? and (2) What is the qualitative content of Southern pride among white and black community members respectively? This provides several research gaps ripe for a micro-view ethnographic study where the Confederate Battle Flag holds powerful symbolic significance for community members both black and white.

A PURPOSIVE FOCUS ON RETENTIONISTS

Members of the Sons of Confederate Veterans, United Daughters of the Confederacy, and ardent supporters of the Confederate Battle Flag were actively targeted for selection for interview and de-selected from the white community member population. They were immediately placed in their own respondent category based on their presumed (and later confirmed) support of the Confederate Battle Flag and Southern symbols. As presented earlier, members of the Sons of Confederate Veterans and so forth make up the cluster of Retentionists. Although I was able to gather data from twenty-six Retentionists, this can give the false implication that they are a significant portion of the community. They are not. Review of rosters and discussions of membership, along with Confederate Battle Flag display and head counts of attendees at Retentionist functions, indicate that membership within the county is very small and estimated at less than 1 percent of the overall county population. However, the powerful sentiments that they epitomize for contentious Southern symbols is critical for analysis, and it is important to get adequate representation to understand the greater social tension within the Lexington-Rockbridge community. It is imperative for me to present the investigative method for which I gathered data on Retentionists for methodological context. The original intention of my research was to study, understand, and present the religious-like sentiments of Retentionists, like the members of the Sons of Confederate Veterans and United Daughters of the Confederacy, and why they hold such passionate commitments to contentious symbols such as the Confederate Battle Flag. However, as with many studies, strategic research objectives modify once in the field. I began to see additional interesting social interplays between all the clusters that offered opportunities to present findings of larger and more generalizable sociological value.

As part of my objective research strategy, it is essential for me to focus on the least understood, and often villainized, perspective of Retentionists so as to objectively present all collective facets of this community. The "*natu-ralistic* investigation," and the "exploration and inspection" of this cluster "constitutes the necessary procedure in direct examination" of their social world (Blumer 1969):

> Symbolic interactionism is a down-to-earth approach to the scientific study of human group life and human contact. . . . If it wishes to study religious cult behavior, it will go to actual religious cults and observe them carefully as they carry on their lives.
>
> If the scholar wishes to understand the action of the people, it is necessary for him to see their objects as they see them. Failure to see their objects as they see them, or substitution of his meanings of the objects for their meanings, is the gravest kind of error that the social scientist can commit. (Blumer 1969, 46–47, 51)

As such, I spent over 200 hours, observing, interviewing, and interacting with a variety of Retentionists.[4]

The method I chose is not necessarily a popular approach within the sociological academy where the preference is to generally study the *oppressed* as opposed to the presumed *oppressors*. There is a risk to the researcher of being "stigmatized" for investigating those deemed "politically marginal . . . loathsome" or "unloved" (Blee 2018, 28, 34, preface). However, *sociological villains* must be objectively studied along with the *sociological victims* in any "performance." In order to fully appreciate the Goffmanian "performances," we must study each "performer . . . as he can be sincerely convinced that the impressions of reality which he stages is the real reality" (Goffman 1959, 17). Only by studying all the performers in the performance can the "sociologist or socially disgruntled . . . have any doubt about the *realness* of what is presented" (Goffman 1959, 17). Studying and presenting Retentionist perspectives in direct juxtaposition with Reformers places me at great risk of being *stigmatized* by my fellow sociologists as being a Retentionist sympathizer. However, I positioned Reformers and Retentionists this way because that is how the majority of respondents see these clusters in their community. Although my analytic method appears unique, I am not alone in recognizing the similarities of the polarized Left and Right in this milieu. In her work concerning organized white supremacy, Blee recognized the "seductiveness of self-righteousness and violence in politics" and the "foolhardy acts of the far Left" (Blee 2018, 14). In an interview with David Duke, she illustrates the similarities shared between Left and Right leadership. "I was struck by how similar his cautious, measured talk was in form, although certainly not in content, to the wary, yet self-aggrandizing tone I had heard in leftist groups when [male] leaders confronted unsympathetic outsiders" (Blee 2018, 16).

Retentionists actively exclude and denounce traditional white supremacist groups in meetings, on social media, and at public events. All Retentionists

I interviewed were white, but the Sons of Confederate Veterans and United Daughters of the Confederacy claim they are not racially exclusive by policy. Retentionists state that they do not espouse a white supremacy ideology and they believe that they actively disassociate from these conventional hate groups. No respondents identified as being part of the Aryan Brotherhood, Nazis, or the Ku Klux Klan. Most respondents felt that few if any of these conventional white supremacist groups could be found in Rockbridge County, but that membership could be found in the more rural counties south and west. Jesse advised that the Klan is "not that strong" in Rockbridge County. "But go to Franklin County, hmm . . . Danville. . . . They don't like anybody." However, Klan literature was anonymously distributed in the spring of 2016 which "prompted a group of professors and faith leaders to form an advocacy group, the Community Anti-Racism Education Initiative" (Dickerson 2017). Some feel that white supremacist influences still exist but have gone *underground*. Jesse provided, "They don't call themselves the Klan anymore. They call themselves militias. . . . But you not going to get them to admit it." That does not mean that Retentionists do not harbor racist sentiments, rather they did not indicate any association and most vocally disassociated from these extremist groups. Ideologically, VA-Flaggers[5] fall into the cluster of Retentionists. However, most Retentionists consider the VA-Flaggers as more radical and ruder in their presentation and demands concerning the Confederate Battle Flag. Some community members indicated that VA-Flaggers were not a local group. No respondents identified as VA-Flaggers.

Information was gathered from a total of 26 Retentionists out of 107 total community respondents. Of the interviews conducted nine were formal, nine were informal, and I engaged with eight speakers during the Lee-Jackson Weekend. Retentionists are predominately Republican, with a few members that were Independent or Libertarian. Retentionists generally identified with the county, Buena Vista, or held a dual identity between the county and Lexington. The Sons of Confederate Veterans and United Daughters of the Confederacy share a sibling like relationship, but they are not identical organizations that are merely separated by gender. Both share a focus of honoring Civil War veterans, but the United Daughters of the Confederacy are generally more understated and do not share the same vigorous interest in reenacting. My first contact with a Sons of Confederate Veterans member was with Larry (SCV: Judge Advocate General), a retired Virginia State Trooper, in November 2019. After the interview Larry invited me to the 2019 Sons of Confederate Veterans (SCV, Stonewall Camp, #1296) Christmas party. At the gathering I had the opportunity to interact with other Retentionists belonging to the Sons of Confederate Veterans. This included Jack (Commander), Cole

(First Lieutenant Commander), and Tucker (Second Lieutenant Commander/ Media Spokesman).

From this social gathering I was then invited to attend monthly Sons of Confederate Veterans meetings and the functions of Lee-Jackson Weekend. A review of the Stonewall Brigade Sons of Confederate Veterans member roster indicated approximately thirty-six members with six associate members in the Lexington-Rockbridge area. I attended several meetings which were open to the public. I observed an average of eight to fifteen attendees per meeting. I also spoke with Jesse, a former member of the Stonewall Brigade and avid supporter of the Sons of Confederate Veterans in general. Lexington also has a local chapter of the United Daughters of the Confederacy (Chapter #2568). I spoke with four members or former members of the local United Daughters of the Confederacy: Liz (former President), Lauren (Current President), Rita, and Diane. Roster membership information received indicated about forty active and inactive members within the community.

When studying Southern symbols and their sacred relevance as "collective representations" for Retentionists, it is critical to observe "cultural interaction" while they were engaged in events as part of "group setting" (Eliasoph and Lichterman 2003, 737). The *holy days* of Lee-Jackson Weekend on 17–18 January 2020 are significant events. Two major functions were sponsored over that weekend. The first was the Lee-Jackson Symposium on Friday, 17 January, at the Lexington Hampton Inn Col Alto. There were approximately seventy-seven people in attendance at the Lee-Jackson Symposium. Almost all were white males (45) and white female (30) with two people of color. The symposium provided for the following speakers and presentations:

1. Ethan—*Stonewall Jackson's Military Family: The Best Staff in the A.N.V.*
2. Logan—*The Friendship of Lee and Jackson*
3. Owen—*The Second Fall of Richmond*
4. Henry—*What the Newspapers Said: Black Confederates "Myth" Examined*

At the start of the symposium, Sons of Confederate Veterans (SCV) Jack and Tucker (SCV: Camp 1296) welcomed attendees. Rev. Frank (SCV: Camp 1296) provided opening invocation and closing benediction. There were several tables set up by presenters for book purchases and a Sons of Confederate Veterans table with literature and T-shirts. Literature included:

• *Sons of Confederate Veterans: Heritage and Honor*, Applications
• *Sons of Confederate Veterans Information Card*: Symbol preservation and Southern Heritage Organization

- *National Civil War Chaplains Museum* brochure
- Religious Christian Pamphlet, *How Can I Be Saved?*
- Memorabilia:
  - *Save Our Monuments: Save Our History and Honor*, decal
  - *My Heroes Wore Gray! Men That Answered the Call of Their States*, card

The second function held over Lee-Jackson Weekend was the Lee-Jackson Commemoration held at the Stonewall Jackson gravesite on Saturday, 18 January. The Commemoration ceremony began around 10:00 a.m. There were approximately 300 people in attendance, and approximately one-third of the attendees were in period garb. Many forms of the Confederate Battle Flag were exhibited. I walked around and spoke informally with some of the attendees. The Sons of Confederate Veterans and United Daughters of the Confederacy sponsored the Commemoration and both groups spoke of their "heroes who wore grey" at the gravesite of Stonewall Jackson. The Sons of Confederate Veterans and United Daughters of the Confederacy appeared to collaborate actively and amicably. The Sons of Confederate Veterans were gathered in military style with period uniforms and weapons. The United Daughters of the Confederacy were subtly gathered and rather demure. Members of the VA-Flaggers may have been present, but they were hard to distinguish from Sons of Confederate Veterans and other observers. No overt white supremacist groups were noted in attendance although they could have been there in covert status.

INFORMATION GATHERED AND
EVIDENCE ANALYZED

My research utilized a combination of nonprobability sampling tactics to include cold call, snowball, quota, and purposive sampling techniques as part of a larger sampling strategy to approach arguable representativeness. The challenge with nonprobability sampling is that the sampling error is unknown, and thus the representativeness of the data is questionable. However, even "probability samples cannot guarantee representativeness" (Lavrakas 2008b, 2). Cold call sampling was accomplished by asking for respondent input without referral but based on building quick rapport in a store like Walmart and Lowes or neighborhood proximity. Snowball sampling was conducted as a form of referral sampling based on the local social networks. In a "limited geographic area such as a county, snowball sampling may be successful as a rare population frame-building technique" (Lavrakas 2008c, 1). Such chain-referral sampling has been proven to be especially useful when conducting research in marginalized environments (Cohen and Arieli 2011, 426). Quota over-sampling was utilized when seeking additional black respondents and gathering added perspectives to confirm or deny previously gathered data so as to make productive conclusions after analysis. Purposive sampling was used as a method to gather *deep data* on Retentionists. This required a greater understanding through embeddedness "of the population to select in a non-random manner a sample of elements that represents a cross-section of the population" (Lavrakas 2008a, 3).

My sampling strategy also embraced Cohen and Arieli's *Snowball Sampling Method* in conflict environments (Cohen and Arieli 2011) and Adedeji's "5-wave-approach" (Adedeji 2019, 1, 5) in an attempt to approach greater non-statistical representative plausibility and approximate randomization. Nonprobability methods have validity limitations for not being statistically random or necessarily representative. However, "it is possible to increase representativity by sufficient planning of the sampling process and goals, initiating parallel snowball networks and using quota sampling" (Cohen and Arieli 2011, 428). These scholars provide that in addition to utilizing a methodological planning strategy, it is paramount that the researcher does not create a challenging or unpleasant interview experience and that they "behave according to the social, religious, and cultural norms of the target population and adopt an empathetic approach towards the respondent and his/her milieu" (Cohen and Arieli 2011, 432). In his research of Sub-Saharan African migrants, Adedeji presents a 5-wave approach "as a method capable of easing access" and "producing a sample that reflects population demographics characteristics" (Adedeji 2019, 1, 11). To approximate random sampling the model utilizes 5-waves or stages of data collection: (1) community leaders, (2) community outreach, (3) chain-referral, (4) systemic multiplication, and (5) natural multiplication. I incorporated this wave-strategy into my research. Wave 1 was my initial interview approach with community leaders such as the mayor, former mayor, vice-mayor, and police officials. Wave 2 was simultaneously conducted with Wave 1 as I engaged in community outreach efforts through Habitat for Humanity, food pantry work at Church of God Church, Lexington Community Church volunteer work, and other community service. Wave 3 chain-referral snowballing took advantage of contacts made in Waves 1 and 2. Wave 4 systemic multiplication directed purposeful and quota techniques toward black community members and Retentionists so as to gain insights of numerical minorities. Wave 5 natural multiplication "involves observation without interference from principle researcher" (Adedeji 2019, 6). Lee-Jackson Day interactions, Sons of Confederate Veterans and United Daughters of the Confederacy functions, Martin Luther King Day parade, and observations of other social festivities and volunteer assignments allowed for reception of data in their respective *group settings*

(Eliasoph and Lichterman 2003, 737) with little or no researcher interference beyond that of mere presence.

Information from a total of 107 respondents was collected and are presented via three tabular perspectives to maximize clarity and analytic purchase. The first perspective is illustrated in Table 1.2. Here data is represented by demographics with a focus on how respondent information was received. For this study, a respondent is defined as any individual who provided pertinent, live input. All respondents had rooted interest in the Lexington-Rockbridge area and generally resided in the area for over twenty years. Community members predominately identified as being from the cities of Lexington and Buena Vista or from Rockbridge County. Some held hybrid or dual loyalties

Table 1.2: Data Description (Author created)

Respondents	*107 Total*
Type 1 (Formal)	87
Type 2 (Informal)	12
Type 3 (Speakers)	8
Highly Productive Observations	13 Total (100 hours+)
SCV/UDC Related	10
Other Formal Gatherings	3
Respondent Demographics	
Gender & Race Identification (ID)	
Male	74
Female	33
White ID	84 (60 Male; 24 Female)
Black ID	22 (13 Male; 9 Female)
Other (of Color) ID	1 (Male)
Age	
80 and Above	11 (2 Black; 9 White)
60–80	56 (13 Black; 43 White)
40–60	27 (3 Black; 24 White)
Under 40	13 (4 Black; 9 White)
Community Ties	
City of Lexington	33 (10 Black; 23 White)
County of Rockbridge	38 (8 Black; 30 White)
City of Buena Vista	6 (2 Black; 4 White)
Hybrid (County-City)	18 (3 Black; 15 White)
Outside	12 (White)
SCV, UDC & Supporters	26 Total
SCV Total (Formal/Informal)	9 (4/5)
UDC (Formal)	4
SCV & UDC Members & Speakers	8
Ardent Supporters (Formal/Informal)	5 (1/4)

(SCV: Sons of Confederate Veterans)

(UDC: United Daughters of the Confederacy)

between Lexington and the County. Respondents that classified as *outside* are those that have an affinity to Lexington (i.e., Sons of Confederate Veterans speakers) but do not reside here. Lastly this table illustrates data collected specifically from the Sons of Confederate Veterans, United Daughters of the Confederacy, and Supporters. The data lack significant representation from minorities other than black because they reside in limited numbers in this community. This did not inhibit me from studying the data gathered and drawing empirical conclusion for the groups that were represented. Type 1, Formal Interview respondents are those that actively engaged with me via formal questioning. Type 2, Informal Interview respondents are those that actively engaged with me via informal questioning normally as part of a participant observer setting. Type 3, Speakers are those that presented or spoke at public functions such as Lee-Jackson Weekend and that I personally interacted with after the presentation. I attended many community functions as part of this study. Of these, thirteen are classified as highly productive observations in that they provided particularly useful data.

As stated, the population in Rockbridge County is approximately 23,000 and in the city of Lexington city, approximately 7,200. The black community make up only 3.4 percent of the population in Rockbridge County and only 6.4 percent in the city of Lexington. However, black respondents make up 21 percent of this study. I increased the quota sample for black voices to ensure better representation as some of the findings were unexpected and I wanted more data to corroborate earlier findings. A weakness of this study may be that the data illustrate the vast majority of responses from those between the ages of thirty-five to eighty. As such the arguable representativeness is perhaps limited only to that age group as the young may have different viewpoints. There is also a preponderance of male input for my study. However, the data represent the views of almost a third of the respondents being female, and responses did not appear to be gendered. The majority of subjects are white with most claiming a Scotch-Irish, English, or German heritage. A few respondents identify from other backgrounds such as Italian, Nordic, Native American, and South Asian. Most white respondents were interviewed before the George Floyd killing on 25 May 2020, but half the black respondents were interviewed after. Interestingly, no noticeable change in reporting trends was observed as it related to individual sentiments of Southern symbols. That does not mean there were no indications of heightened racial tensions within the community but rather it did not appear to reflect directly on responses about Southern symbols at that time.

Evidence is provided, and it firmly demonstrates the attitudes of the cohort studied, and that the sampling is arguably, imperfectly representative, and somewhat randomized for the local population. My study does not make the claim that it is absolute or definitive in its findings as unequivocally representative. However, it very well may be. I strongly suggest, at the very least, that there is evidence enough to consider a pause from the vitriol of conventional narratives presented by the media and many in the sociological academy, and ponder for just a moment, other feasible perspectives and potentials when analyzing contentious Southern symbols.

Table 1.3 illustrates the second data perspective. Data were initially collected utilizing three mutually exclusive categories of interview respondents as part of my organizational and analytical strategy: (1) non-displaying white,[6] (2) black,[7] and (3) members of the Sons of Confederate Veterans, United Daughters of the Confederacy, and ardent supporters of the Confederate Battle Flag. Non-displaying white respondents were selected based on willingness to participate as were black respondents. Black community members were quota sampled to ensure adequate ethnographic representation. Sons of Confederate Veterans, United Daughters of the Confederacy, and ardent supporters of the Flag were purposively selected for interview to glean their unique perspective. It is important to recognize that the numbers of respondents in each category are not representative samples of actual category size in the community population. However, the sentiments gathered are presented as being representative for each respondent category.

Respondents generally provided replies via prompts, or they made unsolicited statements of interest concerning Southern identity and Southern symbols. Prompts were provided in context to the situation and generally open-ended such as, "Why is Lee-Jackson Day important to you?" Follow-up questions were asked, "How do you feel about . . . ?" These questions sought sentiments concerning: (1) political affiliation, (2) Southern identity, (3) opposition to the 2011 ban of Confederate Battle Flag, (4) Confederate monument removal or modification, (5) removal of the name Lee from local institutions, (5) offensiveness of the song "Dixie," and (6) sentiments toward the Confederate Battle Flag. Respondent information was generally gleaned by allowing them to freely speak with prompting used only if a topic was not naturally addressed in conversation. It should be noted that not all respondents provided responses to all questions. Greater clarification on sample size for a particular topic is provided in the narrative. Table 1.3 illustrates percentages of support by respondent category. The numbers in parenthesis indicates the percentage of community members who held mixed, conflicted, or ambivalent feelings on the topic.

The first row of Table 1.3 is bound by a bold outline and exemplifies the rigid convictions and homogeneous responses of the respondent category Sons of Confederate Veterans, United Daughters of the Confederacy, and ardent supporters. They are predominately Republican (and Trump supporters) and identify as Southerners. To a person, they do not support the removal

Table 1.3: Respondent Category Sentiments and Characteristics (*n-total* = 107) (Author created)

Category	Party (D) Democratic (R) Republican (I) Independent	Southern ID	Remove-Modify Monuments	Remove Lee Name	"Dixie" Offensive Song	Oppose 2011 Ban of CBF	CBF represents only Racism	CBF can represent Hearth and Home
SCV, UDC & Support (n=26)	(R) Vast majority	96%	0%	0%	0%	100%	0%	100% Retentionists
Non-displaying White (n=59)	(D) 42% (R) 40% (I)18%	62%	36% (*24%)	4%	65% (*12%)	38% (*26%)	19%	81%
Black (n=22)	(D) 50% (I) 50%	57%	25%	6%	48% (*52%)	41% (*32%)	23%	77%
							Reformers	Forbearers

* Indicates additional % of cluster that had mixed or ambivalent responses)

(CBF: Confederate Battle Flag)

(SCV: Sons of Confederate Veterans)

(UDC: Daughters of the Confederacy)

of monuments, the Lee name, or the Confederate Battle Flag. They do not view the Flag as a racist symbol and claim that it only means hearth and home to them. All respondents agreed that when the Klan, Nazis, or Aryan Brotherhood flaunt the Confederate Battle Flag it is an unacceptable symbol of intimidation and hate.

Non-displaying white and black respondent categories in rows 2 and 3 illustrate more heterogenous responses. Non-displaying white respondents are evenly split between Democrat and Republican with less than a quarter identifying as Independent. Additional evidence collected but not reflected in Table 1.3 indicates that non-displaying white identity by community was about evenly distributed in thirds, with twenty out of fifty-nine identifying with the city of Lexington, twenty-two out of fifty-nine identifying with the county or Buena Vista, and seventeen out of fifty-nine indicating dual loyalties. Respondents that identify solely with Lexington are primarily Democrat (10) with an even split of Republicans (5) and Independents (5). Most that solely identify with the county or Buena Vista are Republican (9), while seven are Democrat, three are Independent, and three are ambivalent or have no party affiliation. Of those that hold dual loyalty to the county and Lexington, eight are Republican, six are Democrat, two are Independent, and one has no affiliation. Regardless of party affiliation, only six out of fifty-seven of non-displaying whites are adamant supporters of former President Trump. Most non-displaying whites (34/57) do not support him at all, and about a third (17/57) hold mixed or conflicted feelings. Black respondents are either Democrat (9/19) or Independent (9/19) with one person declining any affiliation. There are no black Republicans. Information gathered but not illustrated in the chart indicates that most black community members (14/19) do not like former President Trump while a few (5/19) had mixed sentiments. Black community members reside throughout the Lexington-Rockbridge area, to include the incorporated city limits of Lexington and Buena Vista, towns, and the rural settings of the county. Similar to non-displaying whites, community identity for black community members was fairly even in thirds with eight out of twenty-two with the city of Lexington, seven out of twenty-two with the county or Buena Vista, and seven out of twenty-two with dual loyalties to the county and Lexington.

Table 1.3 reflects a striking similarity in sentiments when comparing black and non-displaying white community members concerning Southern symbols and identity. The majority of non-displaying white people and black people identify as a Southerner. Support for the removal of Confederate monuments and the offensiveness of the song "Dixie" is at a greater percentage for non-displaying white than black community members. However, some non-displaying whites hold a positive nostalgic attachment for the song with a few having mixed or ambivalent feelings. No black community members hold overly positive sentiments to the song "Dixie," but half hold mixed or ambivalent views. Attitudes concerning the Confederate Battle Flag are also relatively even between non-displaying whites and black community members. Feelings on the 2011 ban of the Flag by the Lexington City Council provided that most of the non-displaying white and black community members are opposed or ambivalent to the ban. This is not necessarily a signal of support for the Confederate Battle Flag but rather that of support for freedom of expression for one or two days, and a concern that the ban unnecessarily disturbed the status quo perhaps creating greater community strife. Perceptions concerning the symbolism of the Confederate Battle Flag are remarkably consistent between non-displaying white and black community members. The numerical minority of non-displaying white and black community members find the Flag categorically representative of racism and white supremacy. The majority indicate that the Confederate Battle Flag can represent racism and white supremacy, but it can also represent sentiments of hearth and home for themselves or for others in the community. For many respondents, the Flag can be a "red flag[8]" or signal of suspicion, but not necessarily unequivocal evidence of hate or supremacy. For these respondents, context is critical, and more evidence is required before making any firm assessments. Most remarkably, regardless of race within this community, overwhelming support for the retention of the Lee name at institutions such as Lee Chapel and Washington & Lee was indicated. The overwhelming tolerance to the Lee name provides us with insights and clues to what the context of hearth and home, as it is juxtaposed with racism, means in this community. Table 1.3 demonstrates that after accounting for sentiments of the Sons of Confederate Veterans and so forth, community sentiments on Southern symbols are not necessarily racially divided. This finding is contrary to previous research.

Through the use of shading, Table 1.3 reveals the transition from *How data was collected by respondent category* to *How data is analyzed by respondent cluster*. Three main clusters appear based on their unified sentiments towards the Confederate Battle Flag. Columns 8 *(CBF represents only Racism: light shading)* and 9 (CBF can represent Hearth & Home: darker shading), and row 1 (SCV, UDC & Support: bold outline) designate cultural demarcations toward the burgeoning analytic groups or *clusters* using sentiments toward the Confederate Battle Flag as a defining pivot point. Column 8 displays percentages of non-displaying white and black community members that take offense to the Confederate Battle Flag and that for them it only symbolizes hate, racism, or white supremacy. These non-displaying white and black community members make up the cluster of *Reformers*. They recognize no credible contextual argument that the Flag could represent a sentiment of hearth and home. Row 1 depicts the views of the Sons of Confederate Veterans, United Daughters of the Confederacy, and ardent supporters as belonging to the cluster of *Retentionists*. They use and view the Confederate Battle Flag solely as a symbol of hearth and home. Retentionists recognize that the Flag can represent hate, racism, or white supremacy, but they consistently disavow such groups and emphatically state that it does not mean such to them when they display it. They vociferously denounce white supremacy and actively distance from those groups. However, they do not care that the Confederate Battle Flag, as a symbol, is potentially offensive to others. Reformers and Retentionists epitomize a numerical minority of the community and are polar opposites in their perceptions of the Confederate Battle Flag and other contentious symbols. Lastly, column 9 represents the percentages of non-displaying white and black community members that do not categorically see the Flag as a symbol of hate, racism, or white supremacy and recognize the potential for it to represent sentiments of hearth and home for themselves or for others. Their sentiments lie between those of Retentionists and Reformers and make up the cluster of *Forbearers*.

The final analytic perspective is presented in Table 1.4. Analytic purchase is advanced by organizing the data by collective sentiment and providing a platform for discussion in the substantive chapters to follow. Within the cluster, data is subdivided by racial self-identity and re-analyzed to determine if there is a significant racial divide within the cluster concerning symbols of the South. Table 1.4 illustrates that when viewed as a cluster Reformers exhibit the following characteristics: (1) black and white community members (2) Democrats, (3) mixed in their identity as Southerners, (4) not opposed to the 2011 ban of the Confederate Battle Flag, (5) most likely to support monument removal when compared to the other clusters, (6) not supportive of removing the name Lee from institutions, and (7) most likely to find the song "Dixie" offensive. As presented earlier, Retentionists have the following characteristics: (1) white community members, (2) Republicans, (3) strong Southern identity, (4) oppose the 2011 Confederate Battle Flag ban, (5) oppose removal of monuments, (6) oppose the removal of the Lee name, and (7) do not find the song "Dixie" offensive.

The cluster of Forbearers demonstrate the following characteristics: (1) white and black community members, (2) mixed political affiliation, (3) majority hold Southern identity, (4) evenly split on the 2011 Confederate Battle Flag ban, (5) do not support the removal of monuments, (6) do not support the removal of Lee name, and (7) have mixed sentiments on the offensive nature of the song "Dixie." Forbearers are a diverse group racially and socio-economically and appear to have varied perspectives on some issues. A prime cohesive aspect of Forbearers is their sensitivity and broad-minded ability to recognize both the hearth and home significance and the offensive nature of the Confederate Battle Flag to others. Although they would not

Table 1.4: Cluster Sentiments and Characteristics (*n-total* = 107) (Author created)

Cluster		Party (D) Democratic (R) Republican (I) Independent	ID as Southerner	Oppose 2011 Ban of CBF	Remove-Modify Monuments	Remove Lee Name	"Dixie" Offensive Song
Reformers (n= 16)	White (n=11)	(D) 100%	45%	0% *(27%)	36% *(27%)	9%	91%
	Black **(n=5)	(D) 80% No Party 20%	20%	0%	80%	33% **(n=3)	100%
	Collectively	(D) 94%	38%	0%	50%	13%	94%
Retentionists (n=26)	Collectively (White)	(R) Vast majority	96%	100%	0%	0%	0%
Forbearers (n=65)	White (n=48)	(D) 27% (R) 50% (I) 23%	65%	47% *(32%)	6% (*23%)	0%	62% *(13%)
	Black (n=17)	(D) 36% (I) 64%	65%	53% *(41%)	6%	0%	31% *(69%)
	Collectively	(D) 29% (R) 37% (I) 34%	65%	49%	6%	0%	53%

(* Indicates additional % of cluster that had mixed or ambivalent responses)

(** Indicates sample size is too small to be of analytic value)

(CBF: Confederate Battle Flag)

publicly display the Confederate Battle Flag because of its noxious potential, they respect the rights of others to express themselves and their Cherished Southern identity. None of the Forbearers indicated a lack of understanding of the generalized social implications of these contentious symbols for the community. Their coherence as a cluster is demonstrated in their *collective tolerance* of the Confederate Battle Flag as having the potential to represent hearth and home and not necessarily demonstrative as a definitive symbol of white supremacy or racism. The latitudinarian posture of this cluster to recognize varied potential should not be mistaken as personal acceptance or that the symbol was inconsequential. For many Forbearers, the Confederate Battle Flag could provide clues or signals of potential "redneck" or racist attitude, but more individual evidence would be necessary to reach such a conclusion. Forbearers distinguish themselves from Reformers, even though many demonstrate and identify as progressive in their thinking, because they find Reformers rigid in their anti-racist zeal. This middle-path tolerance of the Flag is characteristic of only Forbearers, as Reformers actively despise it, and Retentionists actively cherish it. Forbearers acknowledge these polarized positions as potentials but they generally find the Flag less consequential in personal assessment of a fellow community member when they conduct daily business via personal interactions.

Using Table 1.4 we can see that as clusters, Reformers are in direct opposition to Retentionists. Forbearers are the majority (65/81) of the non-displaying respondents, both black and white. This suggests that the sentiments of Forbearers potentially reflect the feelings of the majority of community members who balance the symbolic potential of the Confederate Battle Flag to represent racism or hearth and home via context and tolerance.

When analyzing the subdivisions of the cluster Reformers, the very low sample size for black Reformers ($n=5$) makes the comparison and any apparent differences highly tenuous. Southern identity is greater for white than black Reformers. Removal or modification of Confederate monuments was higher for black than white Reformers. However, black Reformers indicate no mixed emotions where almost a third of white Reformers held mixed emotions providing for almost two-thirds who were not adamantly opposed to the removal. The question of the removal of the Lee name when considering racial divide is invalid based on the small sample size ($n=3$). The offensive nature of the song "Dixie" was reasonably consistent between black and white Reformers. What can be suggested is that any significant racial divide within the cluster of Reformers cannot be determined. However, Forbearers have a greater sample size collectively and within the subdivisions that allows us to draw reasonable conclusions. In all categories except political affiliation and the song "Dixie," black and white Forbearers share similar sentiments regarding Southern symbols. Politically, black Forbearers were mostly Independent

(9/14) with some Democrats (5/14). White Forbearers were half Republican and the rest split between Democrats and Independent. About half the white (22/47) and black (9/17) community members opposed the 2011 Confederate Battle Flag ban. The song "Dixie" was found to be offensive by more white (24/39) than black (5/16) Forbearers. However, no black Forbearers liked the song "Dixie" but were rather ambivalent (11/16). Only five out of thirty-nine of white Forbearers were ambivalent with ten out of thirty-nine liking the song. Those issues aside, black and white Forbearers can be seen to share similar percentages of sentiments for issues such as Southern identity, the 2011 ban, removal of Confederate monuments, and removal of the Lee name. Interestingly, almost a quarter of white Forbearers held mixed sentiments concerning monuments, but no such mixed sentiments were held by black Forbearers with an overwhelming majority who did not want to see them removed or modified. Along with this interesting finding, black Forbearers have within their ranks some black community members that self-identify or identify family members as *black rednecks*.

From this analytic purchase, we begin to see several interesting developments. The data gleaned from the responses of the black community suggest that the black community is not necessarily a homogeneous group in their sentiments toward confrontational Southern symbols. From these respondents, who plausibly reflect the sentiments of older black residents (over the age of thirty) of Lexington-Rockbridge area, there is no obvious racial divide concerning contentious symbols of the South. As such, the data can be further analyzed by clusters of *like-mindedness* rather than by race. A clear political divide can be ascribed to the polarized clusters of Reformers and Retentionists. However, the significant number of Republicans (24/65) that make up the cluster of Forbearers suggests that more than politics, the *progressive* nature of Democrats to seek change and the conservative nature of Republicans to maintain *status quo* is epitomized in the clusters of Reformers and Retentionists creating heightened polarization between clusters and a mutual intolerance of opposing views. Forbearers eschew both polarization and intolerance as a cluster and demonstrate such in their daily social interactions.

NOTES

1. Benjamin has three standards for Whitopia: (1) whiter than the nation, its respective region, and its state, (2) At least a 6 percent population growth since 2000, and (3) the majority of that growth is from white immigrants. Arguably the Lexington-Rockbridge area might meet these standards depending on interpretation.

However, with the universities of W&L and VMI, greater heterogeneity of thought is found here than in his areas of study.

2. According to the *Roanoke Times* (3 August 2014), the last man hanged in Lexington was William Lee Wilcher who reportedly was a mean drunk. After Sunday dinner he knocked on the door of a friend and shot him in cold blood when he refused to go hunting. Interestingly, in 2014 there was a reenactment of the event, with descendants, emphasizing the sentiments and learning points of alcohol restraint, contrition, and forgiveness.

3. Johnson is a billionaire businessman and philanthropist. He is the vice chairman of Franklin Resources. a global investment management firm also called Franklin Templeton Investments.

4. NOTE: I take it as my duty as a social scientist and my moral obligation as the community "stranger," to represent Durkheimian perspectives and realities of all clusters with "equal enthusiasm." A good defense attorney defends his client regardless of any personal sentiments. This book is neither an exercise in judgmental assessments nor an effort in the labeling of individuals or groups as racists or exonerating them as such. It bears repeating that this book is about the perspectives of various community members and how they feel about each other and how they socially interact on a daily basis.

5. According to the site, https://vaflaggers.blogspot.com/2020/10/, VA-Flaggers were organized 5 September 2011 and appear to be headquartered out of Sandston, Virginia, which is near Richmond. They provide the following self-description: "We are citizens of the Commonwealth that stand against those who would desecrate our Confederate monuments and memorials. . . . Our weapon is the Confederate Battle Flag. Our enemies are those who worship ignorance, historical revisionism and political correctness."

6. Non-displaying Whites is a categorical name to differentiate from the Sons of Confederate Veterans, United Daughters of the Confederacy, and other ardent displayers of the Confederate Battle Flag.

7. Black community members are those who self-identified as black.

8. Pun intended.

Chapter 2

Reformers

Liberal Crusaders and Anti-Racists

As provided in the preceding chapter, respondents for this study ultimately fell into three clusters: Reformers, Retentionists, and Forbearers. Reformers categorically view the Confederate Battle Flag and other provocative Southern symbols as representative of hate, racism, or white supremacy. The cluster of Reformers is part of the sample of eighty-one respondents from the non-displaying White[1] (59) and Black[2] (22) community members that were interviewed. Reformers are diametrically opposed to Retentionists. The majority of the respondents whose sentiments lie in between these extremes, the Forbearers, feel that both clusters engage in a mutually antagonistic intolerance of each other. There were twenty-six Retentionists purposively selected as respondents making the total number for this study 107. Retentionists belong to the Sons of Confederate Veterans or United Daughters of the Confederacy or were firm supporters and hold a sacred reverence for the Confederate Battle Flag and other Southern symbols. The Southern Poverty Law Center (SPLC) categorizes the Flag as one of several "dehumanizing symbols of pain and oppression . . . of white supremacy" (SPLC 2021b). Reformers embrace this sentiment as the sole symbolic representation for the Confederate Battle Flag.

Reformers are made up of eleven (out of fifty-nine) non-displaying white respondents and five (out of twenty-two) black respondents. Previous analysis of the data did not produce evidence of any racial divide in sentiments toward contentious Southern symbols, so the cluster of Reformers is racially mixed. Thus, Reformers make up sixteen (out of eighty-one) of the non-displaying white and black respondents. The vast majority of Reformers are Democrats with no Republicans, and all held a fervent dislike for former President Trump. They consider themselves well-intentioned, liberal crusaders and anti-racists who zealously seek to eradicate inequality and injustice wherever they perceive it exists. Forbearers generally feel that Reformers can be intolerant of any who oppose their agenda. Reformers can be viewed as *anti-racists* because they demand a firm and explicit stance of agency and they refuse to be subjugated or refuse to dominate based on racial differentiation (Goldberg 2009, 10). As such, Reformers are ideologically anti-racist and socially anti-Retentionist, whom they deem racist. Reformers denounce hearth and home sentiments as a credible argument for display of the Confederate Battle Flag. Reformers are operationalized as a cluster because of the shared sentiment they have that the Flag represents only hate, racism, or white supremacy and, as such, Retentionists are haters, racists, and white supremacists. They condemn Retentionists not only for their support of the Confederate Battle Flag but for their militaristic manner, with period uniforms, marching, and weapons. Reformers find the Confederate Battle Flag and the song "Dixie" categorically offensive, and all were not opposed to the Lexington City Council 2011 ban of the Flag for Lee-Jackson Day. Half feel that Confederate monuments should be modified or removed with an additional percentage of white Reformers having mixed or ambivalent sentiments. Collectively only a few feel that the *Lee* name should be removed from institutions like Washington & Lee University and Lee Chapel. Many Reformers are quite vocal, and over one-third occupied positions of power and influence such as mayor, city council members, community leaders, and pastors. All white Reformers were college graduates and most had advanced degrees. Collectively, Reformers zealously believe in the virtue of their anti-racist cause. They feel that they represent the views of the majority of black community members as a homogenous group who they believe all take offense to the Confederate Battle Flag and other Southern symbols. Reformers generally hold a stronger identification with the city of Lexington rather than with Rockbridge County but not exclusively. Most respect the hard work ethic demonstrated by county residents, but they are very wary of their politics as they feel most are Republican. Many Reformers stated they had few if any interactions with Retentionists and that they generally avoid them if they can. Reformers embrace Southern guilt as a way of distancing themselves from their Southern past, and they use it as an implement of othering Retentionists as racists and as their ideological foes in their anti-racist crusade.

REFORMERS: A SOUTHERNER

Most Reformers (14 out of 16) were born or raised in the South, but less than half identify as Southerners. Most recognize the term as a geographic reference for birth and ancestry. Many do not hold great personal significance in being a Southerner. For many black and white Reformers, the term *Southerner* is a moniker of racism. Many Reformers distance themselves and the state of Virginia from the "real" or "Deep" South. For many white Reformers Southern identity is a source of significant internal conflict and guilt. Francine was a former ranking town official of Lexington. She is a white woman born in the Deep South to a home of substantial economic privilege. Francine and her husband, Joseph, came to Lexington in the 1980s. Joseph was an employee at W&L for many years and held several positions. Francine described her mother as a "Southerner, but not linked to the Confederacy." She feels that Southerners are more conservative and that the term *Southerner* is closely associated with the term *Confederacy* and "thinking themselves better." She said a "good chunk" of family and friends are still supporting the Confederacy. Francine feels that she is "not really" a Southerner, but she is conflicted:

> I would really like to think of myself as a Southerner . . . but on the other hand I don't want to be a Southerner . . . I identify with the beliefs of people in the North. . . . We Southerners are very polite . . . and we have our own kind. . . . They are unbelievable in what they say. . . . Things that they may say may not have the word Confederacy in it, but you can read between the lines . . . and you know why they are doing and what they are doing.

Betty has been heavily involved in Lexington politics for many years. She is a black woman who does not consider herself a Southerner. Betty does not identify with either being a Southerner or a Northerner, but hesitantly as a Virginian. She sees the South as states that are below Virginia. "Virginia is mid-Atlantic, not North, or South. . . . It is unique." Janet is also a black woman who was born and raised in the city of Lexington and worked in the banking industry for many years. She does not consider herself a Southerner or a Virginian. "I consider just me. . . . Southerner is racist. . . . and how badly we were done. . . . It is mostly for landed whites." Cora is a black woman who was born in Lexington and raised in the nearby country town of Glasgow, Virginia. Cora does not identify as a Southerner. "I do not. . . . But I am a county girl."

Milli is a white woman who graduated from Lexington High School in 1963. She attended the College of William & Mary. During the summer after her sophomore year, Milli worked on a project teaching black children to read in another county in Virginia. Because of integration issues, county schools had remained closed for five years. "The schools would rather be closed down than integrate them." The experience was a very rewarding one for Milli that raised questions for her. "It changed my life in a lot of ways. It made me think in a lot of new directions. But I came home, it never occurred to me that Lexington School system is still not integrated . . . it was in 1965. I never quite connected the dots. . . . Because it's home."

Although there were similarities in the segregated situations, Lexington did not appear to have the same racial malice for Milli. "The circumstances and situations were never as intense as what happened in Prince Edward County." After graduating college with a BA in History, Milli moved to Boston. "I needed new horizons." In Boston she got married a couple of years later to a black professor. Her husband, William, was an astronomer and they lived in New York, Boston, Houston, Pasadena, Omaha, and Tucson. Milli does not consider herself a Southerner:

"I think there are a lot of stereotypes and pejoratives to being Southern . . . I kind of took comfort that Virginia was considered a mid-Atlantic state. And that goes obviously against the grain of Lexington being the 'Shrine of the South' when we were growing up."

Noah is a gay black minister who is involved with the NAACP, the Community Anti-Racism Effort (CARE), 50 Ways Rockbridge, and pastor of his church. Noah was born in the Tidewater region of Virginia and moved to Lexington about ten years ago. He is a proud and vocal activist in the community. Noah described a Southerner. "Being from the South, culture, and language . . . accent of the South . . . kale, collard greens, fried chicken . . . a lot slower [pace] . . . more hospitable than the North or New York City. . . . More courteous, more friendly, open, inviting you into their home and to a meal. . . . Black Southerners are friendlier than black Northerners, and white Southerners probably on the same scale as white Northerners." However, Noah does not "really" consider himself a Southerner. "When I look at myself, I see myself as a tall, dark, handsome black man, physically and spiritually I see myself as the righteousness of God in Christ Jesus. . . . I've never considered me, being Southern." Based on Noah's observations, some white Southerners in Lexington exhibit disturbing traits that are "racially degrading" and are a "coded response" to him as a black man. "They come out into the street in dirty clothes. . . . I have never seen that in other parts of Virginia where I lived. I never saw that in Atlanta. I have only seen that here. . . . Sometimes when they [white Southerners] sees a black person coming in their direction, they will spit [in a can]."

Liv is a well-traveled white journalist and photographer who does not consider herself a Southerner even though she was raised in Rockbridge County and born in the South. "I'm not a Northerner either. I'm a Virginian . . . I think Virginia, it's in-between the North and the South." Liv has kinfolk in South Carolina which she feels epitomizes Southern and the Deep South. "I couldn't live down there for all the tea in China. They're Southerners. . . . True Southerners are Mississippi and Louisiana and Alabama, the Deep South. I am deeply uncomfortable going down there. . . . It is not my world. . . . That whole Civil War thing. . . . Put it away folks. Put it away. Move on." Many white Reformers are very conflicted in their Southern identity.

Abby is also a white journalist with strong ties to the city of Lexington. For Abby, to be a Southerner, you have to be born in the South and of Southern ancestry. "I think you have to be born here and I think you really have to be born of a really, really truly Southern family." Abby thinks Northerners look down on Southerners and that both entities *other* each other. "I think a lot of Northerners do. . . . Part of the problem in this country is that people are clinging to their regions and pointing their fingers at each other . . . I think non-Southerners have a very jaundiced view of the South that's really not fair." Abby does not consider herself a Southerner, but she is internally conflicted on the topic. "I was raised as a Southerner. But at a certain point I understood that I was not a Southerner. . . . It had a lot to do with race. I can feel my stomach churning as I say that. I have a sinking feeling in my stomach as I talk about what it feels like to be not from here. To be not part of the place you love the most. To be a Southerner to me, is to be raised with a deep, innate pride in family and land that you will die for." Abby distances herself from being a Southerner but demonstrates the internal turmoil. "I have to because it is not right. It is not right if everyone's not included . . . in the time my generation was raised. . . . We were raised with it, and we didn't question it. I grew up standing up when I sang 'Dixie.' That is just what you did." However, at age eleven, Abby saw the racial bathroom doors and began to disassociate herself from the prejudicial side of being a Southerner. Abby copes with the evils of racism in the South by not identifying as a Southerner at all. She feels there is an associated prejudice with identifying as a Southerner for her, and that the word *Southerner* is a loaded term having its roots in the traditional South:

> I do. . . . In my generation we all grew up believing in the Lost Cause and all of that and revering the people who fought. I will just say . . . there is nothing wrong for fighting for what you believe in, ever. . . . What concerns me is when you use the word Southerner, this could be a loaded term. It shouldn't have to be a loaded term. . . . But that was in my generation. In the generation that is now in the lead . . . we should have gotten beyond all of this. And yet I see that we haven't. When you say "Southerner," I think, "Oh dear."

Abby describes the conflict of Southerner identity for her and the balance between pride in family heritage without being racist. "I think we should be able to, and I should be able to as well. And I feel as if it is not completely fair to judge the past in terms of the present. . . . Yes. I have great pride in my family. I wrote a book about them. I have great pride in the land."

Lexington community members that were not born in the South offer an interesting perspective. Vance is an instructor at W&L and was originally from up North. For Vance, the term *Southerner* has a negative association.

"Southerners see the South as an important part of their identity. . . . If someone feels the need to identify themselves as a Southerner, I'm a little worried . . . radar up. 'Let's see how this goes.'" Here we see that the term *Southerner* is a signal of potential racism for some, well before the symbols of Confederacy are introduced. Kate has resided in Rockbridge County for the past thirty-six years, but she was born out West. Kate does not consider herself a Southerner even though she has lived here the longest of any location in her life. She does identify as a Virginian. Her best friend in Fairfield is "definitely a Southerner" because of "sweet tea, eating grits . . . born in Rockbridge Baths." Kate said a Southerner is born in the geographic South, the *Confederate* South. For her, "Northerners are know-it-alls and Southerners are resistant to change." Kate felt that Southerners are more two-faced and are not as genuine. "Southerners are courteous on this side of their face, but they are going to shit on you the other side of their face." For her, this is characterized by the Southern expression, *Bless your heart*.[3]

Some Reformers do identify as Southerners with reservation. Mike, a white VMI graduate and former professor in Louisiana, thinks of himself as a Southerner primarily because he "grew up in the South." To be Southern is more geographic for him. Mike sees Southern as being about "language" and related that when he moved to Florida, he listened to the Watergate hearings on television. "Senator Sam Ervin [North Carolina], sounded like a retarded Andy Griffith. Man do I talk that way?" Ruth is a black retired home care provider. "I never thought about being a Southerner. I guess I am." Ruth was tentative in her response. She considers herself a Southerner only because of the geographical reference to her birthplace. Being a Southerner is not very important to Ruth. "No not at all." Being from Lexington, Rockbridge, and the Shenandoah Valley is important to her. "That is important to me. I like the scenery." However, Ruth also associates the term *Southerner* with white Confederates. "I do. . . . When I hear Southerner, I always think of Confederates for some reason. . . . Some attitudes, you can just tell that they want . . . to keep us in our place. They were raised to think . . . they had supremacy or authority over us. . . . I don't get it very much now. It might be subtle, really subtle. . . . I can sense from some people that I should be in a certain place."

Todd is a white man and a former pastor. Todd considers himself a Southerner. "I have only lived in the South." Being a Southerner is mostly geographic for him. Characteristics of a Southerner include language, accents, and expressions such as *Bless your heart*, and culinary in food preferences and preparations like collard greens and okra. Courtesy is also a generalized trait of being a Southerner. He sees courtesy as a having a "delicate balance" with honesty. "The quintessential Southerner is honest without being rude. . . . [However,] there are some Southerners I know who, just all their lives they are as rude as they can be . . . they felt it was their divine right." It is not important to Todd to be a Southerner now. Todd thought being Southern "is cultural . . . don't know how you avoid it." Todd believed there were different types of Southerners. "The old families can certainly be snooty." He remembered a saying that "North Carolina was the valley of humility between the two mountains of conceit [South Carolina and Virginia]." Todd thinks non-Southerners see Southerners as "talking slow and pretty dumb." "They think we're racists . . . that we're all members of the Klan . . . and all packing [guns]. . . . Growing up as a kid . . . growing up . . . I had pride for the Confederacy, as a kid. But that is long gone." When asked why, Todd explained that growing up there was "South Carolina history" and school provided a revisionist version of the Civil War and history. "It was everywhere. The racism was everywhere, and I didn't even think about it . . . It seemed odd."

Edna is a white woman who was raised in Northern Virginia and currently owns a local business. She considers herself a Southerner and is proud of it. A Southerner has a variety of different meanings for her:

> That has changed a lot in my life. . . . When I was growing up, I was raised to stand up for "Dixie" when it was sung and be very proud of Lee and things like that. But now, I'm a historian and I can look back on things . . . I'm a Southerner but I'm a Virginian. I would say I'm a Virginian first. . . . Not first before American . . . I have found people who would come and argue with me that Virginia is not the South. And it's not the Deep South. I'm not a Deep Southerner.

Edna appreciates the personal and familial connection the people of the Shenandoah Valley have when remembering the Civil War because she still identifies proudly as a Southerner while distancing herself from the United Daughters of the Confederacy:

> I'm a Southerner. . . . My grandmother, as a child in Staunton, on Confederate Memorial Day, she would . . . take Confederate Battle Flags to the veterans, Confederate veterans in nursing homes in the areas. That's what school kids did. Because they were all around her. The scarred people were all around her . . . I do talks with the United Daughters of the Confederacy. I do a lot of things for them. But I don't want to be a part of them.

Peter is a retired jewelry store owner and gay white man who considers himself a Southerner. For him being born south of the Mason-Dixon Line qualifies someone as a Southerner:

Caring, polite, respectful, proud of their family and their family heritage . . .
religious backgrounds, very appreciative of all the things done for us. I don't
subscribe, you know, to the Confederate waving banner type thing. That's a
different kind of Southerner. . . . That's a different issue all together. . . . The
opposite are the Confederate Battle Flag wavers and the people that think that
blacks are beneath them. . . . "All Democrats should be killed."

When asked if a black man could be a Southerner, Peter replied, "Of course."
When asked about a transplant being a Southerner, Peter laughed, "Let's
see . . . interesting question . . . if a person has been here a few years, three to
four, then he would certainly be eligible."

SOUTHERN SYMBOLS: OFFENSIVE SIGNIFICATION

Francine was part of the leading element, with Betty, for the 2011 ban of
the Confederate Battle Flag. Prior to 2011, Francine said Confederate Battle
Flags were up in Lee Chapel in the basement and flown for the state holiday
Lee-Jackson Day. The Sons of Confederate Veterans petitioned every year to
display Confederate Battle Flags on city light poles for Lee-Jackson Day. For
her the Flag symbolizes "hate, oppression, and slavery." She cannot envision
any other argument for flying the Confederate Battle Flag. She felt that if you
had heritage related to the Confederacy, you should "fly it [the Flag] in your
house, but do not fly it publicly." She confided that some of her extended
family members flew the Flag. When the issue of the Confederate Battle Flag
removal in Lexington occurred in 2011, Francine felt that the entire African
American community in Lexington wanted the Flag banned from public
display. "I think that's true." Francine did not always find the Confederate
Battle Flag offensive. "It just didn't dawn on people . . . I mean, I'm one of
those people . . . that I didn't . . . you don't think about it . . . it is just the way
it is every day." Francine recalled that friends who visited Lexington used to
joke about the Confederate Battle Flag display and say, "Gee, the Christmas
flags are up!" Francine felt Confederate monuments on public property ought
to be taken down. If they existed for historical purposes, they should be in
a museum, and it should be clear that slavery is not supported. She thought
the placement of additional contextual plaques might be fine. At one time
Francine sang the song "Dixie," but not now. She believes the song is just as
offensive as the Flag.

Betty proudly spearheaded, with Francine, the 2011 Confederate Battle
Flag ban. Betty feels she is infamously known as the "lady who took away
the Confederate Flag." For her, the Flag is an unequivocal symbol of hate
and oppression:

White people who perpetuated violence . . . hateful violent acts of lynching, of Jim Crow . . . and all of those things to black people. . . . That flag to black people means lynching . . . that means setting fire to black people. . . . setting fire to black people's houses . . . that means killing Civil Rights leaders. . . . It may have been their battle flag . . . but it was a battle flag of white supremacy and slavery. That was what they were fighting for. If they were carrying that battle flag, that is what they were in battle for.

The song "Dixie" reminds Betty of "being on a plantation." She sees "white women on a porch fanning themselves while overseeing slaves doing work for them." The song is a symbol of "domination."

The Confederate Battle Flag was never a "source of pride" for Todd even when he was young. However, he enjoyed reading history books about the accomplishments of Lee and other Confederate generals. The fact that Jackson taught Sunday school at a church to black children does not impress Todd. "It is a good thing that this is not called Stonewall Jackson . . . church!" Todd did not think it appropriate to use Confederate generals' names on churches. "They need to let it go. . . . By keeping the name. . . . If you were a black person hearing that name, it automatically made you think of certain things." Todd feels he was able to distance himself from the Confederacy as a Southerner. On the Confederate Battle Flag, Todd said, "I just don't want to see it. . . . It means revisionist history. It means people not wanting to move on. It means racism." Todd is disturbed by the Sons of Confederate Veterans marching with the Flag. "It's abhorrent." Todd felt all of the Confederate monuments should come down, regardless of when they were built. "None should stand." However, Todd did not feel there was a need to remove the name of Lee from W&L. "I don't see why they need to do that."

Janet does not see anything good about the Confederate Battle Flag. To her the Flag represents "prejudice . . . that means killing . . . reminds me of the Ku Klux Klan." Janet believes that the history of Robert E. Lee and Stonewall Jackson "has been distorted." She thinks both men were part of how black people were treated, and both "had their slaves." Janet believes that Confederate memorials are "reminders of what was," and represent "prejudice and hate," and are offensive. She said they should "take them down" or put them in a museum. However, she does not care about the name Lee on Lee Chapel or as part of W&L University. "They should leave it alone." Ruth felt the Confederate Battle Flag is the flag of hate and oppression in all circumstances. However, Ruth did not support removing the name Lee from W&L. "We've come this far. I wouldn't want to just drop it . . . I don't think it is necessary." Lee Chapel does not offend her. "It doesn't really offend me." Similarly, Confederate statues do not offend her. "They never offended me either . . . I just look at them and keep going."

Justin is a white, retired businessman and an affluent landowner in the county. He was born in Lexington at the Stonewall Jackson Hospital, but he was raised in the county. His family immigrated to the United States, and he considered his parents "very Liberal Democrats just to make ourselves more weird." Justin recalls that his parents pushed back against the status quo of Jim Crow. He feels that he is still a Southerner, but he actively distances himself from any notion of the Confederacy. "I do, yeah." For Justin, a Southerner means "rural . . . some of the cultural things . . . bluegrass, Americana music." However, when he was younger, he felt different:

> For me, of course it was ignorant, but I had no connection in my mind between the flag [Confederate Battle Flag] and the racism. Of course, I should have but I didn't. To me it was just a symbol and I think that a lot of people who have it on their truck or whatever, I think some of it is the same sort of not connecting the dots ignorance.
>
> Then when I went to boarding school, I identified as a Southerner because I was one of the few kids from the South. To be honest, I had a Confederate Battle Flag on my wall. . . . It was kind of who I was. I was a Southern boy. . . . It meant at the time, that I was from the South. I had an identity. . . . In a million years I wouldn't have one today. Today, I think it is quite an active symbol rather than a passive one . . . I think in many cases it is sort of . . . racist. I think it has racist connotations. I'm embarrassed to of ever had one.

Liv was ambivalent about the 2011 Confederate Battle Flag ban. However, she did take issue with the Flag being taken down in Lee Chapel. "I did have trouble when they wanted to take the old flags away from Robert E. Lee in the Robert E. Lee Chapel because that was a historical reference. . . . That's history . . . it's the past. We are not trying to keep it alive." Liv did not support removing the Lee name from W&L or Lee Chapel. "I have real troubles with this. . . . Where are you going to stop? . . . I think he did a lot of good for the college." Liv was asked what political party she belongs too and how she feels about President Trump. "The only one. The Democrats. I was always raised you don't call food stuff and you never use the word hate. I hate Trump. Every molecule of my body wants him to die. . . . Trump is just an animal."

Peter recognized the Confederate Battle Flag as a "historical symbol" as he was growing up. "I don't recognize it today because today, the symbol is for racist." Peter acknowledges the Flag as Lee's battle flag for the Army of Northern Virginia but feels the Klan has made it racist. He does not like seeing it on Lee-Jackson Day when the Sons of Confederate Veterans march. "I still think it is racist the way they are doing it. . . . What do you hope to gain by that?" As much as he deplores the Confederate Battle Flag, Peter is conflicted about the 2011 ban. "They [city council] missed the boat . . . I don't agree with tearing down the flags or tearing down the monuments. . . . We are missing a learning opportunity. . . . Every Confederate Battle Flag, every Confederate monument . . . needs another monument put up next to it." Peter is ambivalent to removing Lee's name from W&L or Lee Chapel. "I don't have a dog in that fight. . . . I haven't formulated an opinion yet that I can actually live with." Peter feels the song "Dixie" is "a cute song, but I know how hurtful it can be."

Even though Mike identifies as a Southerner he is not a fan of the Confederate Battle Flag. "I don't really know what motivates people to fly that thing . . . I never felt any strong tie . . . that is certainly not something I would ever do . . . I was totally supportive of the city's decision to remove the Confederate Battle Flag . . . I felt that it was obviously offensive to significant number of people and not being able to really understand why it might be meaningful to another group." Mike never really thought about either Lee or Jackson before moving to Lexington. "I can understand how they have become engrained with the two colleges [W&L and VMI]. . . . Jackson is memorialized at VMI and Lee at W&L." Mike is not attached to either man, but he does not want Lee's name removed. "It's a tough issue . . . I don't want to see him erased from the name W&L. . . . He made important contributions to Washington College at the time. . . . Even though he led an army for a cause that we think now is totally unjust, he was very much admired and was a hero and I don't see a reason to just wipe it out." Mike favored leaving the Civil War monuments. He views them more as "works of art" or for their historical significance. "I just hate to see them taken down . . . I favor leaving things as they are." Mike does not see the memorials as supportive of the Civil War or the Confederacy, but to "memorialize soldiers." "To me, it is important that that stays."

Abby believes the Confederate Battle Flag should be put in the museum as part of history. "It needs to be retired. . . . You should not ignore history." Abby supported the removal of the Flag from Lexington town flag poles in 2011. "Definitely flying the Confederate Battle Flag is over with. We can't do that anymore." On the Sons of Confederate Veterans and Lee-Jackson Day, Abby stated, "I don't enjoy seeing it, but it is absolutely their right, and we can't deny that. It is their right. . . . Let's remember, these guys [Lee and Jackson] are buried here." However, Abby is very conflicted about Confederate monuments especially in Lexington. "I think Monument Avenue is a huge problem. . . . It's extremely painful for me. . . . It is painful for us to imagine this town without those three statues: (1) in front of Jackson Arch, (2) Stonewall Jackson Cemetery, and (3) in the Lee Chapel. . . . The statues are very visceral. . . . The ones in my town, I can't envision my town without them. It's a very personal thing." Abby does not support removing the *Lee* name from Lee Chapel or W&L. Lee and Jackson and related symbols hold great significant relevance for her and the town. "They do." Even for Abby these things are sacred. "Yeah, they kind of are. . . . We can't abandon history . . . I would be pained. . . . He [Lee] probably saved the place [W&L] . . . I refuse to condemn Thomas Jefferson. I truly do. It makes me mad."

Milli has divided loyalty regarding the monuments between her white family and her black husband. Her parents and grandparents are buried at Stonewall Jackson cemetery where Jackson's monument stands. "I don't want to be buried there. It's less, it's partially because of the name and partially because I'd like my ashes mingled with my husband's. I would never put him there." Milli is highly conflicted regarding the Confederate monuments. She recognizes the significance and context of memorials to Lee and Jackson in Lexington and the offense to others:

> I'm conflicted about this. Part of me, in response to African Americans talking about what an assault it is to their sensibilities to have to deal with that day in and day out. I thought, "Take them all down. Take them down everywhere." And then I thought, we shouldn't be in the business of erasing history. We should give context . . . and also add other statues . . . I could see tearing some of the statues in other places down. Whereas I would be reluctant to do it here because there is such a strong connection here with those two [Lee and Jackson] . . . more legitimacy.

Edna's view of the Confederate Battle Flag changed from when she was younger:

> Again, I have changed a lot on that. I was raised by my grandmother and my great grandfather, this [Confederate Battle Flag] was the best flag ever. Even though they were American patriots too, that was a wonderful flag, but the Confederate flag was great . . . I don't think it [Confederate Battle Flag] was better [than the American]. It was just part of their American heritage. And I think it is part of our American heritage. But I also think that now that I have a lot of African American friends, when I've gone out with one of my friends when they see the Flag, I see the pain that it causes them. I realize I've been insensitive and not understanding.

Edna feels that the Confederate Battle Flag now only represents white supremacy and the quintessential redneck. "I think it is no longer a symbol of the South . . . I think it has become a symbol of intolerance and hate. . . . It really just symbolizes to me redneckness . . . an uneducated person who is not openminded and white . . . intolerant. I think some people use it for the wrong reasons." Edna's main concern now is not to offend her black friends.

However, Edna still considers both Lee and Jackson "very good men." "I don't define them by the military . . . [Lee] was the President of Washington

College was the greatest thing he ever did in his life. He saved that college, and he worked the rest of his life . . . to bring back the country and to rebuild the South. . . . He saw that education was the key to bring everybody back together." Edna does not support removing the name Lee from W&L or from Lee Chapel. "No. He certainly saved that school." Edna does not think any less of Lee for fighting for Virginia, but she does not idolize him. "No. I think he was a wonderful person, but he is not a god. . . . To some he is. And I was raised that he was. But he is not. . . . My parents would take me down there [Lee Chapel] and they would practically melt . . . I was just raised that way. I think it is much more interesting that they were human." Edna has a friend that changed positions from the Woodrow Wilson museum to Lee Chapel. "I told her you are leaving the museum of a President to go to the museum of a god." Edna was conflicted about the 2011 decision to ban the Confederate Battle Flag. "I was pretty conflicted about that, and I was glad I didn't live in Lexington . . . I have always been conflicted about Lee-Jackson Day." With regard to the Civil War monuments, Edna is supportive of their historical place. "I have been very supportive of not melting them down. . . . To interpret why they were there and why they were important and how we can learn from it. . . . Why would you visit Dachau? Why would you not bulldoze those concentration camps and erase them from the face of the earth? Because we can learn what humanity can do."

Noah feels all Civil War memorials "should be taken down." He did not feel there should be any celebration or recognition for the sacrifice of Confederate soldiers under any circumstance to include the Lee-Jackson Day parade. "Knowing the little bit of history of about why they were put up, that was to promote racism, white supremacy. I think they should be taken down. . . . The Civil War was about the institution of slavery." Noah reflected upon the very first CARE (Community Anti-Racism Effort) Martin Luther King (MLK) parade in Lexington. He shared with me his strategy to disrupt the Lee-Jackson Day festivities in 2017 (Dickerson 2017). The Lee-Jackson Day Parade was typically held on the Saturday of the weekend that celebrates the birthdays of both Confederate generals and MLK. For many in the Lexington community, there was an understanding that Friday and Saturday were for Lee-Jackson Day celebrations and Sunday and Monday were for MLK celebrations. The first year CARE petitioned the city council ahead of the Sons of Confederate Veterans to hold their parade on Saturday instead of on Monday, the federal holiday. Noah said this was an intentional move "to interrupt what they were doing":

We are excited about this because four years ago when we had the first parade, it was done with a lot of controversy. . . . Because on that particular weekend the [VA] Flaggers and Sons of Confederate Veterans were having their event and it had been going on for twenty years. So, when CARE decided to kind of interrupt what they were doing, for lack of a better description, we went to City Council . . . and asked for permission to have the parade. So, people were very concerned about whether or not it would be a conflict or some type of violence between CARE and the Flaggers and the Sons of Confederate Veterans.

I directly asked Noah, "Was the scheduling of the MLK parade an *intentional maneuver* to agitate the Sons of Confederate Veterans and the United Daughters of the Confederacy?" He proudly admitted that it was:

> It was. . . . There were people who were leaving Lexington because they did not want to see the [VA] Flaggers walking up and down the main street, parading in their . . . regalia and carrying their flags. So, CARE just wanted to say, "This is not who we are. We are a diverse community where people can come and enjoy Lexington, in all its diversity" . . . and to commemorate the life of a person who taught and preached loving everybody, caring for everybody, who taught inclusivity. So, that was what that was all about.

Gene is part of the cluster of Forbearers. He is politically involved in the town of Lexington, and he recalled in 2017 when Noah petitioned to intentionally schedule the first MLK parade on the Saturday of Lee-Jackson instead of the Monday of MLK Day. At the time, Gene thought this was an antagonistic and exclusive maneuver. He remembered the application by CARE for a parade permit:

> The Sons of Confederate Veterans always had their parade at 10:00 a.m., Saturday morning of Lee/Jackson/King weekend. CARE raced in and seized that time. . . . We did not have a policy in place that the incumbent would have it, we had the circumstance of, that we needed to grant it to them. At the city council meeting, I remember asking the organizers of the CARE. I said, "What are the qualifications for your parade to participate in your parade?" They responded, "We welcome everyone." I said, "I hope you will extend an invitation to the Sons of Confederate Veterans whose time you've displaced." And they said, "Oh, well they wouldn't be welcome." Okay, if it's a unity?

Justin supported Noah and was part of the first MLK celebration. "I wanted to support the opposite view." Justin also confided that the scheduling of the MLK parade for the Saturday of Lee-Jackson Day was an intentional form of *eye poking* or antagonizing, saying, "We are taking your day." "Yeah, it was." Noah indicated that although the time slot was intentionally taken by CARE there were no violent incidents or responses by either side. "Thanks be to God; it was a peaceful and enjoyable commemorative parade." After the first year, CARE held the MLK parade on the federal holiday. Noah explained why he changed later MLK parades to Monday, "It seemed like the best thing to do . . . on his day . . . on the federal holiday."

Of sixteen Reformer respondents only two (one black and one white) support the removal of the name Lee from W&L or Lee Chapel. Dropping the name Lee from W&L was not personally important to Cora but she is concerned about outside perceptions. "It is not important for me, but I think they should . . . I'm raised in Rockbridge County so I've got accustomed to Robert E. Lee and Stonewall Jackson, but being from Arkansas, would you want to send your kids to a school that supports a Confederate General?"

SOUTHERN GUILT: A SELF-REMEDY AND AN IMPLEMENT OF OTHERING

Steel provides that white guilt is an absence of moral authority because the white race is associated with racism (Steele 2006, 24). I tender that *Southern guilt* can be viewed as a two-pronged device in Reformers' well-intentioned, anti-racist crusade. First, it can be used by whites, particularly white Reformers, as a self-inflicted cathartic remedy to depurate unacceptable elements of Cherished Southern identity in themselves as they attempt to gather individual moral authority while distancing themselves from offensive Southern symbols. Second, Southern guilt can also be deployed as a strategic implement of *othering* by black and white Reformers to deny any moral authority for Retentionists because they fail to renounce inflammatory Southern symbols such as the Confederate Battle Flag. Here, Reformers use Southern guilt as an implement to label unreconstructed Retentionists as collective racists and foes, in furtherance of practical symbolic interactionism.

White Reformers demonstrated various degrees of internalized conflict in attempting to reconcile tensions between their current liberal philosophies and remnants of individual nostalgic fabric from their past Cherished Southern identity. As such, white Reformers were prime candidates for Southern guilt as a self-imposed cathartic tool of purification. Over half (5/9) came from an affluent Southern upbringing that employed black nannies or black help in the milieu of Jim Crow. None indicated any conditions of economic scarcity in their childhood. As previously noted, all white Reformers are college educated and many held advanced degrees. Most (7/11) have additional close associations with academia and pedagogy. Those that did not (2/11) were associated with traditionally liberal occupations such as working with the media as journalists or photographers. Of the remaining two, one was a minister and the other an affluent businessman. Many Southern white Reformers shared common attributes. All felt they were liberal, very open-minded, tolerant, and inclusive of diversity except Retentionists. Almost half (4/9) of white

Reformers that came from a Southern heritage actively and vocally disassociated themselves from the Flag and Confederate symbols by renouncing or greatly diminishing their Southern identity. However, most of those that were born in Lexington immediately and proudly stated that they were "born in the Stonewall Jackson House."

Francine came from a privileged and prominent Southern family. Her grandfather, on her mother's side, was wealthy and gave money to her and her sister to attend college. Her grandfather did not monetarily fund her brothers as he expected her brothers to "make their own way." Recollecting her Southern upbringing was an emotional and painful experience for Francine. She wept several times during the interview. Francine acknowledged that she is a daughter of the Confederacy but not in group membership. The Confederacy "was so prominent" in her family. Francine demonstrates her internal conflict and inconsistency when attempting to reconcile her past. She stated that her ancestral lineage on her father's side links directly to a ranking Confederate general. "I have that name in . . . I have [his name] in my name. Which sometimes I use it and other times I don't . . . I still have things in my house that would reflect that . . . They were very important to the family."

Francine recalled that when she asked about being slave owners in the past, it made people in her family very "uncomfortable." Her parents never talked about it. Growing up her family had one black maid named Bernice and her grandparents had a "black man and a black woman" work for them. Bernice came to Francine's childhood home every day but Thursday which was her day off. "She was like a mother to me. She would fix my lunch every day and we would chat. It's hard to think about what that meant to other people, because to me she was like another mother, and I liked her a lot." Although Bernice was part of Francine's family life and was "well into the family," she did not eat with the family, and she lived in a "separate world." Bernice lived on the "edge of town," and Francine never played with or knew Bernice's children. "That was not done in the South. . . . That would just not have occurred to anybody." There was a "black bathroom" in her childhood home. Francine said it makes her "sort of sick now." "Those were different times with different context." But Francine deeply regrets never thinking about Bernice's situation and the separation of races when she was a child. Francine recalled returning home for Bernice's funeral. "Bernice never blamed anyone . . . She just took what came." Francine wept again.

Abby was born at the Stonewall Jackson House hospital in Lexington. "I am from a military family. . . . Both of my grandfathers were military. This is the only house my family ever owned." Abby's ancestors are English and came to Massachusetts in 1636 to escape religious persecution. "Actually, I am a Colonial Dame."[3] Even though Abby was born in Lexington she disassociates herself completely from the South and her Southern upbringing. "So, we're Northerners. I am not from here. I am a damn Yankee . . . I would simply say my grandfathers were on the wrong side of the war." Abby's maternal grandfather was a VMI superintendent and a highly decorated veteran. "He was the most decorated man [of his time]." Abby had a black nanny named "Nanny Pat" who worked for her grandfather and cooked their meals. Abby traveled extensively throughout the United States on the East Coast. Abby spent a couple of summers in France, and visited England, Scotland, Ireland, and the Philippines. Abby described her relationship with her parents. "They were raised by Victorians. They were military. We are expected to toe the line and show up on time and get the job done. We grew up understanding what our duty was. . . . Mother told me, 'It is always easier if you marry someone from your own class.'" Growing up, her parents had no black folk to the house for social visits. Nanny Pat did not eat with the family. "They had Nanny in the kitchen. . . . She served us." Abby stated she was taught the *n-word* was "rude and disrespectful" and that her parents engaged regularly in an aristocratic *noblesse oblige*. Liv was raised in the Lexington-Rockbridge area since she was two years old. Her father was a colonel in the US military. Her mom was British, and her parents met during WWII. Liv does not identify as a Southerner, but she finds a strong link to her English roots and being of European descent. "From the DNA, I am 100 percent European: 63 percent British, 23 percent Scandinavian." Her connection to Virginia is through the land and being raised in Rockbridge County and the Valley. "Very much so because of the Shenandoah Valley . . . that's home." Being Southern is not a direct part of her identity but it is a part of her heritage. "Not directly. I recognize it as an important part of my heritage." Confederate identity and lineage are also part of her past. However, it is not very important to Liv. "No. I think the Civil War was so heartbreaking, so heartbreaking. Again, there is a chord in me because of my lineage." Liv feels a personal connection with Robert E. Lee because of her father. Liv described her dad on his deathbed. "He looked like Robert E. Lee in repose in Lee Chapel. He looked just like Robert E. Lee!"

Liv described her upbringing as "frugal but relatively well-off compared to other families in the county." Her father was from an "affluent family" in the Deep South. "He comes from a family that was not monied, but that was of very good quality. Everyone went to college. Daddy went to Clemson, as did grandfather." She enjoyed a special relationship with her father. "Daddy and I would fox hunt on Wednesday afternoons." When Liv's family lived in Alabama, they had live-in black *help*, a black gardener, and black maids. Liv believed her mom was "completely unprejudiced" but perhaps privileged. She compared her mother's relationship with the black help to her grandmother's relationship with the indigenous help in India:

It's like my grandmother that was living in India in the height of the Raj. I said, "Granny, did you ever wonder what the Indian community members thought about England coming in?" Granny was born in 1883 in Victoria's London. I knew her until I was 32. She lived to be 100. . . . So, I asked, "Did you ever feel that this wasn't the right thing to be doing to this country?" [Liv mimicked in falsetto British aristocratic accent] "Oh darling, they loved us."

Peter was also born in the Stonewall Jackson House. He was raised and educated in Lexington and attended Lexington High School. Peter's mother was from up North and her family moved to Buena Vista when her father started a company there. Peter's father was from the county and was part of the Zucker family who immigrated from Germany in 1743. Peter relayed a Zucker family quote, "When the Indians arrived, [we] were here to greet them." Peter was raised by three black nannies. "When I was a kid my very first recollections of black people, were my nannies. . . . They were wonderful people. They taught me so much, who I am today. . . . There was a wonderful give and take there. I never realized there were problems with blacks and whites. It didn't make sense." In 1963 when the schools were integrated, he knew all the black kids. "I knew them. They would come to our store all the time." When black families came to town, many were his friends and he hung out with them. While there were Jim Crow laws, Peter "would break lines" and sit with his black friends in the balcony of the theater. Peter indicated that his relationship was that of equal status and friendship between families. His family were friends with several black families, and they would comingle regularly to include eating and socializing. In his family, black community members sat at the same table and came to the front door. The nannies served the family but according to Peter they were not treated as lesser folk.

Many Southern white Reformers recalled significant conflict within the family, their friends, or the community as it related to race relations and racial or gendered divides. Francine said that many in her extended family identified with the South and the Confederacy. However, her parents did not, and they were much more liberal in their thinking. Francine remembers seeing relatives who had the Confederate Battle Flag. "We looked down on that." When she was very young, the Confederate Battle Flag was just a flag. As she got older, she became more sensitive to "what it meant to other people." Over time, the Flag "was a bad thing" for Francine. Francine was greatly influenced by her father "because he was very liberal." He was disturbed by the social boundaries between black and white in the Deep South. Their family church was all white, and they gave her parents a hard time for their liberal leanings. Francine said people in their church were "biased and very conservative." It was clear to Francine that her parents were shunned by the church for their racial liberal thinking. Francine related a story of a time when some African

Americans came to their church on a Sunday and sat in the back. People in the church said "Oh, there are your father's friends." Francine said both her parents were "very much involved in the Civil Rights" movement. Her family participated in the Selma to Montgomery march with Dr. King. She recalled the hateful sentiments and being very afraid. After the march, "When we were trying to find our car, this man was saying, 'Why don't you come into our house, and you can tell us why you are here' and we ran . . . we were scared."

Peter advised all of the men in his family belonged to the Knights of Pythias Lodge.[4] "When I came along, it was just something you were supposed to do. And all of a sudden, I noticed, something is wrong with this. This was not [just] a black/white thing. This was a male/female thing. . . . Why don't we have women?" Peter was concerned about the racial and sexual exclusivity of the group. He felt the organization should change in order to expand. The group members were in their eighties and nineties and exclusively white male and did not want to change. "I decided it wasn't the thing for me." Abby described her parents as "polite racists." Abby remembered when her sister was traveling with several classmates back to Lexington. One of the classmates was Thomas, a black male student. "She asked if they could stay here, and mother said that Thomas couldn't stay here. This was after my father had died." Abby is also conflicted about the Sons of Confederate Veterans. She understands that they value their ancestry and heritage very much as part of a "pride in family and legacy and heritage." Abby could not recall if she knew any Sons of Confederate Veterans or United Daughters of the Confederacy members personally. However, she concludes that Retentionists such as the Sons and Daughters are racist because they value their ancestry and heritage:

> In my heart of hearts, I think they are racists . . . but not at the level of the KKK. It is my opinion that there is a smidgen of racism in that. It is hard for me to say there isn't because otherwise, we would all have gotten past how valuable our ancestors are . . . as opposed to anybody else's ancestors. . . . If they are that attached to who their ancestors were, there is a risk of racism. . . . At the same time, I do understand pride in family and legacy and heritage, and I do respect that. Of course, it is meaningful to me if somebody's great-grandfather died on the field of battle in this country regardless of which side they were fighting for. To me that has sacredness.

Mike advised he was not always liberal. He became more aware of social injustice as he has gotten older and has shifted from some conservative views to more liberal ones. Mike "was a registered Republican since the 1960s but I haven't been supportive of the candidates for the last twenty years. I don't know if I changed, or the Republican party changed." Mike attended a segregated school in North Carolina, and he cannot recall dealing with the issues of slavery in school. Mike advised that he was "initially not in favor" of integration. He feared "potential conflicts . . . that fortunately didn't materialize." Mike stated, "At that time, my attitude towards blacks was different than it is today." He was raised that separation of the races was preferred. Looking back, Mike didn't pay much attention to race issues. "That was pretty much my attitude up to the 1960s . . . I didn't pay enough attention." Mike recalls viewing a PBS series that presented news clips about Birmingham and other places during the Civil Rights movement. "I should have seen when I was there . . . and they seem so atrocious now but during the time I just tuned them out."

Liv recalled high school racial integration in Lexington. "We integrated when I was in the tenth grade. It never occurred to me to think anything different. But my father would not let me go to dances." This was because of the potential of Liv dancing with a black man. "In his world that was just unthinkable." School clubs could not meet at her home because there were black students in the club. In her childhood home black community members did not come to the home unless it was to work. However, her father was never rude and could be very generous and paternal. "A black person's house burned down in Lexington and my dad drew up the plans and oversaw it. It was that very strong patriarchal. . . . Daddy had wonderful manners." Conduct and etiquette were paramount for her father. "Very important. Daddy said, 'I don't care if you get As but there is no reason not to have an A in conduct. Good behavior was above all else." Her mother and father did not feel the same about racial distancing. "My father was very patriarchal. There wasn't any 'damn niggers.' There was none of that. I never heard that word [from him]. It was all patriarchal. But naturally they are, like granny, 'these people are lesser by default.' That's how daddy felt." Liv described a very different scenario with her mother. "Mother would sit down . . . and my grandmother came in, my very Southern grandmother. My father's mother came in and my mother was sitting down having lunch with the black lady who came to clean. My mother was always respectful, and she would be cleaning along . . . The black lady got up and very quietly left [when grandmother came into the kitchen]. She would feel the vibe."

Liv was conflicted with some of her heritage. She identified the beautiful sideboard in her dining room that was made by slaves from an Alabama plantation. "Ironically it is the most expensive piece of furniture we own in our family because it's completely unique. I have funny feelings about that." When she had her first horse, a black man, Jed, would come hay the field with his two sons. Her father was polite but actively engaged in social distancing which was not limited to race but also included economic status. "Mother would have us all in for milk and cookies. My dad would have been lovely to Jed and completely respectful as he would be to anybody. But Jed would not have been invited to have supper with us. . . . But there probably would not have been, with lower . . . socio-economic white folk either. So, it would have been the same with whites too."

Todd's father was a minister in North Carolina. The family moved to South Carolina where his dad ministered at the Presbyterian Church. Todd described the town as a Southern town, and he resided there for eight and a half years. Todd remembered that the Freedom Riders came through town. The leadership in his father's church wanted to lock arms and keep black people from coming into the church. His father said. "If you do this, I'll quit [as the preacher]." The Freedom Riders came into the church and there were no problems. His father's resilience in this situation left an indelible imprint on him. When Todd moved to Virginia, his senior year was the school's first integrated class. "We had all sorts of racial things, and I was very engaged in working with them." Todd was president of his class and worked closely with a "number of his black friends" on harmonious integration. He believes his view of the Confederacy changed because of the example he saw in his father as his father challenged racism in his own congregation. Todd saw the history he learned as revisionist history for what was called the "War of Northern Aggression."

Interviews provided that reconstructed white Reformers initially use Southern guilt as an emetic tool to renovate their white image to disassociate themselves from a conflicting past and so as not to appear racist by today's standards (Dew 2016, 62). These Reformers embraced their new cleansed position with a religious fervor. The excommunicative exercise of reconstruction and disassociation filled the void of moral authority with a righteous zeal in their crusade against racism. Additionally, black and white Reformers embrace Southern guilt as a tool of othering and labeling, against the cluster of Retentionists who fail to disassociate from the contentious Southern symbols like the Confederate Battle Flag. Southern guilt is used as a tool of *othering* through sweeping accusations of racism by association via practical symbolic interactionism; comparisons are made with other contentious symbols of racism such as the Nazi flag, with traditional white supremacist groups that display the Flag, and generalized statements and sentiments of distrust or dislike based on ideological collective identity. Reformers exhibit a great tolerance and inclusion for those like-minded. However, in their personal application of *anti-racist*, they appear intolerant to many community members. They are actively exclusive of Retentionists as a cluster and label them as foes. Reformers feel that the ideological animus is reciprocated if not initiated by Retentionists.

Francine was a town leader in Lexington in 2011 and she was active in forwarding the agenda for banning the Confederate Battle Flag. This was an unpopular move with Retentionists and other groups that adore Southern symbols and the Flag. Many protests against the ban were directed at Francine and Betty and they were both understandably frightened by the experience. Francine places all the protestors of the 2011 ban to include the Sons of Confederate Veterans, the VA-Flaggers, and Ku Klux Klan as one unpleasant, "disgusting" lot. She did not think there should be an organization that supports the public display of the Flag. Francine's only contact with the Sons of Confederate Veterans was with them and others standing in her yard with flags. She did not separate the groups "when they are standing in my yard" with their Confederate Battle Flags.

Betty feels, "To this day, we did the right thing" to remove the Confederate Battle Flag. They ultimately had to go to Federal court, and she endured a lot of anguish for many years. For five years following the vote, Betty received hateful telephone calls on or about Lee-Jackson Day. Betty stated that during that troubled time, people in trucks with Confederate Battle Flags flying would yell "nigger," mostly at the elderly, and it was very upsetting to her. Betty said, "The Mayor got the worst of it. . . . Protesters would come to the house and sing 'Dixie' all hours of the day and night." For a couple of years, the protesters hired a plane on Lee-Jackson Day weekend to pull a banner saying, "Shame on You Lexington." By the third year, Betty would leave the weekend of the parade because an airplane would be constantly flying over her house. "It was really grating on my nerves . . . because I knew that they were coming over here, over my house . . . because of me." It bothered Betty that because of her decision the plane was harassing the entire black neighborhood. "It really hurt, because of me . . . because of what I did, it is hurting them now." Betty stated that these harassing antics have since abated.

Betty is unique as a Reformer in that she has had personal interactions with Retentionists such as with Tucker of the Sons of Confederate Veterans and Liz of the United Daughters of the Confederacy. She does not dislike them personally, but she views the Confederate Battle Flag as a symbol of white supremacy and members of the Sons of Confederate Veterans and United Daughters of the Confederacy as white supremacists. For her, they are of a lower order of racist than the Klan, but white supremacists nonetheless because of their ideology. In our discussions, Betty referenced a black church in town that feeds an offensive white male displayer of the Confederate Battle Flag across the street from them. Betty stated, "The church feeds him!" When asked why they feed him if he is offensive, Betty smiled, "It's a process." Betty was referring to Richard the Retentionist and the Church of God. I later found that Betty's sentiments toward Richard were not the same as the church elders, Arthur, Carla, and Faith.

Noah said he has never spoken with anyone belonging to the Sons of Confederate Veterans, United Daughters of the Confederacy, or the VA-Flaggers. For Noah, because the Sons of Confederate Veterans carry a racist flag, they must be racists. When asked if the Sons of Confederate Veterans were welcome to march with the CARE in the spirit of inclusivity on the next MLK Day as Gene suggested, Noah said, "I don't know if we would let Flaggers . . . or the [Sons of Confederate Veterans] now that I think about it, because of their history . . . their racist history." Noah deeply distrusts Retentionists. During Lee-Jackson Weekend[5] in Lexington, I attended the parade on Saturday as an observer. The final leg of the short parade was up a back street and returning to the graveyard which is home to the Stonewall Jackson memorial and burial site. Noah was parked in an alley off the street in defilade. When I first saw Noah, I thought he was waiting to get out of the alley, so I paused, smiled, and waved to him giving him right-of-way. He ignored me as he was solely focused on the parade going past his church, with his sweatshirt hood up. I found this curious, so I walked up thinking he did not see me and said hello, but he did not return the salutation. Instead, he moved his car farther down the ally in deeper defilade. It struck me that he was keeping a watchful eye and surveilling the parade incognito. When I saw Noah at the MLK parade that Monday, he immediately recognized me but made no reference to his surveillance activities on Saturday.

As previously discussed, Justin liked the Confederate Battle Flag when he was young. Now it only "means white supremacy." He believes that neo-Nazis throughout the world have coopted the flag as a symbol of hatred. "Early, it never offended me. I just thought it was part of the Civil War. Now I can see why people say it symbolizes hate. . . . It's like they are making a statement. . . . 'We want to keep you as a slave.' . . . In a lot of places in Europe where they are banned from flying a swastika, they fly the Confederate Battle Flag." Kate also compares the Flag to the Nazi swastika. "I just don't understand any of that. Are the Germans celebrating . . . Hitler . . . [the Swastika] yeah? . . . I didn't know a lot about the Confederate when I moved here. . . . These people want to go back to that. . . . When Trump says, 'Make America Great Again..' . . To me that means let's go back to when it was all, only white men. Women had to stay in the home." Justin has "deep problems" with the Confederate Battle Flag as a symbol coopted by neo-Nazis. "The current meaning . . . has been coopted by white nationalist groups . . . it is currently a neo-Nazi symbol. There is no way around that. It simply is that. . . . It is currently a symbol of neo-Nazis. So, you can't use it. . . . Don't wear it on your shirt when you are in the mall."

Edna is highly conflicted on what the Sons of Confederate Veterans and United Daughters of the Confederacy symbolize today. She feels that the earlier versions of the United Daughters of the Confederacy initially raised money to bury the Confederate soldiers and to put up monuments. "They did it out of loss . . . rebuilding their lives. . . . It was not a racist agenda. They were trying to bring bodies home. The valley was burned . . . to stop food and munitions coming from the valley. Sheridan cut it off. He won in the valley by burning it . . . Soldiers who fought for the Confederacy were no less American patriots than those who fought for the North." It is hard for Edna to reconcile her sentiments that they are heritage groups and that they perpetuate white supremacy. Edna is not a member of the United Daughters of the Confederacy because they currently are responsible for perpetuating racism and white supremacy:

> I'm not. I have friends . . . they bug me about it . . . and I tell them no . . . I don't wish to be. I don't want to be a part of it. Because they, looking back now at history, I see that they have helped perpetuate white supremacy. . . . They are a heritage group . . . [long pause] but inherently I think they are white supremacists. Not in the way that the Klan is. Not in the way the people who marched in Charlottesville are. But they perpetuate things.

Liv could be part of the Daughters of the Revolution or United Daughters of the Confederacy, but she is not inclined to join because she classifies them as *redneck*:

> I feel that the Confederate Battle Flag and this nonsense of Flaggers, still fighting the Civil War . . . I tell you I find it nauseating . . . I think it's nuts. . . . It doesn't put you up in some sort of elite group. I think it is absurd. . . . My father would have never been. . . . If I see a Confederate Battle Flag, I think redneck. I think close-minded, narrow-minded. Redneck to me is a pejorative. . . . A redneck is kind of the Tea Party, throwing beer cans out of the truck, shooting up stop signs. Rabble rousers, people who have no dignity people who have no respect for other people's property, without moral integrity. They are not just country people. Country people are lovely human beings . . . simple, good community members, can fix anything and they are smart.

Ruth is offended by the Confederate Battle Flag and feels that Retentionists are racists because they honor the Flag:

> Early, it never offended me. I just thought it was part of the Civil War. Now I can see why people say it symbolizes hate. . . . It's like they are making a statement. . . . "We want to keep you as a slave." . . . I think of them some honestly think they're celebrating their tradition, their heritage. But underneath it all, it only stood for one thing. . . . It [Confederate Battle Flag] means hate. It does not have respect for human life. We were supposed to be servants and do the labor for nothing.

For Cora, the Confederate Battle Flag always represents racism and is unacceptable in any situation even if the displayers are black. "Always . . . I automatically believe they're racists. It is a racist symbol and that they are comfortable losing. . . . They're underachievers. You're proud that your great-grandfather lost . . . I believe the black people who wave the Confederate Battle Flag want to fit in. . . . Coons. . . . Uncle Toms. . . . They want to be a 'good ole boy' for those white guys." Lee's position as president of Washington University after the Civil War did not provide any redemption for Cora. She compared Lee to the mass murderer Charles Manson. "Manson . . . did some great things along his life. We don't recognize him for those. . . . The bad outweighs the good." Cora has no tolerance for the "Heritage not Hate" argument. "Absolutely not." Cora believes the groups such as the Sons of Confederate Veterans, United Daughters of the Confederacy, and VA-Flaggers are all duplicitous "white supremacists." She feels that the Sons of Confederate Veterans were just as violent in their racist hatred as the Ku Klux Klan. "The Sons of Confederate Veterans do that too. But they are just not publicly doing it." Cora thought she *might* have met a few Sons of Confederate Veterans or VA-Flaggers at Lee-Jackson Day but she did not know any personally. "A few. When they did the little walk down the street [Lee-Jackson Day]. Oh yeah. They were hostile and confrontational like you wanted problems." Cora trusts the Klan more than the Sons of Confederate Veterans:

I trust the KKK more than the [Sons of Confederate Veterans]. Oh yeah, absolutely . . . because I know they don't like my black ass. The Sons of the Confederacy and the American [VA] Flaggers they're racists. But they are more, "Oh hi. How are you doing? I don't want you to know I'm racist. But at the end of the day my white skin is better than your black skin." I respect the ones that are honest about it.

As a cluster, Reformers embrace the powerful collective memory of "enemy-memory" related to the Old South (Steele 1991, 150–51). They connect the present display of contentious Southern symbols such as the Confederate Battle Flag and the song "Dixie" as "objective correlatives" to "powerful memories of the enemy" (Steele 1991, 153). Using Cooley's understanding of sympathy as a "sharing of mental state" (Cooley 1998), Reformers are highly sensitive to the perceptions of the black community, as they imagine them, and hold compassionate sympathies. White Reformers utilize Southern guilt as an emetic to gain moral authority as they embrace this sensitivity to black collective pain, as they perceive it, toward Confederate symbols. However, when Reformers *sympathize* with Retentionist sentiments, they feel hostility toward them. "That is to say, we enter by sympathy or personal imagination into the state of mind of others, or think we do, and if the thoughts we find there are injurious to or uncongenial with the ideas we are already cherishing, we feel a movement of anger" (Cooley 2018, 116).

Reformer hostility is manifested as a generalized intolerance for the cluster of Retentionists based on their inability to renounce the Confederate Battle Flag and their general insensitivity to the collective pain of black people (Steele 1991, 154). Reformers identify a *racist* as someone who is insensitive to the racial vulgarity of the Confederate Battle Flag or other contentious Southern symbols. Reformers feel a heightened "sense of the enemy" which gives them license to deploy Southern guilt as a tool of othering and to deny any moral authority to Retentionists (Steele 1991, 152).

Reformers find Retentionists *guilty by association*, through their use of practical symbolic interactionism, because of Retentionist attachment to controversial Southern symbols. They classify the nostalgic fabric of Retentionists as merely a strategy of expedience and as a posture of anti-racialism to conveniently forget and gloss over (Goldberg 2009). At best, Reformers view Retentionists as *laissez-faire* racists that wish to maintain the racial status quo of white dominance under the veil of heritage (Bonilla-Silva 2018; Haney Lopez 2006; Lavelle 2015). Reformers see the heritage argument as a conservative strategy of convenience and ignorance that constructs a "historical imagination" for Retentionists in their nostalgic fabric of the Confederate Battle Flag (Fleming 2017). For Reformers, belonging to the Sons of Confederate Veterans or United Daughters of the Confederacy is evidence enough to sustain a collective *ad hominem* argument. Few Reformers personally knew many, if any, individual Retentionists. If they did, the ideological and political alignment of Retentionists outweighed any positive personal attributes and, as such, they eschewed social interaction with them. For Reformers, the individual is subsumed by the cluster; the Confederate Battle Flag is always a symbol of hate, racism, and white supremacy. This demonstrates that ideology and sociality are generally not separate spheres of interaction for this cluster. Through Reformer application of practical symbolic interactionism, anyone who publicly displays the Flag is a hater, racist, and white supremacist and must be *othered* as a foe. Reformers differentiate other community members as they embrace *Verba non Acta* social protocols of distinction.

NOTES

1. Recall non-displaying Whites are community members not belonging to the Sons of Confederate Veterans, the United Daughters of the Confederacy, or other ardent displayers of the Confederate Battle Flag.

2. Black community members are those who self-identified as black.

3. The Colonial Dames of America is comprised of women who are descended from an ancestor who lived in British America from 1607–1775.

4. Peter provided that the Knights of Pythias Lodge was a fraternal organization founded by Supreme Court Justice Justus H. Rathbone. Peter said it was the only fraternal organization sanctioned by Congress. It received a charter under an act of the US Congress and was founded in 1864.

5. Lee-Jackson Weekend was held on 17–18 January 2020. MLK functions were held on 20 January.

Chapter 3

Retentionists

Conservative Crusaders and Faith Keepers

Who are Retentionists and why are Southern symbols such as the Confederate Battle Flag so important to them? Retentionists epitomize those community members that revere the Flag as a Durkheimian *sacred symbol* (Durkheim 1912). The national motto of the Confederate States of America was *Deo Vindice* (With God, our Defender). Through the Confederate Battle Flag Retentionists unify as an ethnic cluster in their *civil religion* of Cherished Southern identity (Bellah and Tipton 2006; Wilson 1980). Using the Durkheimian model, my findings suggest that attachment to the Flag is not only cognitive and affective but also *religious* in fervor for Retentionists. As such, the Confederate Battle Flag is the *sacred totem* supported by religious *beliefs and rites* within the *church* of Cherished Southern identity for Retentionists. Robert E. Lee and Stonewall Jackson are *saints* of that church who are feted on the *holy day* of Lee-Jackson Day. Lexington is recognized by many as *holy land* as it is the final resting place for Lee and Jackson and thus *sacred ground* for the church of the Cherished Southern identity. The continuous battles that Retentionists have with Reformers over the Flag are in furtherance of their *crusades* to retain their moral authority seeded in tradition. Analyzing Retentionist sentiments of hearth and home and Cherished Southern identity using (and advancing) a Durkheimian model of religious attachment provides for greater analytic purchase that transcends our understanding beyond mere logical or affective devotion.

Retentionists are generally made up of those belonging to the groups, Sons of Confederate Veterans (SCV) and the United Daughters of the Confederacy (UDC). The Southern Poverty Law Center (SPLC) places the SCV and the UDC within the spectrum of *neo-Confederates* because they "advocate for the continued display of the Confederate Battle Flag (CBF) and statuary devoted to generals like Lee, Davis and Jackson," and the SPLC believes that these groups exhibit other intolerant characteristics based on their core "values" of white superiority:

> Neo-Confederacy incorporates advocacy of traditional gender roles, is hostile toward democracy, strongly opposes homosexuality and exhibits an understanding of race that favors segregation and suggest white supremacy.. . . Neo-Confederate refers to a specific subset of American white nationalism predominant in the Southeastern U.S. which fuses the typically strong nativist immigration policies, Christian dominionism, Confederate "heritage and pride," and other supposedly fundamental values of the "heritage crowd" with belief in inherent superiority of whites of European descent. (SPLC 2021a)

However, the SCV and the UDC are not designated on the SPLC Extremist Files or Hate Groups list like the League of the South or Identity Dixie. The SCV and UDC officially represent themselves as apolitical heritage groups that denounce all bigotry. "The Sons of Confederate Veterans . . . shall be strictly patriotic, historical, educational, fraternal, benevolent, non-political, non-racial, and non-sectarian. The Sons of Confederate Veterans neither embraces, nor espouses acts or ideologies of racial and religious bigotry, and further, condemns the misuse of its sacred symbols and flags in the conduct of same" (SCV 2021).

When discussing modern white supremacy, Blee cautions about generalizations concerning the topic due to the heterogeneous ideologies espoused with these groups. However, her research provides for four general characteristics for modern white supremacists: (1) highly secretive, (2) extreme antagonism toward people of color, Jews, and those who engage in alternate sexual lifestyles, (3) the US state is viewed as the enemy, and (4) "fear and desire an apocalyptic race war" (Blee 2018, 4, 167, 170). Retentionists in this study are not highly secretive and openly welcome the public to their functions and meetings. There certainly may be secret agendas, but participation at monthly functions and important gatherings where emotions ran high did not illustrate antagonisms toward nonwhites, Jews, or gays. Interestingly, many attempts were displayed to include elements of these groups as *like-minded*. Although Retentionists hold a Cherished Southern identity toward the Confederacy and the Confederate Battle Flag, they demonstrate a great patriotism toward America, albeit a conservative America where their enemies are liberal Reformers. Lastly, male Retentionists firmly embrace traditional masculine identities such as their trucks and guns (Carlson 2015), but they do not espouse an offensive posture to incite violence along racist lines. Retentionists fear change and sense a pending doom of anarchy and lawlessness they associate with liberal agendas. As such they feel that they are the last defenders in the conservation of traditional values as they see them.

Retentionists can easily be labeled by race scholars as *racists* of varied sorts and dimensions. Retentionist adoration for the Confederate Battle Flag and their support of the Confederacy as a *Lost Cause* define them as racists for Reformers beyond a doubt. Retentionists, however, see themselves as anti-racists because they actively disassociate themselves from traditional hate groups. That disentanglement is not significant enough for Reformers. Retentionist adoration of the Confederate Battle Flag does not provide an active enough or vocal enough *disassociation* from America's racist past or from traditional white supremacists (Steele 2006). This failure to disassociate allows them to be *de facto* charged by association as racists, haters, and white supremacists by Reformers via Southern guilt. However, most respondents, the Forbearers, did not feel this way because of mere attachment to the Flag. They see both Retentionists and Reformers as those with different perspectives that deserve consideration.

In this chapter I present the religious-like commitment Retentionists share in their *beliefs, rites, and holy days* that unite them in the *church* of Cherished Southern identity (Durkheim 1912). Submitting a religious perspective provides a platform to transcend the nebulous heritage argument and guides us toward a more specific and contextual hearth and home argument which is firmly cemented in conservation and pious commitment to their beliefs that form the cluster of Retentionists. Hearth and home is a principal thread in the *nostalgic fabric* of the Confederate Battle Flag for Retentionists. Nostalgic fabric is a form of reconstructed memory that allows Retentionists and many other community members to have sensible recollections that are comfortable and convenient for them. Metaphorically, nostalgic fabric is used to construct reassuring accoutrements, such as a blanket of reflection, that Retentionists and other community members cling to when embracing their identity. The Flag and other Southern symbols are manifestations of nostalgic fabric. Within this perspective, banning of the Flag, the song "Dixie," Confederate names, and statues represents grave insults and threats to the Cherished Southern identity of Retentionists and others who hold their conviction of hearth and home dear.

For Retentionists, the Confederate Battle Flag evokes feelings of aesthetic adoration and represents freedom of expression. Richard is a simple kind of man or "good ole boy" who adores the Flag. On Lee-Jackson Day, he thought it a "beautiful sight" to see the Confederate Battle Flag lining the street and at every corner. Richard appreciates the balanced beauty of the Flag. He sees the design as "beautiful." "I thought the world of the battle flag . . . it's the color of it . . . the way it stands out." Liz was a ranking member of the local chapter of the United Daughters of the Confederacy and was also heavily involved in Lexington politics in 2011. Liz did not support the removal of the Confederate Battle Flag from city flag poles. "My reasoning was multi . . . You could fly it for 24 hours and if you don't like it leave. Don't look at it [for] 24 hours. By excluding that one flag you have excluded the W&L flag, the VMI flag. If we had a city flag, you couldn't fly it. If we had a high school flag, you couldn't fly it. We can't put up a flag that says, Welcome to Lexington with snowflakes for the winter. We can't have orange leaves for fall. You can't do squat."

Lexington as the burial grounds for Lee and Jackson and home to the universities of VMI and W&L sets the Goffmanian stage of context for presenting why the Confederate Battle Flag and other symbols of the South are so important to Retentionists and other community members in the area. Previous research provides that white support for the Flag can be driven by "Southern pride, political conservatism and blatant negative attitudes towards blacks" (Wright and Esses 2017, 224). Through cluster analysis the authors distinguished four distinct groups of White Southerners: (1) Cosmopolitans, (2) New Southerners, (3) Traditionalists, and (4) Supremacists. Retentionists of my study can be most closely characterized as *Traditionalists* which "are more conservative . . . have strong Southern pride and have positive racial attitudes." "Traditionalists do not display blatant negative racial attitude toward blacks, while Supremacists do. Traditionalists make up the majority of Confederate Battle Flag supporters in our sample, weakening the claim that supporters of the flag are generally being driven by negative racial attitudes towards blacks" (Wright and Esses 2017, 224, 233).

Retentionists of the Lexington-Rockbridge area adamantly insist that they are not associated with hate, racism, or white supremacist groups and most vocally distance themselves from these extremist groups. Interviews and probing follow-up questions found no overt signs of conventional racism via social distancing. During the interview process Retentionists were ultimately asked if they would support a marriage of their children to a black spouse. No abject denial or outrage was expressed. Certain discomfort or hesitancy was expressed in the form of "social taboo" but no more so than with Reformers or Forbearer respondents, both black and white. No "coded talk" which is "central to communication under a colorblind rubric" was unveiled during my investigation (Burke 2012, 91). It can be argued that Retentionists respond with guile. The same could be said for all respondents, and one of the pitfalls of ethnography is the element of response candor. However, interviews with Retentionists and time spent in their milieu illustrated great emotion and religious fervor to include heightened animus on occasion, but none based on race, homosexuality, or democracy as indicated in the earlier description of neo-Confederates provided by the Southern Poverty Law Center (SPLC 2021a). Retentionist ire was focused solely on Reformers and their politics.

As it relates to the symbolism of the Confederate Battle Flag, Retentionists react with a practical symbolic interactionism that directly counters Reformer practical symbolic interactionism toward them. This results in a powerful counter-ideological intolerance of Reformers as foes based on Reformer ideological intolerance of Retentionists. However, Retentionists do not necessarily practically apply symbolic interactionism of the Flag as a mechanism of friendship to others who publicly display it. For Retentionists, a deeper understanding of context and intent is required before conclusions are made.

RETENTIONISTS: A SOUTHERNER

For Retentionists being a Southerner is of powerful significance and can be considered a hallowed membership to the church of Cherished Southern identity. For them, the term *Southerner* transcends the mere geography of being south of the Mason-Dixon Line. It is most associated with *the country* and land, and further defined by Christianity, courtesy, virtue, honor, and tradition. Sentiments of hearth and home thread through the construct of Southern nostalgic fabric and surpass previously documented heritage arguments. Hearth and home sentiments offer greater cultural clarity, context, and positional understanding of the religious-like passion that is embraced by Retentionists in this area. Specifically, it provides locational relevance for Lexington as a sacred site and burial grounds of Lee and Jackson and demonstrates "geography in the life space of individuals" (Wright and Esses 2017). The nostalgic fabric for Retentionists is woven from threads of very personalized attachments to hearth and home. These threads are fashioned from three robust fibers: kith and kin, ancestral land, and conservation of honor.

The fiber of *kith and kin* for a Retentionist is deeply woven in Southern ancestry. They are proud of their European lineages that have been in America for centuries. Of particular pride was pre–Civil War ancestry related to Americans as pioneers. White pride was not couched as supremacy against black people but rather a generalized superiority based on a presumed greater legitimacy of American citizenship because of familial longevity in America and Virginia. Larry stated, "I'm proud of who I am . . . I'm white . . . I'm a Christian . . . and I try to be a good person." Larry's family was from England and were early settlers in the Shenandoah Valley. "The first . . . family arrived in Virginia in 1704." Rita, a resident of Lexington and a former United Daughters of the Confederacy member, described her family ancestry. "The M—[father's side] came to this country with William Penn." On her mom's side, her grandmother's father's family were English and came over on the Mayflower and signed the Mayflower Compact. "I am proud of my heritage. My mother's family was English, and my dad's [side] was all Irish [Scotch/

Irish] . . . I guess I'm proud they were pioneers, and they were willing to try something new. I like change. . . . It makes me feel like I belong to something that has always done this. They were willing to stand up for what they believed in. They were willing to do what is right. . . . It was the right thing. What I believe was right."

For Larry, to be a Southerner is to be "native-born from one of the 13 Confederate States. . . . It's a geographic thing . . . conservative, try to be friendly, try to get along, try to be respectful." For Liz, being a Southerner is based on "good manners . . . honor and heritage." Many Retentionists indicated a sensitivity to insult (Nesbett and Cohen 1996, 39). Jesse, a former Sons of Confederate Veterans member, stated, "They try to be kind, gentle, easy going. But don't get one riled up." Richard is proud to be a Southerner. For him, South is the same as *country*. When asked what *country* meant, Richard said it was "the way I was raised . . . I was raised right . . . you have more freedom in the country . . . relaxing in the country . . . nature" and fewer people. Tucker described a Southerner: "The thing with a Southerner is traditional American Christian. . . . Religion is number one. . . . A Southerner is a geographic reference and good moral values. [Rednecks are] an enemy of mine as much as any because of that stereotype . . . they have poisoned the well . . . I despise the media always runs the most extreme to the forefront for attention. A few bad apples have tainted the barrel."

Lauren does not consider herself a Southerner, but she feels a kinship with them. She joined the United Daughters of the Confederacy as a ranking member of the Lexington chapter as she is proud of her ancestors who hail from the Confederacy. "No. I'm still [Midwest] at heart which is Midwest . . . I think traditional Southerners are very elegant, the yes ma'am, no ma'am thing." She felt that Southerners and Midwesterners are friendly and "laid back." Lauren's motivation in joining the United Daughters of the Confederacy was "to honor" her ancestors who were veterans. Her sentiments on the War Between the States is typical of Retentionists. "Most of the Southerners that fought weren't fighting for slavery. They were fighting because someone invaded their farmland or their homes. Or it was at that time, 'I'm a Virginian. I'm not an American.' It wasn't until after the Civil War that we became the United States."

The fiber of *ancestral land* is a powerful strand in Southern hearth and home sentiments. For Retentionists, the land is connected to the Southern state, and the Southern state is associated with the Civil War and "States' rights and freedom of choice" and, of course, slavery. The Civil War for Retentionists was foremost, "The War Between the States," "A War of Southern Independence," or "A War of Northern Aggression" (Nesbett and Cohen 1996, 6–7). Although Herbert is a Forbearer, his father was a Retentionist. "My father called the Civil War 'the War to suppress Yankee arrogance.'" These tropes are commonly used in furtherance of the infamous Lost Cause argument which is a construct of selective collective memory and part of Retentionist nostalgic fabric. For many with strong Cherished Southern identity they provide the generalized argument, "It was states' rights! . . . The right to leave what we willingly joined.. . . . We only joined the Union with the understanding that we could leave" (Coski 2005, 17). For them, departure of the initial seven states, and ultimately thirteen, was simply an exercising of states' rights even if that right was the institution of chattel slavery. Many references were made by Retentionists that Virginia was forced out of the Union after Fort Sumter was attacked and that Lee was not in favor of secession, but he would take no part in the "invasion of the Southern States" (Korda 2014, 228). Diane, a member of the United Daughters of the Confederacy, embraced the states' rights argument as an issue of freedom for states who "voluntarily joined" the Union, to "voluntarily leave" through secession. For her it was about "federal overreach and reduction of state control." From convenient rationalizing of the strategically offensive maneuver of secession and the attack upon Fort Sumpter, Retentionists also rely upon the sacred reference of defense of one's land, home, and family against invading Yankee marauders (Leigh 2020; Poole 2004; Wilson 1980). This sentiment becomes much more poignant and personal when considering that the land for many rural community members has been in their family for generations and has also served as personal graveyards for their ancestors to include Confederate States of America kin. Jesse, a self-identified gay man and former member of the Sons of Confederate Veterans, has an interesting outlook: "We were the United States of the Confederacy. We were a country. We had our own capital. We had our own Army. We had our own money. Damn Yankees invaded us, and we have been under occupation ever since!"

Retentionists are generally not *apologists* for slavery. However, the issue is conveniently obscured in states' rights arguments. There was never any overt reference to white supremacy or minimizations of that *peculiar institution* by Retentionists. However, reflections of the past, or the good old days, are made with a firm grasp of nostalgic fabric concerning Southern symbols that is selective in its recollection. Some Retentionists, and members of other clusters, admitted to having ancestors who owned slaves. Most claim that their ancestors were born in "grinding poverty" and fought for Virginia as their homeland and country. That does not mean that the issue of slavery was easy for Retentionists to reconcile internally or externally. When asked if "states' rights" were simply those "rights to own slaves," Diane was conflicted and inconsistent. "Well, I think that becomes a human issue more than a states, telling us what we can, you know. I want to keep it at the state level and not let the overall. I'm all about smaller government. Let's let the local entities take care of themselves. I think, slavery to me is so wrong. It's about a human.

We are all people in this world. We should all be treated with the same respect and dignity." Diane was asked if the Confederate Battle Flag and the slavery issue could be disentangled. "I think they are so closely intertwined that it is hard for people and once you have been told something, it is hard to back that out." However, Retentionists do fervently try to disentangle slavery from the threads of Southern hearth and home.

In 2018 a *Statement from the President General* was issued on the United Daughters of the Confederacy website. The statement recognizes the nationally polarized sentiments toward Confederate memorials. The following are excerpts of this statement:

> The United Daughters of the Confederacy appreciates the feelings of citizens across the country currently being expressed concerning Confederate memorial statues and monuments that were erected by our members in decades past. . . . We are saddened that some people find anything connected with the Confederacy to be offensive. Our Confederate ancestors were and are Americans. We as an Organization do not sit in judgment of them nor do we impose the standards of the 19th century on Americans of the 21st century.
>
> We are grieved that certain hate groups have taken the Confederate flag and other symbols as their own. We are the descendants of Confederate soldiers, sailors, and patriots. . . . The United Daughters of the Confederacy totally denounces any individual or group that promotes racial divisiveness or white supremacy.
>
> Join us in denouncing hate groups and affirming that Confederate memorial statues and monuments are part of our shared American history and should remain in place. (Crutcher 2018)

The third fiber of hearth and home for Retentionists is *conservation of honor*. Retentionists wish to preserve their version of virtue of their Cherished Southern identity and tradition through consecrated remembrance, or commemoration. Retentionists identify passionately with the "sublime self-sacrifice" of their kin and especially with Robert E. Lee and Stonewall Jackson (Leigh 2020). They position these veterans as "noble warriors" who were admittedly associated with the ignoble cause of slavery. Common tropes used by them are "Save Our Monuments: Save Our History & Honor" and "My Heroes Wore Grey! Men That Answered the Call of Their States." When entering Lee Chapel, Valentine's "sarcophagus" of Lee in papal repose is striking. There is a vague similarity in positioning to that of the tomb of Robert de Bruce in Scotland, Lee's reputed forefather. Retentionists and other community members of Lexington hold a sacred place for the "saints" Lee and Jackson. References to "St. Bobby" and how "Stonewall taught black children to read in Sunday School at the Lexington Presbyterian Church" were common references. Retentionists have the strongest attachment but not necessarily a monopoly on such ardent sentiments. For many community members, Lee and Jackson are flawed patron saints of Lexington and Rockbridge County. Abby is a Reformer and actively disassociates herself from being Southern and supported reverting the *Robert E. Lee* Episcopal Church name back to *Grace Episcopal* because "Lee would have supported that." Yet, Abby still holds "St. Bobby" in great esteem above and beyond the Confederate Battle Flag:

> Yeah. He was an amazing man. So was Grant for that matter.. . . . He [Lee] put family and the land over country. He was the Superintendent of West Point. He turned down the offer to lead the Union Army and come home. . . . It's a heart-breaking choice. . . . He [Lee] did the best he knew how to do. He was a man of honor. . . . He is a flawed human being but a great man nevertheless. . . . We called our church Saint Bobby's . . . humorously. . . . That is how big Robert E. Lee is in this town.

Retentionists most strongly embrace their nostalgic fabric through tightly intertwined threads of hearth and home that are constructed with the fibers of kith and kin, ancestral land, and conservation of honor in preserving their Cherished Southern identity. Personal affiliation with Confederate ancestry and the perceived nobility and virtue for fighting for what one believes in goes beyond mere ethnic and clan association because there is a direct familial reference. The sacred connections of hearth and home are maintained through family bibles, land deeds, oral stories, myths, and graves of kith and kin marked with Confederate States of America (CSA) grave markers adjoining the patron saints of their Cherished Southern identity. It is in the "kin not the causes" that the long-standing community members of Lexington may be linked (Humphrey 2015).

SOUTHERN SYMBOLS: SACRED TOTEMS OF THE CHURCH OF CHERISHED SOUTHERN IDENTITY

Durkheim described religion as a "more or less complex system of myths, dogmas, rites and ceremonies—they operate as if it formed a kind of indivisible entity" (Durkheim 1912, 33). For the Retentionist, the "indivisible entity" is the church of the Cherished Southern identity and the Confederate Battle Flag "the sacred thing . . . par excellence, that which the profane must not and cannot touch with impunity" (Durkheim 1912, 38). The Flag is "sacred to them because it was representative of the God of battles and the cause of self-defense" (Rumburg 2015, 39). Retentionists feel that the Confederate Battle Flag in particular holds a religious significance and that their Cherished Southern identity has its roots in the hearth and home of the South. During the Civil War, the Flag "was looked upon as that which represented the essence of life" (Rumburg 2015, 38). The *sacred* derivation of the Confederate Battle Flag has been related to that of the Saltire or St Andrew's Cross (Coski 2005, 9, 11, 19, 33). St. Andrew is the Patron Saint of Scotland, and the flag of Scotland is the Cross of St. Andrew. The following is an excerpt from a pamphlet titled *The Truth About the Confederate Battle Flag* written by a Retentionist pastor in Georgia: "The Confederate battle flag is based upon the national flag of Scotland. The national flag of Scotland is the cross of Saint Andrew and the cross of Saint Andrew is a symbol of Christian faith and heritage of the Celtic race" (Weaver 2000).

Retentionists particularly revel in that Lee is reputed to be the "17th direct descendant of Robert de Bruce of Scotland" (Rumburg 2020). Robert de Bruce led Scotland during the First War of Scottish Independence against England and is revered in Scotland as a national hero. The correlation between the *Roberts* is important when considering esteemed causes and connections.

The deified connections of Cherished Southern identity serve as constant reminders of duty to commemoration and preservation of tradition as part of hearth and home. Larry felt that Lexington, with the graves of Lee and Jackson and his ancestors, was *hallowed* or *sacred ground.* "Absolutely." He reiterated that his great-grandfather was buried in the Stonewall Jackson Cemetery. Larry was baffled why they couldn't have allowed the Confederate Battle Flag for their memorial service for Lee-Jackson Day, one day, each year. Retentionists believe that their main objective is to preserve their Cherished Southern identity and to be left unmolested. They fear change. Jesse succinctly stated, "I don't want people to change me or our way of life!" As such, Retentionists felt that the Confederate monuments should be left intact, but many were not opposed to adding other monuments to honor notable black figures. Retentionists share a sense of being categorically misunderstood, a sense of pending doom and loss of what they hold dear. Diane had conflicting feelings about being a Retentionist as she did not want to appear offensive. She exhibited a deep melancholy that the Flag legacy was apparently coming to an end. "It is just matter of time before the 1st Confederate Battle Flag and 2nd Confederate Battle Flag, and other, you know there are other flags that are a part of the United Daughters of the Confederacy? I am sure that all of them at some point will have this negative connotation because it is part of the Confederacy. And the only thing anybody hears when you say 'Confederacy' is . . . slavery."

In the church of the Cherished Southern identity, both the Sons of Confederate Veterans and the United Daughters of the Confederacy engage in formalized rituals related to the Confederate Battle Flag that can be disconcerting and offensive at face value and rather suspicious to the casual observer. At the beginning of their meetings, the Sons of Confederate Veterans engage in a ritual where they stand, pledge allegiance to the flag of Virginia, and salute the Confederate Battle Flag. No pledge of allegiance or salute was made to the US Flag. Tucker advised that the pledge to the US Flag was changed after the Civil War to include the word *indivisible* to address Southern rebellion, thus the Sons of Confederate Veterans chafe at this reference. This is a point of contention for the Stonewall Brigade of the Sons of Confederate Veterans. Cole stated, "I say the pledge of allegiance all the time. I don't care for that particular word [indivisible] because of my Southern heritage." Tucker was asked about the lack of pledging allegiance to the US Flag at Sons of Confederate Veterans meetings. He provided coyly, "By pledging to the state you vicariously pledge to the country." Cole provided more background stating that not pledging allegiance to the American Flag was unique to the Stonewall Brigade of Sons of Confederate Veterans camp. Having the American Flag present at Sons of Confederate Veterans meetings but without a pledge of allegiance was a "compromise" to an internal dispute:

> We do not say a pledge of allegiance to it. This caused some controversy. We had a big who-do over that. It was pretty interesting. . . . That is not the context for why we are there. We are there specifically to honor our ancestors who fought in that war [Civil War]. . . . We had members who were adamantly opposed to the flag being there. Even being there. Let alone saying the pledge of allegiance.
>
> I didn't want the US Flag at our meetings. . . . That is not why we are here tonight. We are here to promote our own ancestors and what they did, for that two hour, once a month. . . . Under that context, that [American Flag] was the flag of the enemy . . . the flag of oppression. . . . But at the same time, the moment I walk out that door, it is totally different.

The following are salutes and pledges by the Stonewall Brigade of the Sons of Confederate Veterans as provided by Tucker:

THE SONS OF CONFEDERATE VETERANS
PLEDGE TO THE VIRGINIA FLAG

I [pledge allegiance] to the flag of Virginia with affection, reverence and patriotic devotion to the Mother of States and Statesmen which it represents the Old Dominion where liberty and justice were born.

THE SONS OF CONFEDERATE VETERANS
SALUTE TO THE CONFEDERATE BATTLE FLAG

I salute the Confederate Flag with affection, reverence, and undying devotion and to the cause for which it stands.

The Sons of Confederate Veterans salute consists of an outstretched right hand, similar to that of a handshake with the palm up. Tucker advised that the Sons of Confederate Veterans "pledges to the Virginia State Flag" and "salutes the Confederate Battle Flag." When asked what *the cause* was specifically, Tucker replied, "I always tell everybody, you got to look at it in context. . . . American liberty, all of what Washington fought for and Lee defended." Tucker referred me to all that we have spoken about up to this point in the interview. That *cause* was characterized as "resistance to federal tyranny and the preservation of states' rights and individual liberty." Retentionists argue that the *cause* was about independence and choice, more than slavery. Tucker was queried about the fact that Lee *let go* of the Flag after the war. Tucker stated, "He [Lee] was a military man. He obviously knew he was defeated." After the pledge and salute rituals, a recognition of veterans of all wars is made. Interestingly, for the functions that I attended, most Sons of Confederate Veterans members did not identify as veterans.

I was unable to personally witness United Daughters of the Confederacy rituals at their meetings. I was invited to part of a UDC luncheon to present my research, but afterward I was politely dismissed before any rituals were presented. Fortunately, Liz described the United Daughters of the Confederacy opening ceremony. Their meetings are usually held at a local restaurant in a private area. The UDC president places three small flags on the table: the American Flag, the Virginia Flag, and the Confederate Battle Flag. They salute each one and she described the ceremony as "very religious based." I obtained a copy of a United Daughters of the Confederacy handbook that had chapters on "Standing Rules," "Chapter Bylaws," "Pledges," and "Opening Ritual." The UDC "Pledges" are made to three flags, the US, the Virginia, and the Confederate Battle Flag. Below are the pledges and salutes:

PLEDGE OF ALLEGIANCE TO THE FLAG
OF THE UNITED STATES OF AMERICA

I pledge allegiance to the Flag of the United States of America and to the Republic for which it stands—one Nation under God, indivisible, with liberty and justice for all.

SALUTE TO THE FLAG OF VIRGINIA

I salute the Flag of Virginia with reverence and patriotic devotion to the "Mother of States and Statesmen" which it represents—the "Old Dominion," where liberty and independence were born.

SALUTE TO THE CONFEDERATE FLAG

I salute the Confederate Flag with affection, reverence, and undying remembrance.

The Opening Ritual for the United Daughters of the Confederacy is of particular interest as it demonstrates the religious context to their nostalgic fabric woven with various strands of virtue to include duty, valor, and sacrifice to create a UDC *ceremonial robe* of Cherished Southern identity.

OPENING RITUAL

President: Daughters of the Confederacy, this day we are gathered together in the sight of God to strengthen the bonds that unite us in a common cause; to renew the vows of loyalty to our sacred principles; to do homage unto the memory of the Confederate defenders, and to perpetuate the fame of their noble deeds unto succeeding generations. To this end we invoke the aid of our Lord. Hear My prayer, O God; attend unto my prayer.

Response by all Present: From the end of the earth, I will cry unto Thee when my heart is overwhelmed; lead me to the rock that is higher than I.

President: For Thou, Lord art good and ready to forgive and plenteous in mercy unto all of them that call upon thee.

Response by all Present: Give ear, O Lord, unto my prayer; and attend to the voice of my supplications.

President: Almighty God, our Heavenly Father, we adore Thy love and providence in the history of our country, and especially would we thank Thee for our Confederate history. We thank Thee for its pure record of virtue, valor, and sacrifice; and for the inspiring reflections that, despite it(s) bitter disappointments and sorrows, it proclaims for us, to all the world that we came through its years of trial and struggle with our battered shields pure, our character as a patriotic and courageous people untarnished and nothing to regret in our defense of the rights and the honor or our Southland. Give us grace, our Heavenly Father, faithfully to accept Thy will concerning us, and make us all to glorify Thee in a sincere obedience to Thy holy commandments through the merits and mediation of Thy Son, our only Savior, Jesus Christ. Amen

If the United Daughters of the Confederacy and the Sons of Confederate Veterans have a sibling relationship in their church of the Cherished Southern identity, the Children of the Confederacy has a filial one to them. Retentionists believe it is vital to "teach the truth" and to inspire "many little ones to learn more about Southern history" (Pitre 2002). The Children of the Confederacy is "a children's organization, begun as an auxiliary" to the United Daughters of the Confederacy in 1897 (Allen 1990). I came across three *catechisms* concerning the Children of the Confederacy: (1) Pre-Junior Catechism, (2) Catechism, and (3) Senior Catechism. The "Catechism" was initially compiled and printed in 1954 with the purpose "to teach the truths of our Confederate history and to convey the objectives" of the United Daughters of the Confederacy and Children of the Confederacy (Allen 1990). The "Pre-Junior Catechism: A Symbolic History of the Confederate States of America" (Pitre 2002) is a small pamphlet that shows pictures of "Heroes & Heroines," "Flags of the Confederacy," and "Other Southern Symbols." The following is a portion of the Preface:

> In order to "Teach the Truth" which was the national theme for the 2001–2002 General Organization of the Children of the Confederacy, it was apparent a pictorial catechism for our younger members was needed . . . I pray this symbolic history of the Confederate States of America inspire many little one to learn more about Southern history and the Children of the Confederacy. Proverbs 13:22 says, "a good man leaves an inheritance to his children's children." It is with great Southern Pride that I compiled this catechism. May each member of the Children of the Confederacy grow up to share it with their children's children as an undying remembrance of our Confederate ancestors who fought for what they believed in.

The other two catechism pamphlets are organized in Q & A format. They reference topics like "How it All Began," "Secession and the War," and the importance of the United Daughters of the Confederacy and the Children of the Confederacy. The Senior Catechism has 161 questions, and the following is the final question:

> Q. Why should the United Daughters of the Confederacy consider the Children of the Confederacy organization important?

> A. Because the members of the Children of the Confederacy are the logical ones to perpetuate our Southern heritage and the future of our Confederate Organizations.

KEEPING THE FAITH: THE HOLY DAYS
OF LEE-JACKSON WEEKEND

In 2020 the Lee-Jackson Weekend functions provided a unique opportunity to witness the passion and intensity of the holy days and the religious-like characteristics and sentiments demonstrated by Retentionist speakers and attendees in group-setting. The weekend consisted of two functions for Retentionists. The first was the Lee-Jackson Symposium held on Friday, 17 January, at the Lexington Hampton Inn, Col Alto. The following accounts of presentations are summarized to highlight key points made by speakers to illustrate a focus on religion and virtue in protection of conservative values and hearth and home. These accounts represent the views of the speakers and, judging by the positive affirmations, the views of the general audience.

Ethan is a published historian. In his presentation Ethan focused on the virtues of Stonewall Jackson and his staff officers. Jackson wanted "the right sort of man" and had "the most educated staff in the Confederate Army." Jackson did not surround himself with those that would mimic in his own image. He wanted a staff that offered a spectrum of skill sets but would also "do what was right" and those who were diligent and reliable. Jackson held four specific criteria for staff officers: (1) unique and valuable talents, (2) exceptional courage, (3) desire to excel, and (4) Presbyterian faith. Kinship and personal friendship were not relevant factors in Jackson's selection. It did not matter to Jackson if an officer came from the North as long as the officer was loyal to the cause and met his criteria. The famous autodidactic mapmaker Jedediah Hotchkiss was from New York and was ordered by Jackson, "Make me a map of the valley." No better mapmaker would be found during the Civil War. For Jackson, "courage matters more than knowledge, that determination means more than talent and self-sacrifice achieves more than ambition."

Logan is a Sons of Confederate Veterans chaplain and part of the Society for Biblical and Southern Studies. He authored books on Confederate signification. Logan quoted Scripture throughout his presentation as he focused on the friendship of Lee and Jackson and that these were both "men of great integrity." For Logan there is a correlation between conventional religion (Episcopalian and Presbyterian) and the military greatness for Lee and Jackson. The two were "driven together because of the catalyst of war." Their friendship grew during the "War of Aggression." Logan felt that Lee and Jackson had much in common. "They were brothers in Christ . . . men of prayer . . . men who loved the word of God." They were also both West Pointers, Virginians, and great believers in the US Constitution. They were "honorable and unusual men." There was great trust between these two friends. Lee referred to Jackson as his "right arm." Jackson stated that "Lee was the only man he was willing to follow blind-folded." Logan stated, "They were unbeatable . . . by the grace of God." Logan felt Lee was the "consummate Southern Christian gentleman" and that in old Virginia textbooks, the word *Christian* was used "without apology." "Character is invincible." Lee considered his first duty as a "Virginia gentleman." Jackson was a "soldier saint." When speaking of Lee's and Jackson's deaths, Logan became emotionally moved. "Any nation would be grateful to have just the Lee or just the Jackson. But to think of the double blessing that we had of having both. Thanks be to God for such examples of Christian, manhood and friendship. I do believe that these two men would be better role models for our kids today than some of these ball players that are multi-millionaires and live lives deserving of the wrath of God." Logan provided an apocalyptic warning to the audience: "If we do not continue to remember our heritage, it is going to be erased. Think of ancient Egypt. A new pharaoh would come along . . . they would chip off all the great exploits of the previous pharaoh and write their own. We are being written out. We are being chipped off. They want to remove all vestiges of our heritage and what God gave us. We must not allow that."

Owen is a member of the Sons of Confederate Veterans (Norfolk County Grays/Camp #1549). His business card reads, "Past Virginia Division Commander, Past Chief of Heritage Defense, Commander of the Army of Northern Virginia." Owen's presentation focused on threat and loss to Cherished Southern identity. Owen stated, "We are now facing a situation worse" than the four years of the Civil War, and this may be the last Lee-Jackson Day ceremony. The losses he referred to consist of monuments, guns, freedom of expression, and truth. Lee and Jackson were the epitome of "Christian men." "The same people that hate us, hate Christians . . . We are Confederate Christians." Owen felt that the Southern states succeeded over state rights and that slavery had existed in all of North American for 200 to 250 years. Owen refers to the "lie":

The biggest lie . . . the war was over slavery and nothing but slavery. . . . The war was not about slavery for the first two years. . . . There were no "Join the Union Army and Free the Slaves" recruitment posters. There were "Preserve the Union" posters. If it were a true concern for Lincoln, why did he not grant the Emancipation Proclamation the first day in office? . . . Nobody gets any blame but us, Southerners. Slavery was a terrible thing, and it was an issue. We all agree that slavery was bad. We are all glad that it ended, and we don't want to bring it back. . . . The Emancipation Proclamation had nothing to do with freeing slaves. . . . Lincoln is the enemy. Was then, still is. . . . Before Lincoln entered politics, he was a lawyer.

Owen describes the enemies of the Retentionists as "the liberals and we need to reach the community members in the middle." These "enemies" blame Southerners for all the wrongs of the Civil War. "Slavery was a terrible thing. Nobody here wants slavery, and everyone here believes that slavery was bad . . . I think the most racist thing there is, is for a bunch of white liberals to running around and decide what is best for African Americans . . . and they haven't asked one African American yet . . . they make decisions for other people. . . . Our enemies of today are all liars." Owen declares that today's enemy are "not blacks, but the liberals, the black-faced Minstrel"[1] trying to "destroy every bit of our heritage." Owen defends this heritage and focuses on the positive and progressive attributes of Lee and Jackson. "Lee gave up his house, his US military career, and slaves. . . . Lee graciously took communion with a black man after the war. . . . Lee did not own slaves, but he inherited some from his father-in-law based on the gendered law. Lee freed those slaves. . . . Jackson taught slaves Sunday School and gave up his life. . . . Both fought in defense of Virginia. Lee and Jackson gave everything up for Virginia."

In an effort of inclusivity Owen refers to Jewish Confederates, Judah Philip Benjamin,[2] and Moses Ezekiel.[3] "I know why the South lost. We just didn't have enough Jews!" Owen felt that he and those like-minded were under attack as indiscriminate racists. "This is contemporary. We are white racists. We hate American Indians. We hate blacks. We hate Jews. This is just not true. . . . Stand Watie was a leader of the Cherokee Nation and held a general's rank in the Confederate States of America during the American Civil War." Owen defends Confederate monuments. He referenced that just like the McArthur statue should not be considered anti-Japanese, neither should a Confederate statue be assumed to be anti–African American and antisemitic. He provided that there is law in Virginia which protects all war monuments:

> There are proposed versions of the law which would remove protection for all monuments, not just Confederate but also ones like the Vietnam veteran's monuments. . . . They want to take down every monument on Monument Avenue. . . . They want Richmond, the Old Confederate Capital to fall. . . . It is not just a Confederate thing anymore. It is an attack predominately on the South. . . . They got rid of our state song. They got rid of our pledge to the flag . . . there is nothing in there about slaves, or darkies or plantations, it's to the Old Dominion, the mother of states and statesman where liberty and independence were born.

Owen prognosticated a dismal future for those with strong Cherished Southern identity. "It's like *1984*![4] All he did was put the date too early . . . it's coming." [Quoting Orwell] "'Some ideas are so stupid that only intellectuals believe them.' The most effective way to destroy people is to deny and obliterate their own understanding of their history. . . . There will not be a Lee Highway. There will not be a Dixie Caverns. They want every school, every road, every-everything."

Henry is a reenactor and a member of the Sons of Confederate Veterans (Camp SC). Henry does not claim to be a professional historian or a professional speaker. He is currently engaged in a "research project" concerning the "accuracy of black Confederates." He became interested in black Confederates four years ago after the church shooting in South Carolina and the close scrutiny of the Confederate Battle Flag. "Among the other places I went, I started looking online and started looking for people of like-mind to discuss the history with." His references include CivilWarTalk.com, articles, and archives to include the Library of Congress on the topic of black Southerners and black Confederates. "People get angry about this, and people say, 'There were none.'" Henry's objective was to gather and investigate all the contemporaneous news articles he could find. In four years, he has accumulated 1,915 articles with 1,200 unique stories from the Civil War. Starting with December 1860 to July 1861, Henry cites many articles with the theme that the free-black population of the South "voluntarily contributed to the efforts of the Confederacy and to the fight against Yankee invaders." Henry goes on to cite numerous articles from Charleston, Columbia, Richmond, Norfolk, Baton Rouge, Savannah, and Pensacola which document offers by "free-colored people to contribute, fight or protect their community and state."

The second function held over Lee-Jackson Weekend was the Lee-Jackson Commemoration on 18 January 2020, the day after the symposium. It was convened at the gravesite of Stonewall Jackson in the cemetery formally named Stonewall Jackson Cemetery. Along with the change of cemetery name, time would demonstrate that this would be the last state-sanctioned holiday. The official program: "Lee-Jackson Day, Lexington in Old Virginia: *Here We Find the Homes and Shrines of Famous Men*" provided the following interesting background on the holiday in Lexington:

> Lee-Jackson Day is a holiday recognized in several States of the American South. The holiday is celebrated in Alabama, Arkansas, Florida, Georgia, Kentucky, Louisiana, Mississippi, North Carolina, South Carolina, and Virginia. In Texas, it is known as "Confederate Heroes Day." In Virginia it is a state holiday which falls on the Friday before the third Monday of January.
>
> The holiday was originally created in 1889 to celebrate the birthday of General Robert E. Lee who was born on January 19, 1807. The holiday was put into effect by Governor Fitzhugh Lee who was nephew of the general and had been a Confederate general himself. In 1904 the holiday was changed to include a tribute to Thomas J. "Stonewall" Jackson who was born on January

21, 1824. The change was made under the administration of Governor Andrew Jackson Montague.

Lee-Jackson Day has been honored in Lexington since the late 19th century. It seems only befitting that various celebrations and events have been held to honor the birthdays of the generals in their final home and resting place. The United Daughters of the Confederacy, United Confederate Veterans and the Sons of Confederate Veterans have sponsored events to honor Lee and Jackson in Lexington. Typically, such events were held on January 19th, Lee's birthday. Today the event is held near the state holiday.

In 2000, the first large scale celebration of Lee-Jackson Day in nearly 25 years was brought back to Lexington. The following year, the newly reformed Sons of Confederate Veterans camp, The Stonewall Brigade, continued the basic format with a program focused on Godly character and ideals of men which are an inspiration for our time and future generations.

The Commemoration ceremony began around 10:00 a.m. and there were approximately 300 people in attendance: 180 white male, 120 white female, and 3 community members of color. It was about 30 degrees, grey skies, with only occasional freezing rain. The conditions were predicted to be much worse and precluded the attendance of the Wickham Camp, Sons of Confederate Veterans, Pipes and Drums, and perhaps other potential attendees. Upon my arrival at 9:45 a.m., approximately 150 people were at Stonewall's gravesite. By the end of the function, 150 more would arrive. Approximately one third of the attendees were in period garb. Most displayed various forms of the Confederate Battle Flag. The overall atmosphere could be characterized as a combination of Veteran's Day and Mardi Gras as the occasion had mixed elements of reverence and revelry. I walked around and spoke informally with some of the attendees. The following are quotes in response to the basic question: *Why is this function important to you?*

Luis (SCV, Texas): "My son is a soldier . . . I am very proud of him. My family fought and died for this. . . . If anybody knows anything about this flag, this is the cross of St. Andrew. This is one of the most holy symbols there are. People who will sit there and traipse this are lower than dog shit as far as I'm concerned."

Evan (Reenactor): "They [Lee and Jackson] were great men. They loved God. They were very Christian, a lot of respect for that. They were great leaders. . . . They made a couple of mistakes there but, they were great men. Truly, I respect them just for that."

Sam (Confederate Battle Flag bearer): "They loved God, and they were great Christians."

Buck (Reenactor, Stonewall Jackson): "It means a lot to me because it is my ancestry, my people."

John (SCV): As a reenactor, somebody that appreciates this kind of thing, we're out to promote specifically generals Lee and Jackson. . . . We're here to honor Civil War soldiers."

Kit (Mounted reenactor): "Used to do it in Richmond. This won't last much longer. It will be stopped. . . . Ask any white person. . . . Ask any white person. . . . If blacks have their way, it will be against the law to have a Confederate Battle Flag . . . I think Robert E. Lee and Stonewall Jackson are the greatest men that ever lived. See you next year if we still get to do this."

Halley (Attendee with her children): "There's two sides to each issue, and I'm teaching my kids that the biggest thing is to research and learn from history."

At approximately 10:30 a.m. the Commemoration formally began with the Invocation given again by Reverend Frank (SCV). Welcoming remarks were provided by Jack (SCV Ranking member, Stonewall Brigade). He was followed by Chris (SCV, Ranking member, Virginia Division), Terri (Virginia United Daughters of the Confederacy), and Sonya (Children of the Confederacy). After these opening remarks, "Amazing Grace" was sung by all attendees. Multiple wreaths were laid by a variety of representatives from all over Virginia. Once completed, the Lord's Prayer was said in unison followed by an Honor Guard military gun salute by the 5th VA Inf., Botetourt Artillery. The ceremony was concluded with "Taps."

Public statements were made during the official commemoration. The following are relevant excerpts:

Rev. Frank (SCV): "In this hour we remember Stonewall Jackson because he was a mighty man of God. Because he was brave in the face of the enemy. Because he taught us how a Christian man should die."

Jack (SCV, Stonewall Brigade): "To keep our heritage, especially everything that is dear to us. We must be proactive. This is our annual memorial service."

Chris (SCV): "We must hold the ground and hold the faith as our forefathers did. We are here to celebrate these two brave men. Not only them but . . . all the other brave men who are buried here. . . . They made us very proud. These are our ancestors . . . and hold the faith. As you know we are in the middle of a fight. They are trying to change state law . . . and the history of VA. We need your help to battle the undesirables that wish to do away with our history and heritage."

Terri (UDC): "To honor the memory of two great men . . . among the great military leaders of all time. . . . They preferred to be remembered as men of great Christian faith and principle . . . [quoting Lee] 'There is a true glory and a true honor. The glory of duty done and the honor of integrity of principle.' General Jackson was known for his deep Christian faith. In 1855 he taught Sunday School to slaves in Lexington. . . . Money was raised years later by those related to the same Sunday School students for a memorial in Roanoke. Likely making Stonewall the only Confederate general to have a memorial in an African American Church."

Sonya (CoC): "To honor two great gentlemen. Not only men of the South but men of Virginia . . . great men of God who led men into battle during the War Between the States."

Liz (UDC): "Honor our generals. Which is why we love Lexington. We want to make sure that they stay here and that we always honor them. I was a member of City Council. My claim to fame was that I cast the vote, 'Yes, we can keep these flags.' As you can tell, I was voted off council."

Shortly thereafter the parade formed, and many people who attended the ceremony marched down Main Street. The group marched from the cemetery down Main Street, making a right on Washington and then an immediate right on Randolph Street. They ended the parade at the east side of the same cemetery. We trailed the approximate route of the parade and watched the revelers. Following the parade there was a Sons of Confederate Veterans luncheon at the same Hampton Inn and a final speaker, Jason—"Defending Confederate Memorials." A similar Order of Service for the luncheon was provided by the same speakers, with very similar sentiments as they had at the cemetery. Frank provided another Invocation and Benediction. After the opening remarks the Congregational Hymn, "Nearer My God to Thee" was sung. The final speaker of the weekend was presented.

Jason is an author of a book on the South. He begins the presentation describing a Southerner as it relates to collective memory, hearth and home, and kith and kin. He quotes William Humphrey, the Texas novelist:

> If the Civil War is more alive to the Southerner than the Northerner it is because all of the past is, and this is so because the Southerner has a sense of having been present there himself in the person of one or more of his ancestors. The war filled merely a chapter in his . . . [family history] . . . transmitted orally from father to son [as] the proverbs, prophecies, legends, laws, traditions-of-origin, and tales-of-wanderings of his own tribe . . . It is this feeling of identity with the dead (who are past) which characterizes and explains the Southerner.
>
> It is with kin, not causes, that the Southerner is linked. Confederate Great-grandfather . . . is not remembered for his [probably undistinguished] part in the Battle of Bull Run; rather Bull Run is remembered because Great-grandfather was there. For the Southerner the Civil War is in the family.
>
> Clannishness was, and is, the key to his temperament, and he went off to war to protect not Alabama but only those thirty or forty acres of its sandy hillside, or stiff red clay, which he broke his back tilling, and which was as big a country as his mind could hold.

Jason does not defend the institution of slavery but rather the institution of duty for the Confederate soldier. He warns of the "vocal" numerical minority:

> Statue critics say the Confederate soldier fought for slavery. But fewer than 30 percent of Southern families owned slaves. In truth, according to historian William C. Davis, "The widespread Northern myth that Confederates went to the battlefield to perpetuate slavery is just that, a myth. Their letters and diaries, in the tens of thousands, reveal again and again that they fought because their Southern homeland was invaded." Moreover, when their impoverished families were finally able to collect enough money to erect memorials, they honored the soldier for his battlefield sacrifices.
>
> Today a vocal minority holds Confederate soldiers in contempt, much like the many Americans who sneered at returning Vietnam veterans in the 1960s and 70s. Mixed in with chants of "Hey, hey, LBJ, how many babies did you kill today?" some civilians mocked the soldiers. . . . Dishonoring such monuments demeans later generations of American warriors who were inspired by the Confederate soldier.

Jason warns of *presentism*, the "mob sport" of vandalism, and "censorship" initiatives comparable to the former Soviet Union:

> Finally, toppling Confederate statues has evolved into a mob sport, with impunity for the vandals. . . . Anti-statue activists are behaving much like the leaders of the former Soviet Union where censorship and rewritten history was part of the states' effort to ensure that the correct political spin was put on their history. In response, George Orwell warned, "The most effective way to destroy a people is to deny and obliterate their own understanding of their history."

Jason offers alternatives from the perspective of a Retentionist. "Rather than taking down Confederate monuments, we should be adding new ones that address the subjects of slavery, the Underground Railroad, black soldiers, and Reconstruction as well as the Jim Crow and Civil Rights eras. Adding new monuments for more recent heroes while keeping the old ones in place provides a tangible record of how our society evolved."

After Jason's presentation the Congregational Song of "Dixie" was sung prior to the Benediction and the official closing of the Lee-Jackson Weekend functions. In a follow-up email with Ethan after his presentation, he indicated his concerns about the "fading holiday" of Lee-Jackson Day: "I trust you enjoyed Lee-Jackson Day in Lexington. It is a fading holiday due to the rejection of Christian virtue by the educational establishment and the depraved and ignorant cultural ethos of modern America. Re-writing of the past by destroying the parts they don't like . . . sending them down the memory hole . . . has a long history among tyrants."

As epitomized by the sentiments expressed by those presenting and attending Lee-Jackson Day 2020, the Confederate Battle Flag and other Southern symbols are powerful constructs of nostalgic fabric for Retentionists and a sacred symbol of efforts to preserve "our way of life and our country" against that which is deemed unholy and un-Christian. It is also a rally point in their crusade to retain any moral authority and their very existence as acceptable community members. This refers not just to the South and the Confederacy but also to a virtuous Christian America as Retentionists envision it. The feeling of loss of virtue and desperation is palpable. Tucker provides: "I would say right now 50 percent of the Christians to me are lost, regardless of race or color. They are not really Christians. They have adopted social justice warrior mentality. . . . It's not Christian anymore. It's humanism."

Above all else, Retentionists fear anarchy, chaos, socialism, and communism as roots of liberalism and progressivism that destroy the things they wish to protect and conserve. To allay their fears male Retentionists maintain strong attachments not only to their God but also to their guns. Several of the Sons of Confederate Veterans monthly meetings had lively discussions on gun control. Guns along with tractors, trucks, chainsaws, and motorcycles serve as "tools in the gendered toolbox to assert masculine identities" (Carlson 2015, 167). Jesse's Confederate Battle Flag with the large silhouette of an AR-assault weapon and the logo "Come and Take It" epitomizes male Retentionist blended passion for their Flag, their guns, and fierce independence. These sentiments closely resemble Carlson's description of the moral worldview of gun-carrying "citizen-protectors":

> The concept of citizen-protector refers to a moral disposition regarding life and death. Citizen-protectors consider using deadly force against another human being, under certain circumstances, to be a morally upstanding response to a violent threat . . . the willingness to take a life is tantamount to a civic duty. In gun carry culture, however, this civic duty is not just a prerogative of a public servant (policemen or soldier); it is the mark of full citizenship. (Carlson 2015, 66–67)

The citizen-protector constructs a "brand of citizenship" that provides for "rights, duties and obligations" to participate in the public sphere as a gun carrier as they blend their sense of "self-made individualism" and their duty to protect what they deem important as part of group "cultural belonging" (Carlson 2015, 67). Male Retentionists create a similar sense of cultural belonging in their Cherished Southern identity as they embrace their sense of full citizenship via "rights, duties and obligations" through powerful nostalgic attachment to the constituent elements of hearth and home: kith and kin, ancestral land, and conservation of honor.

There are several recurring concerns for those who carry a strong Cherished Southern identity, who support the display of the Confederate Battle Flag and memorials and who feel their civil religion, their Cherished Southern identity is being attacked. As of 2021 Lee-Jackson Day is no longer a state holiday for Virginia. "Virginia's state holiday celebrating two Confederate generals has officially been scrapped in favor of making Election Day a state holiday" (Stewart 2020). With the loss of the official "holiday," the 2011 ban of the Flag, and the current trend of public miscorrelation between police brutality and Confederate symbols, Retentionists feel they are fighting a retrograde battle and are further victimized. Many Retentionists wonder where the *blasphemy* will end. Will their patron saints, Lee and Jackson, be entirely obliterated from history as attempts are made to rename Washington & Lee and Lee Chapel?[5] Will their names be struck from the history books in an effort to be politically correct? Will Northern/liberal revisionism conveniently forget facts like Northern slavery and black Confederate soldiers? (Interestingly, Retentionists rarely offered recognition of previous Lost Cause revisionism.) Retentionist feel they are under siege in the holy land of Lexington and that they are engaged in a final consecrated crusade to save their Cherished Southern identity. At a closing benediction of the monthly Sons of Confederate Veterans meetings, Rev. Frank offers a prayer. "Heavenly father, as we dismiss this evening, let divine protection fall upon the Confederate Monuments in such ways to bring honor and glory to Christ. In his name we pray. Amen."

Their perceived crusade is a real one for Retentionists. Utilizing practical symbolic interactionism, the infidel and foe for Retentionists are the Reformers and they comfortably invoke God in their holy cause as demonstrated in the Sons of Confederate Veterans mantra, *Deo Vindice* ("With God, our Defender" or "God will Vindicate"). Reformers are represented as "the enemy," "liberals," "Communists," Democrats," "Northerners," and "outsiders who want to make changes." Like Jerusalem, Lexington is a holy land for two competing religions, and a "memory battle" between Reformers and Retentionists is ongoing (Whitlinger 2020). Along with being sacred ground, Lexington is perceived by Retentionists to be a hotbed of liberalism with W&L at the nexus of liberal thought. Tucker feels that liberal agendas found in colleges and churches today only propagate "the virus" of progressive thought against Retentionist conservatism. Jesse feels that Lexington was ruined by "damn Yankees." "City folk . . . rich, educated, hotsy-totsy . . . liberals . . . bullies . . . I can't stand them. . . . They are liberal Democratic Socialists and that is what the town is." Jesse feels displaced. "They're here and you can't do anything about it." Jesse used to be a Democrat but he "had to switch over to Republican." "They got too far left." Jesse felt abused by rigid-minded Reformers in Lexington, and he aligns more closely with conservatives even though he is gay. "I'm up front with them. I tell them I'm here, I'm queer, get over it. If you don't like me, you go your way, I'll go mine." He thinks the local conservatives are more tolerant even as a gay man. "After they get to know me. Everybody knows and accepts me as I am. No problems." Jesse feels that the liberals did not accept him because he identifies as a Southerner, a Confederate, and "a fag." Retentionists feel that progressive inclusivity is only demonstrated toward like-minded liberals and not inclusive of truly diverse thought that might include Retentionists. They generally feel as if they are aberrant community members and scorned by academia. Cole stated, "It is so insulting to be demonized, or somebody who doesn't know me or never interacted with me, classifies me as a racist or a hateful person. What an ignorant assumption." Liz, a former United Daughters of the Confederacy member, felt that being a Southerner is "absolutely" under attack. "I believe that Southern traditions and Southern persona . . . I believe it is under attack right now, politically, and socially. . . . Members of 50 Ways Rockbridge, the faculty at W&L, liberals, people . . . that claim they are lovers of diversity, inclusive but are actually haters of diversity and are non-inclusive."

Jason directly challenges liberal academia and entities like the SPLC who draw singular conclusions of the intentions of those erecting the memorials as being solely racist. In his public presentations he offers counterarguments to why Confederate memorials were erected when they were.

The academic community is at the forefront of those wanting to remove Confederate statues, which they characterize as racist. In doing so they violate the American Historical Society's warning against "presentism," which is defined as an uncritical tendency to interpret the past in terms of modern values. It fails to recognize that racial attitudes throughout America 150 years ago were different than they are today.

The Southern Poverty Law Center (SPLC) wants Confederate statues removed from public spaces. Several years ago, they published the chart above depicting the dates when Confederate statues were erected. As you may see, they attempt to associate the construction of Confederate statues with three eras they claim correlate to white hostility toward blacks. . . . In truth, four factors that the SPLC evades caused the building surge during the 1900–1920 interval. First, since the old soldiers were dying-off family members wanted to honor them while they were still around. A twenty-one-year-old who went to war in 1861 was sixty years old in 1900 and seventy-five in 1915. Second, the Civil War's semi-centennial commemoration was a major factor motivating statue construction. Nineteen-eleven marked the fiftieth anniversary of the start of the war and 1915 was the fiftieth anniversary of its end. Third, both of the preceding points contributed to a simultaneous surge in the number of statues erected to honor Union veterans. It is only natural that Confederate descendants wanted to follow suit at the same time. Fourth, post-war impoverished Southerners generally did not have enough money to pay for memorials until the turn of the century. Notwithstanding its population growth, the region did not recover to its pre-war economic activity level until 1900. (Leigh 2019, 14–15)

As stated earlier in the chapter, Retentionists did not outwardly display negative sentiments toward black citizens or those of African heritage. Most stated that they were unconcerned if their kin married a black spouse. Jesse proudly acknowledges his African heritage. He advised he had his DNA recently tested. He can trace back to 1630 when there was a "Sub-Sahara East African who married an Asian." His namesake kin came from Germany and married Jewish folk. "[We] came to the US and married Scotch/Native American. . . . When they get on television and speak of people of color . . . I got it all." Jesse showed me an old family portrait as proof of his diverse background. Jesse stated that if he had children, he would not be opposed to them being attached to black folk. "If they love each other and take care of each other and take care of the kids, and he don't beat her, I don't care. . . . They can come in here any time and eat, and I can go over there." Lauren has a friend who is married to a black man. "He's great." Lauren credits such open-mindedness to her association with the military. "It was very common." She would support her daughter if she wanted to marry a black man as long as he was "treating her well." Diane stated, "You are going to fall in love with whoever you fall in love with. You can't direct the heart . . . I would happily welcome a black man into the family as opposed to a white jerk."

Sons of Confederate Veterans Retentionists make great efforts at their brand of inclusivity to combat racist allegations by Reformers that only WASPs were soldiers in the Confederate army. At Sons of Confederate Veterans meetings and symposiums, there was much discussion about Jewish, Italian, Native American, and black Confederates. Along with these very small minorities in the historic Confederacy, there do exist a few black members in the ranks of the Sons of Confederate Veterans throughout the country. Respondent information provided that Teddy is a black Sons of Confederate Veterans member who resides in southern Virginia. I attempted contact with that Sons of Confederate Veterans group but had no success. H.K. Edgerton of Asheville, North Carolina, holds great notoriety as he is a Sons of Confederate Veterans member and a former president of the Asheville branch of the National Association for the Advancement of Colored People (NAACP) (SPLC 2000). Sons of Confederate Veterans Retentionists do not try to represent that there were significant numbers of black Confederates, but rather it is important to them that it is recognized that they existed. As Press Officer, Tucker takes great pride in the *racial inclusivity* of the Sons of Confederate Veterans in the Lexington Black Confederate Sites/Tour at Evergreen Cemetery. The following is an excerpt from the site:

Lexington Black Confederate Sites/Tour—

No topic is more hotly contended over than the role of slavery and Black Confederates during the Civil War. There is no doubt that many slaves were used against their will in during the contest, but there are plenty of examples of others who voluntarily served or at least looked at their service fondly post-war. Lexington was located in the more mountainous region of Virginia and was therefore not heavily populated with slaves. In fact, the region was moderately abolitionist, however, just like the rest of Virginia, when Lincoln called for an armed invasion of the South, the area voted to secede from the Union. When the local troops marched off to war, a number of free and enslaved blacks accompanied them. Among those were the likes of Jim Lewis, James Humbles, Levi Miller, and Jefferson Shields. You will find their graves at Lexington's historically Black Cemetery, Evergreen with the exception of those buried prior to the 1880's in the Old Colored Cemetery which was obliterated by a housing development in 1945.

Charles H. Wesley, a distinguished black historian who lived from 1891 to 1987, wrote "The Employment of Negroes as Soldiers in the Confederate Army," in the *Journal of Negro History* (1919). He says, "Seventy free blacks enlisted in the Confederate Army in Lynchburg, Virginia. Sixteen companies (1,600) of free men of color marched through Augusta, Georgia on their way to fight in Virginia," according to (Dr. Walter E. Williams) (SCV 2020).

Retentionists recognize the co-option of the Confederate Battle Flag by white supremacy groups such as the Ku Klux Klan, Aryan Brotherhood, and Nazis. This is a massive frustration point for Retentionists and many Forbearer community members. Although Retentionists practically apply the symbolic interactionism of the Confederate Battle Flag toward Reformers as foes, they do not necessarily apply the status of friendship to other groups who fete the Flag. In many cases they label them as foes. The Sons of Confederate Veterans has gone on record to distance themselves from hate groups and even the VA-Flaggers who they describe as "offensively aggressive and militant." Tucker emphatically stated, "The KKK carries the American Flag, the Confederate Battle Flag, and the Christian Flag. They co-opt everything I like. . . . They act like animals."

LOSING THE FAITH AND SOUTHERN GUILT

It is important to note that Liz, Rita, and Diane are now former or fading Retentionists and have distanced themselves from the United Daughters of the Confederacy because of the argumentative sentiments in the community and Southern guilt. For them, the United Daughters of the Confederacy and the Confederate Battle Flag are not worth the time, the effort, or the angst.

They exhibit a distancing characteristic of disassociation from the United Daughters of the Confederacy and the Flag and greater sensitivity for black community members. Liz is a former ranking member of the local chapter of the United Daughters of the Confederacy and serves as a ranking member of other local Lexington organizations. She joined the United Daughters of the Confederacy years ago and is also a ranking member of the local chapter of the Daughters of the American Revolution. Liz found her duties were a lot of work as the United Daughters of the Confederacy maintained gravesites for Confederate States of America soldiers. Liz described a former UDC president as a member of the old guard and as a "dumb, old *bitch* mean lady." Although the United Daughters of the Confederacy was changing, there are still the "old stalwarts." She described that generation as, "so close to Jim Crow." "Writing the textbooks that . . . were influencing children [through] tainted history." Liz joined the United Daughters of the Confederacy to more closely connect to her Cherished Southern identity. However, internal politics of the United Daughters of the Confederacy and personal conflict drove her away. For Liz the sacred aspect of the Confederate Battle Flag is more closely related to conventional patriotism and freedom of expression. The Flag as a specific Confederate symbol is not necessarily important to her. Instead, Liz displays the Bonnie Blue Flag.[6] She flies it as a "poke" or statement to say, "You don't know what you're talking about." Liz advised for women of the current generation, the United Daughters of the Confederacy is predomi-nately about lineage and heritage. Liz feels that she doesn't glorify or identify with the Confederacy or its associated politics, but she does hold a strong Cherished Southern identity.

Rita's and Diane's introduction into the United Daughters of the Confederacy was through their mothers. Rita stated, "Mom was in the United Daughters of the Confederacy and the Daughters of the Revolution and all the proper things." Diane describes her inculcation:

My mother was very proud of her Southern heritage. She was a part of the United Daughters of the Confederacy and of the Daughters of the American Revolution. [She] got my children involved. . . . She signed me up for every-thing. . . . She always paid for my sister and myself to have our dues paid. I didn't know there were dues for those groups until she passed away and they started calling saying, "Aren't you going to pay your dues?" I went to all these conferences and events with my mother because she was partially handicapped. She needed somebody to push her around and let's be honest, to get her a glass of wine and cigarettes. . . . People heard that I went to these conferences and people thought I was really into this. . . . Not so much.

Growing up, Rita was "rebellious" toward her parents. She was raised in an exclusive and protective environment. "Mom and I didn't always see eye to eye." Rita was not allowed to play with black children. Her father and his brother had been punished as kids for playing with black kids and were sent to Fishburne Military School. "I never really saw black kids growing up." Rita described a heated dispute with her father when she was a teenager. Dr. Patterson was a black doctor in town whom everyone loved. The doctor wanted to buy a house on Overhill Drive, which was a new subdivision where the wealthy built. Rita's father strongly disagreed, and he was under pressure from the city council to keep this neighborhood white. "My dad and I had a big fight about it. My dad said, 'This can't happen. We can't have him moving into the neighborhood. It's going to ruin property values.' I said dad, that is just crazy. Times have changed. We got into a big argument of this." Dr. Patterson and his family were economically barred from obtaining the home as neighbors collectively bought the lot to block his purchase. Rita now considers herself "a tree hugging conservative." "I am Daughters of the American Revolution. I am letting United Daughters of the Confederacy go. . . . It's just, it's too controversial. I'm getting tired." Some of Rita's friends believe in the current conspiracy about "evil Democrats":

> What I am finding is that my friends have totally different opinions and that scares me a little bit. I have never run across this as much as in the last years with the situation in the government. . . . Some of their comments make me not want to be around them as much anymore. They are believing in the whole great conspiracy thing . . . "the media is forcing us to do things . . . these evil Democrats . . . " And I'm going, nobody is evil. They are just trying to do what they think is right . . . I feel very alone today.

Diane's mother signed her up for the United Daughters of the Confederacy and Diane "participated to have a relationship with her mother, to support her in her endeavors":

> It would go back to my mother with the whole UDC thing. . . . For her it was very much a Confederacy thing. She loved the history. She loved the research. She loved the genealogy.
>
> Me, not so much . . . I don't cling to the Confederacy . . . I like more about Southern charm. I like good manners. I like a gentleman. It is not to me, "Let me carry my Confederate Battle Flag" or let me say "I had slaves or didn't have slaves." It is more about an attitude and upbringing and good manners. You know, taking care of your mamma. Raising your babies. . . . God fearing. Good manners. Be a gentleman.

On the Confederate Battle Flag and the United Daughters of the Confederacy, Diane stated:

> My mother was a part of this group and we used to put them out in the cemeteries. . . . With the Confederate soldiers in there, we used to put the Confederate Battle Flag out during Confederate holidays and things of that nature. And then it got a negative taste and people didn't like the Confederate Battle Flag. . . . Because everybody associates it with slavery . . . and the Klan. All of it is bunched in together. It makes me question, "What did I learn? Is it right or is it wrong?" As part of the UDC, my kids got involved with the CoC, Children of the Confederacy. Part of that was to learn the catechism. . . . There was a spelling bee, and my kids won a lot. They were smart. Not because I am such an advocate of the Confederacy, but because we drove from Texas a lot. In the car, what else did we do? We studied the catechism, and we memorized the catechism.
>
> I fear that when I die, people are going to think that I am this big Confederate . . . [laughing], I am leading the revolt. It's kind of funny. I don't see the flag as that. I just see it as a Southern heritage thing. . . . It's about Southern rights. . . . Yet it just screams, "I want to own a slave." I acknowledge that for so many people, I can't change their perception and their belief that that's right because in so many places and ways, that's what's being told. Even in the schools now. . . . We home schooled and we told our own story. Because my mother was part of the UDC, we told that story. But that makes me wonder if that was the right story? I would hope that is the right story.

Although the Confederate Battle Flag can represent the positive aspects of being a Southerner for Diane, she no longer displays it because it may be offensive to others. Diane has lost interest in the United Daughters of the Confederacy and the Flag and has new priorities that focus on the future. "I would never display that now because of all the negative connotations that come with it. It's not worth me carrying that Flag or showing that Flag if it is going to hurt somebody else. I am not passionate about the work that they are doing. Especially since I have a new grandson. I have other priorities. I realize life is short."

Liz, Rita, and Diane have lost the faith as Retentionists and exhibit elements of Southern guilt. Jesse is now a former Sons of Confederate Veterans member, but he is still a Retentionist as he is staunch in his beliefs and display of the Flag. He left active membership because of personality conflicts within the local camp. Jesse joined the Sons of Confederate Veterans in the 1980s. He joined well after he came out as gay in the '70s. The Sons of Confederate Veterans did not give him a hard time for being gay. Jesse left the Sons of Confederate Veterans shortly after the 2011 ban. "No. It got too political. I don't want nothing shoved down my throat. I don't want nothing shoved down the damn Yankee's throat." Jesse felt the commander of the Sons of

Confederate Veterans at the time was overbearing. "His ideas were way out there. . . . He's out there. . . . He got too far. A lot of people quit because of him . . . died, quit, moved away. . . . Just towards the, I guess, it towards the Yankees here in town. They're here. We can't do nothing about it."

For Retentionists the Confederate Battle Flag is the sacred totem supported by religious beliefs and rites within the church of Cherished Southern identity (Durkheim 1912). "Dixie" is a favorite hymn used in unification. Robert E. Lee and Stonewall Jackson are saints of that church, and they are celebrated on the holy day of Lee-Jackson Day. The final resting places for Lee and Jackson are sacred ground, and Lexington is seen as the holy land. With the 2011 banning of the Flag and a generalized antipathy against Confederate symbols, Retentionists feel that they are engaged in a crusade in defense of their church of Cherished Southern identity. From the *heritage* argument we have advanced our understanding of individual Retentionist sentiments, via context, to the hearth and home argument which provides greater cultural clarity, context, and positional understanding. A Retentionist clutches his nostalgic fabric which is woven from very personalized threads of hearth and home. His attachment to the Confederate Battle Flag is that of a "totem that is the flag of the clan" (Durkheim 1912, 222). The threads are reinforced by fibers of kith and kin, ancestral land, and conservation of honor "from which faith and dogma originate" (Coski 2005). These constructs are woven by the individuals and the collective locational space, the adoration for their home, the South, and their history (Wright and Esses 2017, 226). The church of Cherished Southern identity provides sanctuary for individual constructs of nostalgic fabric to coalesce into a cluster of Retentionists. Through beliefs and rites, they unify in an effort to preserve their collective nostalgic fabric and to express kindred effervescence as they hope to be understood and even accepted as community members. Retentionists *believe* in the sanctity of their Cherished Southern identity even if it is imperfect and inconsistent. Durkheim provided that there is "perhaps no collective representation that is not in a sense delusive; religious beliefs are only a special case of a very general law" (Durkheim 1912, 228).

Critics, and others like the Reformers, can easily label Retentionists as racists across the sociological scholarly spectrum of racial taxonomy as their rhetoric and ritual can appear frighteningly similar to those of the traditional Ku Klux Klan. However, Retentionists do not consider themselves racists because they actively disassociate from traditional white supremacist groups and do not engage in racially prejudicial or distanced individual social interactions. As such, they see themselves as *anti-racists*. Yet, they refuse to accept that "racism is deeply embedded in the fabric of our society" and to distance themselves from contentious Southern symbols (Diangelo 2018, 22). According to race scholars, anti-racism requires a commitment to remembering and accounting for historical conditions of racial degradation whereas anti-racialism suggests "forgetting, getting over, and moving on" (Goldberg 2009, 21). Retentionists effectively embrace an "anti-racialism" posture, but they do not make excuses for the institution of slavery embraced by the Confederacy. However, by emphasizing states' rights arguments they expediently disassociate slavery as an unpleasant collateral occurrence in the fight for white Southern freedom from Federalist oppression. This anti-racialism conveniently utilizes a collective memory that is particular in interpreting the past as a mechanism for Southern identity maintenance (Lavelle 2015). Retentionists do not deny the "historical conditions of racial degradation" but their collective memory "is selective in interpreting the past" (Fleming 2017; Goldberg 2009; Lavelle 2015). Their perspective of hearth and home is deeply imbedded and appears incongruous to non-believers as do many religious beliefs to those looking from the outside.

Retentionists feel that Reformers are insensitive to their religious-like sentiments. Of course, Reformers would argue that Retentionists are insensitive to the vulgarity of their totems to others. Retentionists find Reformers *guilty by association* because of their animosity toward them and toward hallowed Southern symbols. Their religion is one of conservation, and liberal progress as espoused by Reformers is a core threat. Retentionists do not see themselves as *offensive* but rather *defensive* in their ideology. The erosion of traditional moral authority in their nostalgia of kith and kin, ancestral land, and conservation of honor is beyond their comprehension. Retentionists feel that they are in the vast minority and that they are being prejudiced against. They retaliate in a counter-crusade against Reformers not only as infidels but as active defilers of tradition. Through Southern guilt, Reformers charge Retentionist as intolerant racists and haters. Retentionists counter-charge Reformers as being self-righteous and intolerant of any view other than their own. They view Reformers as non-representative of the black community but also as perpetrators of an "intellectual blockade." "This post-1960s black identity intolerance—promoted by white intellectuals as well as black leaders and activists—is a painful parallel to the post-1830s intolerance among white Southerners against anyone who questioned slavery in any way" (Boorstin 1965, II:213; Sowell 2005, 59).

Unlike most Reformers, Retentionists are familiar with individual Reformers through business interaction but collectively group them as the opposition, as communists, socialists, and anarchists. They generally avoid socializing with Reformers outside business dealings. Although Retentionists engage in practical symbolic interactionism in labeling Reformers, they cautiously interact with them in the course of doing business. However, they view them with great suspicion as they *other* them as "pagans." In his business, Tucker separates his moral code, religious zeal, and personal preferences from his business transactions. "I separate out the business side. I find with the 'cancel culture' those folks don't want to do business with you. Which I am fine with. I never say no to anybody that calls me to do a job. It may make my stomach churn, but I will not say no on that basis . . . I have a different view of tolerant. I look back, what would Jesus do? They never, Him or Paul, never failed to interact with the pagans."

For Cole interacting with Reformers during business dealing, such as W&L administrators, requires caution so that he can reach his "objective." "Tread lightly . . . for the objective . . . For them to stop shitting on my ancestors. For them to stop shitting on Robert E. Lee. For them to stop being publicly ashamed of the man who if it wasn't for him, they wouldn't exist today."

As with Reformers, Retentionists utilize practical symbolic interactionism to subsume individuals into the cluster they are ideologically or politically associated with. Again using Cooley's understanding of *sympathy* as a "sharing of mental state" (Cooley 1998), Retentionists are sensitive to the perceptions of the black community, as they imagine them, and appear to hold limited compassionate sympathies. However, they refuse to abandon their Cherished Southern identity because it is sacred to them even if it offends some. When Retentionists *sympathize* with Reformer sentiments, they feel *hostility* toward them ideologically and socially as Reformers try to deny Retentionists any moral authority regarding the Confederate Battle Flag. As with Reformers, Retentionists manifest this hostility into intolerance for the opposing cluster. This demonstrates that like Reformers, ideology and sociality are generally not separate spheres of interaction for this cluster unless business prudence dictates otherwise. Thus, Retentionists view Reformers as anti-Christians, anarchists, and enemies of the church of Cherished Southern identity, but they will conduct business with them. Like Reformers, Retentionists distinguish themselves from others as well as differentiate opposing community members through *Verba non Acta* social protocols.

NOTES

1. Reference to former Virginia Governor Ralph Northam (D). Northam confirmed in 2019 to CNN that he was in a yearbook photo showing one person dressed in blackface and another in KKK white hood and robes. He apologized for "the decision I made to appear as I did in this photo and for the hurt that decision caused then and now."
2. Secretary of State of the Confederate States of America.
3. The first Jewish VMI cadet.
4. Referring to George Orwell's book *1984*.

5. Lee Chapel was renamed University Chapel in June 2021.

6. Unofficial banner of the Confederate States of America at the start of the Civil War.

Chapter 4

Forbearers

Acta non Verba

For the cluster of Forbearers, neither the "presentations" of Retentionists nor those of Reformers are completely satisfactory (Goffman 1959). Forbearers are the third and largest cluster in this study making up most of the sample of sixty-five out of eighty-one non-displaying White[1] and Black[2] respondents. Forbearers are a racially mixed cluster like Reformers. Previous analysis of the data provided no evidence of a racial divide concerning sentiments toward contentious Southern symbols. Forbearers do not categorically view provocative Southern symbols like the Confederate Battle Flag as representative of hate, racism, or white supremacy as Reformers do, nor do they retain the same intense religious-like reverence for these items as Retentionists do. Forbearers do not designate *others* via the practical symbolic interactionism of the Confederate Battle Flag. For them it could signal caution, but not firm conclusion. Although most Forbearers feel limited attachment to the Flag, they do support the freedom of expression for others to display. They distinguish themselves from both the opposing clusters of Reformers and Retentionists by their tolerance of these clusters and other community members even though they do not share their ideological zeal. As a cluster, Forbearer political alignment is relatively evenly dispersed with one third identifying as Democratic, Republican, and Independent although no black Forbearers identified as Republican. Most Forbearers do not like former President Trump, or they have mixed sentiments toward him. Half oppose the 2011 Confederate Battle Flag ban with even more indicating mixed or ambivalent sentiments. Few supported removing the Confederate monuments, and none felt it necessary to remove the Lee name from Lee Chapel or Washington & Lee University. Over half the Forbearers find the song "Dixie" offensive and even more indicated mixed or ambivalent sentiments. Only a few white Forbearers had any nostalgic fondness for the song "Dixie," and none of the black Forbearers did.

131

Forbearers do not consider themselves crusaders for or against controversial Southern symbols. They abhor racists, haters, and white supremacists but do not judge Retentionists as such based solely on their association with the Sons of Confederate Veterans, United Daughters of the Confederacy, or the display of the Confederate Battle Flag. Forbearers require more direct evidence. Forbearers do recognize hearth and home sentiments as a credible argument for display of the Flag and many hold varying degrees of such. However, Forbearers are suspicious of over-zealous fondness or scorn of Southern symbols especially outside a normative context such as Lee-Jackson Day. Forbearers are generally not vocal, and occupy various positions in the socio-economic, and educational spectrum. Collectively, Forbearers feel fairly confident that their views are reasonable, progressive, and representative of the community at large. Most indicated that they knew some Retentionists, and they would not eschew them based on their affiliations alone. Forbearers attempt to be collectively tolerant of the myriad sentiments toward Southern symbols as they also negotiate an anodyne position for those who do take offense. Both white and black Forbearers attempt to balance their various individual Cherished Southern identity through retention and modification of their nostalgic fabric while accounting for Southern guilt as a technique to negotiate an Aristotelian "middle way" for themselves, but they do not use it as an implement of labeling or othering via practical symbolic interactionism of contentious Southern symbols.

FORBEARERS: A SOUTHERNER

Approximately two-thirds of the Forbearers identify as Southerners. There were three reasons why the other respondents do not strongly identify as Southern. The first is that a third of those were not born in the South nor was their family from the South and therefore they feel that they could not identify as such. Half feel that their identity lay more with Virginia, the Shenandoah Valley, Rockbridge County, or Lexington rather than with the *South*. Here we begin to see varying degrees of disassociation from the South as this group actively balances their Southern guilt with their nostalgic fabric. Although they disassociate themselves from the monikers of racism, redneck, and/or ignorance that is associated with the South, they also retain some semblance of Cherished Southern identity in the context of Lexington as the Shrine of the South for the burial grounds of Lee and Jackson. The remainder of those who did not identify as Southerner simply do not care or had mixed sentiments.

Samuel was my first point of contact in Lexington as I began my research. He is a retired white professor from VMI and a veteran. Samuel "definitely

considers himself a Southerner." "My parents were never very racially motivated" but his extended family members in the Deep South were not racially
tolerant. "[My folks] took people as they came. I've learned to do that. But,
in my early days, the family beyond my own parents were Southerners, and
they had those Southern beliefs, very [long pause] racial in many aspects.
Fortunately, my mom and dad were not." When his father came home from
WWII in 1945, his dad went to northern Virginia to look for work. Samuel
was raised in a "very mixed neighborhood," and his best friend was "a young
black fellow who lived down the street." As a result, he felt that he never had
the "racial tendencies" that the extended family members had. For Samuel,
a Southerner is much more than just geography as people from Florida are
not Southerners. The term Southerner is a "tough question" for him to define
because he "does not think in those terms." "There is a lot of stuff . . . that
goes into being Southern . . . attitude and general behavior. Southerners, to
me all tend to be, I like to think at least, ladies and gentlemen."

Samuel is very proud of his Southern heritage. His ancestors landed in the
Carolinas in 1665 and were active "very heavily in the American Revolution."
His *kin* fought for the Confederacy and his great-great-grandfather was killed
at Antietam. Samuel is a member of the Sons of the American Revolution and
could be a member of the Sons of Confederate Veterans. "I appreciate what
they did . . . they fought for what they believed was right . . . I am proud of the
family members who fought in the war but can't agree with the cause." That
is why Samuel is not a Retentionist. Samuel stated that nowadays both black
and white people who reside in the South can be Southerners. "In the past,
blacks might have been considered Southern, but they were not Southerners"
because of racial differentiation. "I'm hoping that has gone away." Samuel
advised me that he was "born into being a Southerner" and that transplants,
like this author, can never be true Southerners. Over coffee we discussed
Southern heritage, the Confederate Battle Flag, and Cherished Southern identity. Samuel emphatically stated, "It's so much more than heritage. People
who aren't from the South don't understand. It's about hearth and home!"

For those Forbearers who identify as Southerner the constitutive elements
of being a Southerner were fairly consistent among all interview subjects.
Most believe first and foremost that it is a birthright based on Confederate
geography. Karl, a white state employee, considers himself a Southerner since
he was "born and raised below the Mason-Dixon Line." For him the title is
geographic not political. He sees Virginia as a Southern state and ascribes
to the "conservative family ideals" but not the "racism" of the Deep South.
Austin is a white man who was born in Virginia Beach and attended VMI. He
considers himself a Southerner based on the same geography. "I was born and
raised in Virginia and that is part of the South." Faith is a black woman who
grew up on a farm in the county. She is a retired food preparation specialist.

Faith considers herself a Southerner. For Faith, being a Southerner is where one is "born and raised" as well as other attributes such as accent, cuisine, and hospitality. "I think we're more hospitable." She feels that Northerners are different than Southerners. "They are more standoffish." Bridget is a black retired administrator with General Motors. She was raised in Buena Vista, but her father's family came from the county. "We have quite a history with my dad. My grandmother, his mother, was a slave." Although Bridget worked up north in New York for many years, she returned to Buena Vista and generally considers herself a Southerner. "I hadn't even thought about it. I guess, yes, I could be. I'm friendly . . . I think it's a good thing."

For Forbearers, a Southerner has a type of *honor* that consists of courtesy, God-fearing, industriousness, chivalry, and patriotism. After geography, *courtesy* was the next prevailing Southern characteristic that respondents named. Char is a black health care worker. She proudly considers herself a Southerner. For her, a Southerner is "Me . . . down home, good honest . . . likes good Southern food . . . manners, respect of others and their thoughts." Nia is a retired white teacher. She described Southern as: "It is a way of life. But I don't mean the hateful part of the way of life . . . I guess . . . courtesy, friendliness, being willing to talk. Willing to help." Nia felt that Southerners appreciate courtesy even at the cost of candor. "They may not be candid with you about things. They may smile and nod and agree with you and all, then walk away and say, 'Oh my gosh that guy is crazy.'" She acknowledged that Southerners sometimes demonstrate a lack of "forthrightness" particularly with the expression "Bless your heart." "A Southerner. . . . 'Bless their heart.' . . . They can dismiss someone, but that person might not ever know that they were dismissed. You know how Northerners are more forthright and that may be why Southerners kind of perceive them as rude because they come right out and say it. Southerners beat around the bush, *aaaallll* the way around, and saying the same thing. . . . It is a cultural thing." Kevin, a retired white Army officer, stated, "So when I think of Southerner, I think of somebody who has got manners, hospitality. I think of people that are good, just good-natured. Somebody willing to give a hand." On the topic of Northerners Kevin stated, "No offense, but I think they are more direct where I don't think a Southerner would be . . . lacking tact. I find they can be rude. . . . Basically, 'Get out of my face, I don't want to talk to you' kind of thing. Where a Southerner, 'Bless your heart' . . . when I think of Northern, I think of New York." Harvey is a man of color who did not identify as black. He was born outside the United States, but he sympathizes with Retentionists and lost causes as his country of birth has similar contentions in a "traditional warrior culture." Harvey considers himself liberal and described Southern characteristics as a "culture of honor, not always in a good way . . . the notion that I stand for something that is more than just me." Bart is a white man, and he described what a Southerner is to him. "Well, I guess somebody who grew up in the South or was raised in the South. But I think it's just the way you was brought up anyways. I was brought up old-fashioned kind of style."

Many Forbearers feel that Virginia Southerners are more tolerant and easygoing. Carla is a black woman who is a retired security specialist. She feels that being Southern is about the country and "how you look at the life around you." She did not feel that being a Southerner was limited to whites but rather a pace of life. "To me, I am in no rush to go anywhere and do anything . . . and that's country . . . it's not just a white thing." Fred is a black retired professor and was born and raised in the town of Lexington. "I adamantly identify as a Southerner." Mark is also a retired black educator. For Mark, being born in Buena Vista makes him a Southerner. He remains here because of the tolerance. "I'm born here . . . I'm proud to be a Southerner. . . . One of the key attributes of being Southern is tolerance. . . . For me it's tolerance, I guess. . . . To an extent I think they are pretty tolerant . . . I think people around here will work with you. You get to know them, and they get to know you. When you get to know them. Of course, you've got your extremes . . . I think people around here are generally tolerant." Max is a white VMI graduate and a retired Air Force officer. He was born in the Deep South and moved to Lexington when he was four years old. Max believes there are positive attributes to being Southern. "I think Southerners are very, very patriotic. I think they are more likely to serve in the military." For Max a Southern tradition is immersed in a nostalgic *chivalry*. "Chivalry was definitely a part of it . . . I think Southerners tend to dwell too much . . . on the past. I think there is a healthy way to do it and a not so healthy way to do it. You can dwell on the past and appreciate the beauty of a place like this."

Herbert is another white VMI graduate and veteran. He was born and raised in North Carolina. Herbert "absolutely" considers himself a Southerner and at times misunderstood:

> The day I was born, my father put a Confederate Flag over my bed and a portrait of Stonewall Jackson at the foot of my bed . . . I was raised on the biographies of Lee and Jackson . . . Both sets of grandparents were raised during Reconstruction and some of that bitterness, especially from my father's mother, kind of came through . . . kind of colored my upbringing. I . . . wouldn't say we Southerners are a victim group, but . . . we proudly feel victimized.

For Herbert, to be a Southerner "you have to be born in the South." Herbert used *truth in humor* when speaking with me. As with others, he affectionately referred to the interviewer as a "damn Yankee." A Southerner for Herbert is: "Being a gentleman, I associate that with being a Southerner. I'm not a Lynyrd Skynyrd kind of Southerner. I'm kind of an old. . . . That's more of a beer-drinking redneck kind of Southerner. . . . *Free bird.* . . . It's chivalry and being a gentleman that's what comes to mind." Herbert feels there are different kinds of Southerners depending on the state and that there is a pride based on where in the South you came from. He describes the stratification. "There is an arrogance that comes from Virginians. . . . My mother was real arrogant about being a Faa-ginian. . . . The arrogance of Virginians is palpable. . . . You got to go to Richmond and find the blue bloods . . . they feel they are a cut above."

Half of Herbert's VMI class was from Richmond. "There was the Richmond group and pretty much everybody else." However, Herbert does not think Richmond, which historically held the aristocracy of Virginia, looks down on Lexington because of VMI and the "holy ground" of Lee and Jackson. For Herbert, North Carolina is considered "less sophisticated" by Virginia standards. "My father always said, 'North Carolina was the valley of humility between the mounts of conceit [South Carolina and Virginia].'" Continuing in his vein of humor, he noted North Carolina was "clearly better" as a Southern state than Louisiana who were just "poor white trash." For Herbert, Georgia no longer counts as a Southern state, because they "have been invaded by Yankees." Herbert described South Carolina Baptists as having "hell, fire, and brimstone" religious fervor and maintaining a tremendous pride in being the first Confederate State to succeed from the Union. "South Carolina . . . is too small to be their own Republic, and too big to be an insane asylum . . . That whole state is different, people from South Carolina are different." Herbert proudly showed me his VMI class patch which displayed the Confederate Battle Flag and the American Flag.

Not all Forbearers identified as a Southerner. Bob is a black repairman who does not consider himself a Southerner. He feels it is more important to be an American. "Just me. . . . Bob." Bob is conflicted about what a Southerner is. Generally, he categorizes a Southerner as white, "somebody that walks around and just walks past and doesn't speak . . . heads up high." However, Bob does not think that "Southerner" is necessarily a bad term and doesn't necessarily have to do with race but more about class status and money. "It's a lot of things . . . arrogance . . . I'm better than you . . . or I got more money than you." Harold, a white 90-year-old former paratrooper, returned back to Rockbridge County after worldwide service in the Army. Harold does not identify as a Southerner. "No. I'm [Harold]. I've been around too much." Harold identifies as a "mountain man." Harold's father was from Rockbridge Baths, but he died in a car accident when Harold was three years old. Harold was raised by his German grandfather. "[I] look like my grandad, George. . . . He was born right over here on the hill . . . in the little hut." Harold pointed across the road, where his mom was born in a little brick building that was the former slave cookhouse on that farm. His mother, Grandmother Hanna, and Grandfather George helped on that farm and did odd jobs and housecleaning for the owner. They were poor and lived "hand to mouth." Harold took pride that his ancestors date back to the Revolutionary War. Harold has the manifest of the ship when his father's family arrived and keeps it in the family bible. Harold spoke about his racially integrated upbringing on the farm as one of several poor manual laborers. "On the farm we had blacks, and we swam together, we hunted together, ate, we did everything together but sleep together and some of them probably did that [laughing]." For Harold, race, creed, and color are not elements that determine friendship, only work ethic:

I'll tell you who I don't like . . . lazy asses. If a man is industrious and tries to do good. . . . He's my friend. . . . The good Lord gives us a . . . yardstick to go by . . . the Bible . . . nothing comes easy. . . . You get on the east side of the Blue Ridge Mountains you find greater dissatisfaction with black and white. . . . But on this side (west) of the mountain . . . it's a . . . human being, it's not a black and white, it's a human being. On this side of the mountain, you have to earn your keep . . . these are mountain people.

Nina is a white retired educator. She does not consider herself a Southerner. "No not really." For Nina there are different kinds of Southerners based on geography. "I don't see our area, Virginia, as being a part of the Deep South." Nina feels she is part of the Shenandoah Valley but where she lives is technically the James River Basin. She identifies mostly as a Virginian. "Oh yeah, I do." For Nina, the Deep South is what constitutes as true Southerner. "People might see me as Southern . . . the stereotypes of Southern women . . . fanning themselves with the vapors, that's not me. Holy-roller religious crap, that's not me." For Nina, a Southern lady is religious to the point of evangelical and takes upon the airs of a *delicate flower*. Nina believes that hospitality is a Southern quality. "I like to think I am hospitable as a Southerner . . . maybe a little friendlier than [Northerners]." However, Nina indicated that a Southerner could display a certain duplicity. "Hypocritical politeness. That's not something I do. Which I think is Southern." Nina identifies more as a "county lady who likes country life who is also very interested in history."

Like Retentionists and some Reformers, many Forbearers, particularly those county community members, embrace a special *love of the land* not just aesthetically but through a direct interaction such as with work or recreation. Harold feels a close kinship to the Shenandoah Valley and the Blue Ridge Mountains. He described the intertwined relationship between country people and the land. "The Germans and the Scotch-Irish that settled in here, they haven't changed a whole lot . . . [close] to the land. Probably, they don't realize it. It's part of them. . . . The Shenandoah Valley is different . . . it's not me and them, but us . . . I love this area . . . all my people are buried here." Karl does not think of himself as a Southerner or just as a Virginian. He considers himself as from the Virginia valley, "I would consider myself . . . someone from Appalachia," specifically a Shenandoah "valley person."

In their descriptions of a Southerner, Forbearers also illustrated their specific fibers of hearth and home: kith and kin, ancestral land, and conservation of honor. Respondents spoke with great fondness for their ancestors while recognizing the serious flaws of the Confederate cause and their kin's potential racial intolerance. Ancestral lands, often referred to as "the valley," "the mountains," "the land," and "the country," were revered as unifying elements for Forbearers but also one of disassociation from being a Southerner for many. The fiber of conservation of honor is demonstrated in references to courtesy, duty, work ethic, and willingness to assist neighbors. Yet, Forbearers recognize and detach themselves from antebellum notions of being Southern and especially the Deep South, such as social dominance and distancing, stratification, and traditional Southern airs.

SOUTHERN SYMBOLS: IT DEPENDS ON THE CONTEXT

Forbearers hold varied sentiments for Southern symbols such as the Confederate Battle Flag and the 2011 Lexington City Flag ban on Lee-Jackson Day. All respondents feel that the display of the Flag by the Klan, and other traditional hate groups, is a symbol of intimidation and hate. No respondent suggested that freedom of expression included public display of the Confederate Battle Flag out of context. Many Forbearers find it acceptable for the Sons of Confederate Veterans to march down Main Street in Lexington as the Shrine of the South. However, no one thinks it appropriate to march with the Flag up on Diamond Hill, which is a predominately black neighborhood, as part of the Sons of Confederate Veterans' rights to freedom of expression. Here, situational context of hearth and home is critical for Forbearers. Since Lexington was home to both Lee and Jackson and now their bodies are interned there, the situational context is given for Lee-Jackson Day as the march starts at the graveyard and gravesite for Jackson, proceeds down the main business thoroughfares, and returns to the graveyard.

Fred, a black professor, began his career at Washington & Lee as a custodian and then became a lab assistant while taking night classes. After obtaining his undergraduate degree he continued his education by attending graduate school at a prestigious university in Virginia. Years later, he returned to his alma mater and eventually became W&L's first black department head. Fred recognizes the "cultural draw" and "cultural identification" the Flag has for some working-class whites in the Lexington area and believes that "working-class whites did not engineer the Civil War." "Working-class whites were drafted . . . and likely, none of those working-class whites were from families that owned slaves. . . . Like all wars, the war was decided by people other than ground soldiers who had to fight." However, Fred felt some of the "cultural identification is also racial" and polarized. "This [Flag] is another thing that is divisive in American culture." Fred felt that Lee's reputation reached saintlike mythical mis-proportions. "Lee the slave owner does not bother me one bit. Lee the man who seems to have some real racial hang-ups does bother me . . . I am numb to the issue of slavery. I am not numb to the issue of racial hatred." Fred was surprised when they took down the Confederate Battle Flags in Lee Chapel at W&L. Fred stated that as a point of historical fact, "The Lee family never wanted the Confederate Battle Flags" on display in the chapel. Yet while Fred was very conflicted about the man, Lee, he did not advocate the removal of Lee from the name Washington & Lee. "It does not bother me in the least . . . I earned a degree here. The school has been very, very good to me. I have never been ashamed to say where I was educated. I have never been ashamed of that fact that I work here." These complicated sentiments reflect patterns of nostalgic fabric where fibers of friendship, institutional belonging, and conservation of what we remember fondly remain deeply embedded in some members of this community. Progress tugs us forward and conservation anchors us back.

Max holds the Confederate Battle Flag and the song "Dixie" close to his heart as he reflects upon his nostalgic fabric through his family and VMI. He retains his version of Cherished Southern identity while recognizing that others may not feel that way. Max described his private display of the Flag:

> I've always had a Confederate Battle Flag. I still do. I don't hang it in view. Sadly, I did at one point, I had it hanging on my wall. But then I got to realize that, you know, if I ever had a black friend come over. I got to a point when I realized I had to put myself in some of my black friend's shoes and think how I would feel about that flag. And I could understand why they would be upset. . . . From the positive side, it represented the Old South, the old planta-tions. When I hear the old tune "Greensleeves," I get a lump in my throat . . . "Dixie," I loved.

Max loves the American Flag, and it is sacred to him. It reminds him of his time in the US Air Force and the caskets draped with the flag. He felt that the Confederate Battle Flag is sacred too. "Yes." The Flag doesn't just symbolize slavery to Max. "To me it didn't . . . I was angry when they took 'Dixie' out of VMI." When asked about the 2011 ban of the Confederate Battle Flag Max stated, "I hated it. . . . They were denying me an appreciation of the history of the Old South . . . I want it shown. It's history." However, Max does not support the Lost Cause. Like modern conflicts such as Vietnam, Iraq, and Afghanistan, Max divests himself and soldiers from the political causes and focuses on the individual soldier's obligation to duty and honor. For Max, the Lost Cause was wrong, but the Confederate Battle Flag retains a certain traditional code of conduct. "Chivalry, bravery, honest, your word is your bond and that is an old-fashioned value that was North and South . . . it was overblown in the South in a positive note. A man would die rather than be dishonest."

Max feels that "states' rights . . . is an excuse." Although he adores the Confederate Battle Flag, Max recognizes that it can be associated with hate and with white supremacy and, as such, reconciliation of nostalgic fabric in the Flag is challenging when attempting to be inoffensive:

> That was probably the excuse if you will. Much like we erred going into Vietnam and erred going into Iraq. I think it was a huge mistake to secede from the Union, huge . . . slavery and states' rights. . . . That's wrong. That is the wrong reason to secede. They made a huge, huge mistake. . . . Slavery to me was very wrong, but it was history. I don't like that Confederate Battle Flag to represent white supremacy by any long shot . . . I'd like to yank the Flag out of their hands and beat them over the head with it . . . I hate to see that. Is it a symbol that I understand why the black people do not like it.

Max recalled hearing a version of "Dixie" that moved him to tears. "My brother sang a version of 'Dixie' that I physically had to leave, I came out here and wept. That is how powerful that song moves me. It still does." When asked if the song moved him in a religious way, Max stated, "Yes because that's the South. It's my South not the black man's South sadly." He recalls singing "Dixie" at VMI. "That used to be our school song at VMI. We would march to 'Dixie.'" He recalled at VMI as the song "Dixie" began during certain intervals the cadets would provide a "rebel yell" as they fall into formation to march. "It still moves me. I'll get a lump in my throat every time I hear that." Max relates to the history of VMI and the cadets that fought in the Civil War:

> Those Confederates, those young boys who were as young as fifteen, marched right in the backyard here. There is an old road back here and that used to be Highway 11. . . . That is the road they used to march to New Market to fight against the Northern command up there. Had it not been for the cadets, they would have lost the battle. . . . They knew they had a good chance of dying and they did it anyway. . . . Fighting the odds against a superior force. . . . That's what that Flag means to me. I take great pride in that and that is one of the historic aspects of VMI that I do cherish.

Paul is a former ranking member of the Lexington Police Department. He is a black man who was raised in New York City and a Marine veteran. Paul said he does not consider himself a Southerner "until I go home and visit my family in NY and then I realize . . . [I am] no longer a New Yorker." He feels that he is a "pseudo Southerner." Paul arrived in Lexington after the 2011 ban of the Confederate Battle Flag. In his official duties, Paul works with many of the polarized entities concerning contentious Southern symbols. On occasion, visitors to Lexington wanted to know, "Why do you have this Flag flying?" Paul felt, "They do not understand the heritage that is associated with this city . . . it doesn't resonate." For Paul, the Confederate Battle Flag significance is held as "beauty is in the eye of the beholder." When he looks at the Flag, he relates to "the hurt that was derived from what that Flag, in my eyes, represents." As a symbol, he recognizes that others see the Confederate Battle Flag differently:

> [They] have some heritage in that Flag, and it means, in totality, something different to [them]. . . . "My great-great-grandfather fought in this war, and I honor his bravery". . . . Yeah, I could certainly . . . I could rationalize that . . . or I could see why someone would honor . . . heritage associated with the flag. . . . Me personally . . . if that was my situation . . . there would be very few times that I would honor the heritage . . . but also associate some of the hurt that may be associated with that heritage. So, I would find good moments that I made that clear.

Paul views the Flag as "another symbol of representation of someone's thoughts and opinions." He works with and is friends with folks who display the Confederate Battle Flag. When asked how it makes him feel, he replied, "It makes me feel that I have a difference of opinion." Ultimately, Paul has very mixed feelings on the 2011 Confederate Battle Flag ban. His concern was for limitations on the freedom of expression especially for a limited time and within what he felt was the appropriate context. "Hmmm . . . I don't know. I think that the jury, for me, is still out on that . . . I think if I wanted to honor my ancestors and I wanted to carry perhaps an African flag, or some-thing like that . . . that, I should have a right to do that."

Austin "grew up a Southerner in Virginia." "I still love the song 'Dixie.' But I no longer like the Confederate Battle Flag." At one time he did like it. For Austin the Flag was a "Southern thing." Growing up, he read lots of books on the Civil War and he was enamored with many of the historical characters like Lee and Jackson. Now Austin is very concerned about the offensive potential of the Confederate Battle Flag to black community mem-bers. "Now the Flag is a symbol of slavery and a symbol of hate." However, Austin is conflicted and also appreciates what the Confederate Battle Flag means to Retentionists. "I know there are legitimate people . . . Sons, Daughters of the Confederacy . . . very, very good folks there . . . but it's time to put the Civil War behind us. The Confederate Battle Flag is a symbol of the South and the Confederacy. . . . It's history also." Austin still holds Lee in high regard. "I think Robert E. Lee was a tremendous role model. He went with his conscience fighting for Virginia and for states' rights. I respect him as a man. You can't change history. . . . Lee was a fine warrior and a very, very honorable man." Austin had mixed sentiments on the 2011 Confederate Battle Flag ban. Initially, he felt it was unfortunate that they had to take down all the flags, to include VMI and W&L as a result. "That's a huge part of Lexington's history and the tourist industry. . . . The city council was in a tough position." Now Austin feels, "That's fine . . . probably correct for the Confederate Battle Flag [to remove it]." Samuel believes the freedom of expression is offset by the offensive nature of the Flag. Herbert feels Confederate Battle Flag display today is questionable. "It has been co-opted by white Nationalists, the KKK . . . I think we should set it aside." When asked about the 2011 ban, Herbert said, "It was a good idea." For Herbert, the Civil War was about slavery, but it was also about "entering into the Federal family voluntarily." "Is it possible to pull out? The war settled that question. . . . I think 99 percent of the Confederate soldiers were defending their land."

Bob is a black handyman and is married to Betty who is heavily involved in Lexington politics. Although Betty belongs to the cluster of Reformers, Bob is a Forbearer. His opinions on the Flag differ from his wife's position because of his association and experience with white people in the county and their display of the Flag. "[I'm] from the county . . . knowing the people, knowing them . . . when either I worked with them or friends with their family or their children . . . We like had no problems and they always treated me with respect, and I treated them with respect." Bob feels that flying the Confederate Battle Flag is a part of being a white Southerner. However, on rare occasion he has seen Lee-Jackson Day marches with black men carrying the Flag. "Why this black man be walking down the street with a . . . Flag . . . and I sat there, and I wondered, wow, where did you come from?" Bob did not feel it necessary to ban the Confederate Battle Flag for Lee-Jackson Day. "I actually didn't see anything wrong with them . . . because it's somebody's heritage. But it's not mine." He stated that he can talk about it, laugh about it, and others can have their own opinions about it. "You can believe what you want to believe in . . . I'm good with it . . . but what if I wave the Black Panther Flag in front of you? . . . So, it's two sides of the fence right here . . . Doesn't really bother me now. It's kind of like, no difference, if you have a Martin Luther King march down through the middle of town. I look at it as the same thing." Bob believes that the Confederate Battle Flag is about "how the things used to be in the old days" and would appreciate greater sensitivity or recognition that the "good old days," were not so "good" for black people. However, Bob does not believe he has the right to say, "I don't like your heritage." When Bob was young, he was indifferent toward the Flag, "didn't bother me at all." "I have no problem with it, as long as they don't get up in my face." Bob was referring to the VA-Flaggers and their aggressive tactics.

Harold is ambivalent and "had no feeling" on the Confederate Battle Flag. "You know what means more to me than the Flag? That yellow flag with the copperhead curled up on it [Don't Tread on Me] . . . independence . . . don't abuse me." His grandfather was "non-political" and never flew the Confederate Battle Flag. When Harold sees the large Confederate Battle Flag on Highway 81, he thinks, "There's another nut-head." He acknowledges the person has the right to fly the flag. "It's alright. It's his thing." However, it is not Harold's thing. In 2011, even as a staunch Democrat and progressive, Nia was not initially supportive of the Confederate Battle Flag ban. "Not really, no." Currently, she remains conflicted. She recognizes the Flag has been co-opted by some, and yet she believes the Confederate Battle Flag can represent a form of heritage and reenacting. "If they are reenacting, why not?" While Nia identifies as "very liberal and an active Democrat," she is "interested in history." She related to the Flag as a "historic thing." She sees the period garb of the Sons of Confederate Veterans on Lee-Jackson Day in Lexington, as adding legitimacy. "This [Lexington] is where it was. They are on-site. This is a historic site." Some community members empathize with Confederate Battle Flag displayers. Harvey, an immigrant man of color who did not identify as an African American, provided, "When I see people waving the Confederate Battle Flag my reaction is not anger. My reaction is pity. Because I understand where they are coming from. You got your ass kicked and I understand your family members were killed. I get that . . . Yet, you want that thing to mean something. You know you are on the wrong side. You still want it to mean something."

George is a white man who was born in Pennsylvania, but he identifies as a Southerner and a Virginian. He is the foreman for several construction sites and a staunch and active Democrat. Robert E. Lee was one of George's heroes growing up and he is part owner of the hotel formerly named the Robert E. Lee. George still admires Lee's "grace in defeat" and that after the war he immediately went to work "fixing the divisions" in the country. George's view on the Confederate Battle Flag changed over time. Initially as a historian George "fought the fight for the flag originally, and now I am fighting the fight against it." As a student and reenactor, George fought for the Flag to be used for Civil War reenactment for the Lexington Regiment as the original battle flag for that unit. Now, he is fighting against it if it is used in the wrong or hurtful context. "Anywhere that the Flag actually was, has to be respected. The Flag was there . . . history happened." For George,

Confederate memorials are important. "Confederate veterans are US veterans by the US government" and should be left up. For George and many Forbearers, the Confederate Battle Flag was a flag for the Army of Northern Virginia. However, the "other meaning of the flag is a problem." George affirms, "The KKK and racist groups co-opted the flag of Northern Virginia as their own symbol . . . they did it in the 1960s . . . as a counterpoint to segregation."

Nina has "split loyalties" because her mom's family fought for the Confederacy and her dad's grandfather fought for the Union and was captured and held at Andersonville.[3] He was one of seven who escaped, and she has a "secret box" he carved while in prison. She finds it "amazing" that there were Confederate Civil War statues in thirty-one states while only thirteen states fought for the Confederacy. Asked if the monuments should be taken down, Nina thinks the decision "should be left up to the locality." "Maybe that's the best way." However, Nina felt a purging of all Southern heritage and reference to the Civil War was not appropriate. "It seems people went overboard on getting rid of anything to do with the war and Southern generals. One example, is the church, the Robert E. Lee Church[4] . . . I understood why community members wanted to change the name, but I just did not want that change. . . . It was named for him after the war. He did a lot of good things for W&L." Nina does not support dropping the Lee name from W&L or Lee Chapel. "It's history. Good, bad, or ugly, its history." She concurs with adding additional context rather than tearing down statues. For Nina, the monuments do not represent the Lost Cause, but rather are memorials to men killed.

Elaine is a white retired academic administrator. She has conflicting views on the Confederate Battle Flag as it has been co-opted by some. "Well, you know, so much has happened around here that is not pleasant, it has tainted that Flag. . . . The Flag itself is a symbol and has become a symbol of something that I think, is mistaken . . . I think it is kind of a hate symbol. It didn't need to be. It's been prostituted." However, she did not perceive a message of hate from the Sons of Confederate Veterans for their desire to display on Lee-Jackson Day. "No. I suppose they should be allowed to [march]." She did not place the Sons of Confederate Veterans or the United Daughters of the Confederacy on the same level as the Ku Klux Klan. Ultimately, Elaine was conflicted about the 2011 ban of the Confederate Battle Flag. "I'm going to say, I don't know . . . I think a lot of this business has gone to extreme especially as it relates to Robert E. Lee . . . I like him . . . I think he was admirable . . . I've often asked myself what I would have done had I been living in Virginia and had to make the choice. Am I going to stay here and fight or am I going North to fight against?"

Thomas is a white resident of Buena Vista and runs a market stand with his brother and his sister. He does not agree with the 2011 ban of the Confederate

Battle Flag. He sees the Flag as history and heritage. "That is what built this town. I don't think they should have done it to satisfy a few people." Thomas believes that if he were black, he would feel the same way. "The black friends I grew up with didn't have no problem with it." Kyle is a farm laborer and served in the USAF. He feels that the Confederate Battle Flag is a political expression or "a statement" of defiance. For Kyle this sentiment is not a statement of racial superiority or hate. It is rather one of freedom of expression and frustration. Kyle does not fly the Flag personally, but he understands that it could be important to others as a symbol of the South and rebelliousness. He also understands that some black community members may object to the Confederate Battle Flag. However, Kyle feels that we as American citizens, do not have the inalienable right, *not to be offended*. "They feel, 'What right do you have to tell me I can't fly this? . . . You aren't going to tell me I can't do it [fly the Flag].' As Americans, we do not have the right, not to be offended. . . . We do have the right of expression." Darrel provided that his cousins are "raucous and drive big trucks with the Confederate Battle Flag flying on one side of the truck bed, and the American Flag flying on the other." He believes some of it is "defiance on the part of young . . . person who is basically saying 'Don't tread on me.' . . . 'Don't tell me I can't do that.'"

Forbearers who support the display of the Confederate Battle Flag or are ambivalent do not see it as a symbol of white supremacy but rather a tainted history. Levi is a white retired car salesman originally from Charlottesville, Virginia. For him the Flag "meant more than a battle flag for the South." Levi doesn't own a Confederate Battle Flag but said he once flew one on his porch railing. For him, the Flag is a "symbol of a group of people in the US . . . it's personal choice . . . you should have the right to do it." The Flag for Levi means "I'm a Southerner." "We all have a history . . . sometimes the history . . . isn't attractive." The 2011 ban of the Confederate Battle Flag from Lexington light posts had mixed sentiments. Dan is a white retired Virginia State Trooper who sees Lee-Jackson Day as an ethnic holiday and disapproved of the 2011 ban. "Thought it was stupid." However, he recognizes that the Confederate Battle Flag as well as the American Flag can be used for hate, by the Klan. He is disgusted by white supremacists and does not recognize them as legitimate displayers of the Flag. "Anybody who sees the KKK and believes them, something is wrong with them. . . . You're honoring Lee-Jackson. It's a Lee-Jackson Day. You're honoring your heritage. It's just like anyone else honoring their heritage. . . . What's the difference with them being Irish and us having a flag?"

Gary is a white car salesman. He grew up in Lexington and the county. For Gary growing up, there was a difference going to school in the Lexington city versus in the county. In Lexington, Gary attended the Lylburn Downing Middle School. In the early 1970s the school was desegregated from the all-black high school and integrated as a middle school. When his family moved to the county, he went to the old Rockbridge, "The Rebels," high school in Fairfield, Virginia. He thought the "county was easier" than being in the city school. He felt that folks in the county "were more country." "Living in the city of Lexington and living in Fairfield [the county] is two different things . . . different folks. Color not being the issue though." Gary reflected on his high school experience:

> We had this little rebel character in the gym waving it [Confederate Battle Flag]. But in the 70s nobody cared. And this was right after the 1960s. You would have thought, maybe they would have cared then. . . . No (one) cared about it. It was just who we are. "Rockbridge Rebels," we're still on the Facebook page. "Rockbridge Rebels," "rebel pride". . . . Even now, and there are plenty of black students who use that Facebook page.

Gary has mixed feelings about the Flag, and he does not display it. "But I'm fine with the Confederate Battle Flag. . . . At the same time, I am not one who is going to put it on my truck and wave it in people's face. But I am fine with it. . . . The flag is not evil. Evil things were done under the flag just out of respect, nowadays some people do take it as being offensive . . . I just don't see a need to do that."

Stephen is a black health care worker. He feels that a single assessment of a man's life, like Lee's, is inadequate. He firmly believes that people are complicated and can change throughout their life. When considering the lives of Lee and Jackson, Stephen feels strongly that a person's life should be viewed holistically:

> How do you judge a person's life? Do you judge him from the beginning, the middle, or the end? Because you could have somebody in their youth, drank, did drugs had multi-children by multi-women. But in the end of their life . . . they are an entirely different person than what they were at the beginning. You look at Robert E. Lee. At the beginning he did what his conscious told him to do, come back to his mother state. He was a Virginian. After the war was over, he became an educator.

Mark also saw two sides to Lee. "I think he fought for the wrong side. He was a brilliant commander. . . . He's capable. I think Lee, from what I have read, was steeped . . . in white supremacy. He grew up in this privileged, slave-based society. So how else could he be? And then he went on to defend a government that wanted to maintain white supremacy." However, Mark also accounted for another side of Lee. "In the end . . . he was in St Paul's Church in Richmond. There was a black gentleman who went to the altar . . . and Lee went with him. And I'm thinking, maybe he did have a different side after all.

Maybe there was another side to him. . . . There are so many facets to him."
Tate is a black retired bus driver and current musician. He does not view Lee
or Jackson as inherently evil. Tate sees Jackson as a "teacher and instructor"
and Lee's choice as a difficult one. "Robert E. Lee's sympathies were with
Virginia because his family was from Virginia. . . . He chose a side. When
we was kids, we used to go see Traveler." Tate did not support dropping the
name Lee from W&L. "I don't think they should. The reason why is because
he became president of what used to be Washington University. You're not
going to take the Washington name off!"

Arthur and Carla are black deacons at the Church of God. Arthur was not
born in the South and moved here later in life. Currently, Arthur is active in
Lexington politics. He volunteers yearly as a marshal for the MLK parade.
Arthur does not see the Confederate Battle Flag as a definitive symbol of racism, but at times he is suspicious. "I don't have a problem with the flag. I have
a problem with the meaning, how they use the flag. . . . The piece of material
has never done anything to me. It has always been the person who is carrying that material." Although Arthur supported the 2011 ban, he wondered if
the decision did not aggravate racial tensions. "That's a mess. That's just a
mess . . . I can't say I'm not happy to see them go . . . I think it was a good
thing to let that go . . . but . . . it started a war." For Carla, the Confederate
Battle Flag does not always represent race, rather it is "how it is presented." "I
don't have a problem with the Rebel flag. I have a problem with the mindset
of [some of] the people behind the flag. . . . You know that is part of their
history. That is part of who they are." Carla sees the Confederate Battle Flag
as a symbol that can represent hearth and home for some and is not necessarily a rally cry for hate. The Flag does not bother her, even when displayed
outside her church, the Church of God, where Richard lives across the street.
While Carla does not own or fly a Confederate Battle Flag, she knows some
community members, black and white, who do fly it. She said simply, "That's
how they were raised."

Faith is a black elder of the Church of God and she likes the Confederate
Battle Flag. "I think it's a beautiful flag . . . I've got one little plastic one that
sticks on the refrigerator . . . I'm going to tell Richard to put it in his will
when he dies, I want that Flag . . . The big one." Faith was asked if she would
display a Confederate Battle Flag outside. "I would love to, but my neighbors
probably wouldn't appreciate that [laughing]." Faith did not feel that the 2011
ban of the Flag served the black community well. She feels that supporters
of the Confederate Battle Flag took to greater and more prominent display
on private property such as the massive Flag on Billboard Hill on I-81. Faith
noted it was "Northern kids . . . black and white liberals" that were part of
the movement to remove the Lee name from structures at W&L. Faith did

not find liberals in town to be very tolerant. "No, they are not." Faith has no problem with Lee-Jackson Day parade. "Well, I would say for the one day it's okay. Like I say, you either go if you want to or if you don't want to, don't."

Oscar is a twenty-one-year-old black student from the county. He has very mixed sentiments on the Confederate Battle Flag. When traditional white supremacist groups display the Flag, it is certainly a symbol of hate. When the Confederate Battle Flag is displayed by local rednecks it *can* symbolize hate. "At the end of the day, it's still hate." However, Oscar Jr. recognizes the potential for the Flag to represent a country style of living without hatred. "Yeah. There's some truth to it." Alex is a thirty-six-year-old black truck driver that loves the country way of life. He describes himself as an American and believes in the First Amendment. The Confederate Battle Flag does not bother him, and he was not offended when they flew on Lee-Jackson Day prior to the 2011 ban. "I may not like what you have to say but I don't have to. I will fight for your right to express even if I disagree." To Alex, Lee-Jackson Day is "just another day" and it is not inherently racist. He feels that it is not so different from Martin Luther King Day. "Some of the very best people I know, and will go to battle for, fly it." When the Confederate Battle Flag was taken off the city flagpoles in 2011, he was ambivalent. However, he did not like that the Sons of Confederate Veterans were restricted in their freedom of expression.

Tate has "mixed feelings" on the Confederate Battle Flag. "I used to tell people that Flag is not hurting me. I just don't want the guy flying that flag to drag me behind his pickup truck or run me off the road just because of the color of my skin." Tate feels that although the Flag can mean hate, often it does not. He related an occasion when the VA-Flaggers came to town and there was a black man marching with them. "He [the black VA-Flagger] said, 'Y'all don't know your own history. It doesn't mean hate. It's heritage.' I try to look at it from their viewpoint. It does mean something to them in a positive sense." However, Tate is also suspicious of the heritage argument and finds the logic convenient at times. "That heritage was built on the backs of my ancestors toiling out in the cotton field." Tate recognizes that the Confederate Battle Flag is also a battle standard. "I can go past the Flag and see it and don't see it." Corbin has a different reason for why he has no issues with quarrelsome Southern symbols like the Flag, Confederate parades, and monuments. He feels it symbolizes loss and "losers." "Let them do it. Again, they still represent a war that was lost . . . 400 years from now they are still losers . . . It doesn't offend me."

Zayn is a black retired Air Force officer who now lives in the county. He does not object to the Confederate Battle Flag. "I've got no problem with that Flag. We had it in several military units I was in . . . Vietnam . . . Afghanistan." The Flag is not necessarily a symbol of hate for him. "When the Confederate Battle Flag is used, then it is for hate. When it is displayed, it is not." Spence is a black truck driver and handyman that also lives in the county. He also has no issues with the Flag. "I tell you; they never bothered me. When I was growing up, a lot of my friend's houses that I went to had them somewhere . . . I'm not a big history person. . . . It didn't offend me . . . Whatever people want to believe or do, that's fine. As long as they don't affect or bother me." Char, the black health care worker, indicated that her best friend is Jesse who was part of the Sons of Confederate Veterans. Char was annoyed that students who were not part of the community interfered in tradition. "You know some black kids at W&L made them take down the Flags in Lee Chapel. I didn't think that was right. No, they have been there for years, that's history. It should have nothing to do with them or what they are feeling or in their feelings. . . . This girl down there, she has one. She has one on her door, one on her flagpole. She hugs me and kisses me. I don't care nothing about that Flag. That Flag docs not make me or break me."

Agnes is a black retired teacher and veteran. She was born in the Stonewall Jackson Hospital[5] in 1948. Agnes informed me that black babies were delivered in the basement and white babies were delivered upstairs. As a teacher, she gave tours of the Stonewall Jackson House to her students and would show them the basement where she was born. "In 1948, it was segregated . . . down in the basement [laughing]." Years ago, Agnes was initially suspicious of the Confederate Battle Flag. She recalled a white man working at the local thrift store who was wearing a bandana on his head. The man helped her load her Christmas tree into her car:

> I spoke with a young man who had a Confederate Battle Flag around his head. You know sweat band . . . white guy. He worked in the thrift store. . . . He was helping me stuff my Christmas tree into my car. . . . And I asked him, "You know that about the Flag you have on your head?" He said, "Yeah that's my heritage." [I said,] "Well, do you understand how it invokes among African Americans? They see it as a symbol of hatred and . . . lynching." When the Klan came in and used it as their symbol, that's what happened. That's the main thing that black community members see.

Agnes continued to have a long conversation with the assistant, and she listened to his position. By the end of the conversation, she felt no racial hate emanating from this man toward her or black community members. "No, he was the sweetest thing. I'd take him home." From that interaction Agnes changed her opinion of the Confederate Battle Flag. "It is a battle flag. That's all it is. I have one. I started collecting." She did not agree with the 2011 Flag ban for Lee-Jackson Day. "For one day? One day? . . . It's not up all year long? It was his battle flag . . . I understand that. . . . Why not?" She wants to educate community members on the different meanings and interpretations. "I know it's a battle flag. That's why I want to teach . . . black community members, yes." Agnes recalled a Confederate function in the past, possibly Lee-Jackson Day. "I remember when the Confederates were here, there was a black family [that] was a part of it." Agnes was asked about how she felt about Lee-Jackson Day and the Sons of Confederate Veterans, United Daughters of the Confederacy, and reenactors. "I love the big [hoop] skirts . . . I watch them in the parking lot and go up there and wave . . . They are people reenacting. Even people I go to church with out in Collierstown. People are people. This is what they are doing for their heritage and lineage and family. They have a right to." The Lee-Jackson Weekend did not offend Agnes, nor did she sense hate in their celebration. "No, no." Agnes was asked if the large Confederate Battle Flags on I-81 and Highway 60 represented hate to her. "I don't think so. No . . . I'm not jumping to hate. . . . That's what they make it as, symbol of the South. . . . They want to be noticed . . . recognized. I think there needs to be education going on."

Bridget is a black woman who retired from working up North and returned to the community. She has never met any United Daughters of the Confederacy members, but she is quite familiar with the Sons of Confederate Veterans. She does not feel that the Sons of Confederate Veterans march on Lee-Jackson Day in Lexington is a display of hate. "No. They have that right as far as I'm concerned." She did not support the 2011 ban of the Confederate Battle Flag. "It's okay with me. . . . Why not? Let them march." She believed that community members should be able to put up the Flag for Lee-Jackson Day and then supporting flags for MLK Day. "Let them be." Bridget is ambivalent toward Southern symbols. "That Flag and those statues aren't doing a thing. They are not doing it. It's the people who are doing it. They don't mean that much to me. . . . To me that meant that was their flag for that time. Now it doesn't mean a thing to me." When asked if the displayed Confederate Battle Flag has racist connotations, Bridget replied, "Some of them do. Some of them don't." The Flag is not necessarily a symbol of hatred for Bridget. "Not necessarily." The meaning of the display of the Flag depends on the surrounding context for Bridget. Bridget recognizes that when the Klan flies the Confederate Battle Flag it is a symbol of white supremacy. "They are a hateful group." Yet, Bridget liked the Sons of Confederate Veterans, and she unequivocally did not categorize them as a hate group. "How can you say? You cannot judge a book by its cover. . . . Yeah, I know of them. They are not [hateful] either. I'll tell you why. The Colored School Group, we used to go to the Labor Day Parade here and go out to the park. Every year, who would help me set up the tent? The soldiers from the Sons of Confederate Veterans. So, who's to say? They didn't have to. And they would talk [to us]." Bridget specifically lauded Jack, a ranking member of the Stonewall Brigade of the Sons of Confederate

Veterans. Jack works at the store where Bridget regularly shops. "He's in the country where my father is from. And he is always talking to me. 'Miss Bridget. What's going on?' Asking about the group . . . the church . . . He's one of the Sons! Now he is my best friend. . . . What else can you ask for?"

Most Forbearers feel no need to remove Confederate memorials. The generalized collective sentiment "Leave them be" was summed up by Spence Sr. "It's history. I think they should just be left alone. It's history." Some respondents felt that additional context could be added to these monuments and some suggested that additional monuments be erected to those black community members that made significant contributions. Spence specified, "If there is an importance. Not just to be putting them—to be putting them." Nick is a white man from the county and a retired salesman. He feels strongly about Confederate memorials, "Don't mess with those. That's history. If you take those things down, you are no better than the Taliban blowing up the Buddhist temples in Afghanistan." Nick suggested, instead, erecting other monuments in addition to the Confederate monuments to recognize contributions of black community members.

Stephen did not support the destruction or removal of Civil War monuments. He felt that it was an important reminder that the Confederate cause was lost and an unpleasant chapter in American history is in the past. "I don't want them [statues] to come down. Because if they come down, then my great-nieces . . . won't know what happened over here. They're a constant reminder of where we've been and don't want to go back. . . . They are important. Leave them up. . . . It's still a reminder that you lost." Agnes did not support the removal of Confederate monuments. "What I'm learning is that it's a history. It is history. When you remove something, you are removing history. . . . That bothers me. For the people who have, think it's offensive, just like the Confederate Battle Flag, we need to be taught our history, understand our history, and learn from our history. Some of its good and some of its bad. Leave them be, the but is to learn about it."

Lee and Jackson are consistently referred to by Forbearers as flawed Christian warriors engaged in a faulty crusade. However, removing the name of Lee was considered insulting and unnecessary by all Forbearers. Karl is a young white man who identifies as a liberal Democrat and state employee. He feels, "It's historical . . . you can't eradicate all names on the wrong side of a conflict." Herbert strongly feels that the Lee name should remain on W&L. He thinks that Lee and Jackson had an important part in the local history. Herbert believes there should be a course of study on the two men's character at W&L. Herbert stated, "If you were going to take Lee's name off W&L, then take Washington's too." He thought humorously the college would just be "&." "To me it has nothing to do with slavery. It has to do with the leadership and characteristics . . . the way I was raised . . . there is God, Jesus Christ, and Robert E. Lee . . . As a Southerner . . . we still have Northern liberalism being impressed." "Leave it alone" was a recurring theme again for many Forbearers when it came to the topic of removing the Lee name from W&L or Lee Chapel.

REDNECKS, BLACK REDNECKS & SOUTHERN GUILT

For Forbearers, the term *redneck* can have negative and positive connotations, but generally it refers to county or country Southerners. Citizens of Lexington city do not usually fall into the redneck category unless they identify as such or moved into the city from the county. As a pejorative, Forbearers view rednecks as ignorant whites that may be racially prejudiced. They are commonly referred to as "white trash" or "ignorant folk," and there is a sliding scale with the Ku Klux Klan epitomizing the ultimate redneck. Display of the Confederate Battle Flag does not automatically signify a redneck, but it is a clue of redneck or racist potential. In a positive reference, redneck means "hardworking," "independent," or simply "country folk."

Jude is a white farmer and was born and raised in the county. He farms for a living as his ancestors have for hundreds of years. The term *redneck* was hard for Jude to describe but it was not complimentary. "What got categorized as rednecks, the ones . . . the Rebel flags, using them the wrong way . . . I guess the people that absolutely don't like blacks because they are black . . . kind of rougher people . . . always fighting. . . . A lot of the people in school . . . categorize us as redneck because we wore jeans. I like to think of myself as country. . . . Most rednecks are country . . . but they are [racist]." Tony is a white man who works for the city of Lexington, and he sees himself as a working man. "Average guy . . . works every day, go home, take it easy, watch TV." For Tony, a *redneck* is a "bad thing." "People I don't like. They got tattoos all over them. . . . I wouldn't want to be a redneck. . . . They are wild, drink all the time, fight and carry on . . . I don't like that. . . . Out in the boonies . . . Collierstown and South River and places like that. Real ruffians." Bart, who lives by himself in the backwoods, considers himself a *good ole boy* or *hillbilly,* but not a redneck. "I don't know. I don't consider myself redneck. I consider myself hillbilly. It's a difference. I think rednecks [are] ones that go out and start fights and stuff. If they get to drinking, they get liquid backbone. They want to fight. . . . I'm not a redneck. I'm a hillbilly . . . I just keep to myself . . . from the backwoods."

Some Forbearers feel that the term had mixed connotations. Austin is a white man and native Virginian who has lived in the area for over forty-five years. The term *redneck* was a very difficult one for Austin to describe but it has mixed potential and could be a "term of endearment." "I think a lot of it comes down to education and opportunity. . . . Education is the key to everything." Austin feels that in the rural parts of the county there are "rednecks" that do not have the "education or opportunity" and prefer a simpler less complicated existence. "It is hard, very hard . . . people make jokes about rednecks . . . you know . . . Jeff Foxworthy . . . 'You know you're a redneck if . . . '" Bruce is a white "damn Yankee" transplant, but he has lived in the county for over forty-four years. When asked specifically what the term *redneck* means, Bruce was conflicted. "Ignorant, country . . . Irish Creek." However, Bruce's friend Gary was a self-styled "redneck intellectual" who embraced his "humble country origins."

For a few white Forbearers a redneck is a positive term, and it is a proud moniker of country in the spirit of defiance expressed in lyrical sentiments by Hank Williams Jr., Charlie Daniels, and Lynyrd Skynyrd. Gary was raised in the county, and he knows lots of rednecks. For him, the term has a more innocent, naïve connotation. "It means countrified." Thomas feels most country folk are "good ole boys" or rednecks. While a Northerner can be a redneck, "Southerners are considered more rednecks than Northerner peoples and I don't know why. They say, 'You from the South? You, just an old redneck boy.'" Kyle describes himself as a "semi-educated redneck," "tradesman," and "aviation electronic technician." He describes what a redneck is. "It's a country thing . . . a country guy, or woman . . . just would rather be left alone to live his life . . . how he sees fit . . . enjoys having a good time . . . doesn't see anything wrong with others having a good time."

Most black Forbearers felt the term *redneck* applied only to whites and could have mixed connotations. Oscar has some good white redneck friends. He did not believe that all rednecks are racist or bad. "No, no. It's weird. It's a fine line." "Yeah. . . . Some are just country, not haters." The line for Faith between good and bad redneck is when it becomes overtly prejudicial and racist. A bad redneck is epitomized by the Klan. For Faith, good rednecks can overtly display the Confederate Battle Flag like her friend Richard who lives across from the Church of God. Faith described good and bad rednecks. "Like we like to say about some of our white friends. . . . Some of them are really out there. And others like Richard, they are as nice as they can be. . . . The ones that we call bad ones are the ones that don't care about calling you the n-word or say something about your momma or daddy and all this stuff."

Mark felt the term *redneck* was not necessarily a derogatory term. "A lot of white people around here wrap themselves around the fact that they are rednecks. That's their identity. . . . You got some rednecks that will probably defend me to the death. . . . Probably would die for me."

Mark recalled a childhood incident where a white neighbor redneck came to his defense:

My mother used to send me to a store about three or four blocks away. I'd walk to the store and, of course, you'd have somebody [white] out on the porch hollering, "Nigger, nigger, nigger" or something like that. This one [white] gentleman, who knew my family, he defended me. He told that person, "You come out that porch and say that [again]. . . . "If you step out in the street here, I'm going to whip your ass." So, you had people who would defend you.

The term *black redneck* is adopted by over a quarter (6/22) of the black respondents. This is a positive term for black country folk who identify as Southerners and embrace country activities such as hunting and fishing. This term closely identifies with the *good* white redneck previously discussed. This is very different from Sowell's use of the term which he defines as those black people belonging to a "less achieving" urban "black ghetto culture." "Much of the cultural pattern of Southern rednecks became the cultural heritage of Southern blacks. . . . Moreover, such cultural traits followed blacks out of the Southern countrysides and into the urban ghettos—North and South" (Sowell 2005, 27, 33).

Black rednecks do not support the 2011 ban, nor do they see the Confederate Battle Flag as being categorically racist. They all had county and country ties and either saw themselves or loved ones, or were referred to, as black rednecks. Wade is a black thirty-nine-year-old aspiring electrician. He proudly considered himself a Southerner, country, and a black redneck. "Oh yeah, oh yeah . . . sweet tea, horseshoes, corn hole, country music . . . a country boy. Black redneck, that's me. . . . Oh yeah, oh yeah. I like mud bogging. I love it. I like four-wheeling."

Spence felt that redneck was the equivalent of country. "I consider it, back, deep back in the hill's country person. . . . Everyone calls me a black redneck. I don't know if I am a redneck, but I am very country." Carla thought she was a "bit of a redneck" as she likes her "cowboy boots and cowboy hat." For Carla, both black and white could be redneck. Char refers to her son as a black redneck. "I call my son a black redneck. . . . He's so country. He listens to only country music. He wears camouflage. He's got big trucks; big toys and he dates a white girl." For Char, redneck equates to country.

Unsurprisingly, black rednecks all were politically Independent, and do not find Southern symbols offensive. Black rednecks are all tolerant of the Confederate Battle Flag and some openly admire it like Faith and Wade. Wade stated, "People ask me about the rebel flag. It's not the flag it's the person. . . . There are people who . . . fly that Flag because they're proud. I have no offense to that. . . . Somebody's proud of that flag . . . I actually was thinking about painting one on the Tahoe." Black rednecks feel a general kinship with good white rednecks because they share the same appreciation for county activities. These groups regularly co-mingle in country activities.

Wade likes to camp, fish, and jet ski with his white redneck friends. Black and good white rednecks share equivalent Cherished Southern identity through a nostalgic fabric of country activities that relate to the land and each other. Laughing, Faith referred to her brothers as "little black rednecks." She described the comradery of rednecks. "We like to call our brothers little black rednecks. . . . They are the same as white rednecks. . . . Cause my brothers all belonged to this hunting group, white people, you know, in with them. Plus, they are family friends like brothers to us."

Southern guilt is a challenge for many Forbearers regardless of race. The reconciling of Cherished Southern identity in terms of nostalgic fabric and progressive anodyne is in constant flux. Darrel is a white employee at W&L who does not own or display a Confederate Battle Flag. He is "conflicted" on the importance of the Flag to him. He is aware that his ancestors are in the graveyard and the gravestones are marked with Confederate States of America markers. When Reformers challenge his conflicted status, Darrel is highly perturbed. "What are you saying to me? That my great-great-grandfather was bad? What am I supposed to do? What are you saying I should do? That the moral decision I have to make is to reject my great-great- grandfather and his background and the heritage? What?" Darrel believes that things should be looked at in "the context of the period," namely the Civil War and slavery. For him, a failure to grasp context leaves Southern symbols vulnerable to the illogic of presentism.

For black rednecks one's racial loyalty may be called into question. Recall Cora's statement as a Reformer. "I believe the black people who wave the Confederate Battle Flag want to fit in. . . . *Coon.s . . . Uncle Toms*. . . . They want to be a 'good ole boy' for those white guys." Yet there are many community members that challenge the unyielding Reformer narrative. Char and Jesse are good friends. They met when they both worked at W&L. Their friendship does not fit the customary paradigm. Char is a black woman, and Jesse is white gay man and avid Retentionist. When interviewed, both indicated a great fondness for each other. Years ago, they would dance the Virginia Reel at social functions at W&L. Some of Char's black friends confronted her. "Why can't I do the Virginia Reel. I can't be black and do the Virginia Reel? What are you talking about? . . . I do it anyway. Just because I want to do it. He asked me to do it with him . . . if he was worried about me being black, he's doing it with me. We're partners. I'm not worried, we're doing it. We're helping each other."

Like some Reformers, some white Forbearers came from economic or stratified privilege and had black nannies that they fondly recollected as they exhibited Southern guilt as a means of self-disassociation from perceived prejudice. Oliver was born in the South. His parents were from upstate New York and moved to Lexington. Yet, Oliver does not consider himself a Southerner. "Never have." He recalled the license plates when he was growing up that said "Lexington—Shrine of the South." Such sentiments hold no significance for him. Oliver is proud and identifies as being from Lexington and Rockbridge County. But he does not identify as a Virginian or a Southerner. "I consider myself to be lucky . . . living here and having the experiences I have. . . . When I was five, we had an African American woman, she just graduated from high school here, she was like our nanny." When he was a boy, his nanny took him to Leggett Department Store in downtown Lexington where there was a drinking fountain labeled "Colored water." Oliver asked, 'Well, what color is that water?' My nanny laughed."

After years in the business world, Herbert returned to Lexington in 2012. Herbert is fond of the Confederate Battle Flag but supports the 2011 ban so as not to be offensive to black community members. Recalling his childhood, Herbert emotionally reflected upon his black nanny, Tara. She generally came for the day and was an important influence in Herbert's childhood. Tara would bring her children during the summer, and he would play with them. "I had two moms. [Tearing up] One umm . . . sorry. There was this wonderful woman that would come to our house every day and help my mom cook and that kind of stuff. She was family . . . she was family. . . . When my parents would go out of town, she would stay with us, and she would cook for us and eat with us. She was family. . . . When she died, we walked in with the family at her funeral."

RICHARD THE RETENTIONIST AND THE CHURCH OF GOD

Early in my interviews Betty, a Reformer, mentioned a situation where a white man was displaying multiple Confederate Battle Flags right across from a black church in town. My first inclination was that this was a fine example of a racist hate statement to antagonize black churchgoers. However, Konrad, a self-identified progressive, personally knew Richard, the Flag displayer, and indicated that there was more to the story. He described Richard as a "nice guy" who loved to hike in the woods but was having health problems due to cancer. Konrad also knew Arthur, the church deacon at the Church of God, and he suggested I speak with him. Konrad stated, "They can always use a hand on food delivery day." In October 2019, I walked up to survey the area. The Church of God and Richard's home are halfway up the hill from town facing across from each other. I stood by the church and gazed across the street to see the small humble home with several flags to include several variations of the Confederate Battle Flag flying on his flagpoles. As I was standing outside the church, I met Faith for the first time. She provided that she was a church elder and that she could introduce me to Carla, a church deacon and Arthur's wife. Later that day, I set up a time to interview Carla and Arthur.

I came back the next day and formally introduced myself to Richard, not knowing what to expect. Richard is an unusual Retentionist in that he does not belong to the Sons of Confederate Veterans, and he does not know his ancestral lineage. However, he still identifies deeply with his multiple variations of the Confederate Battle Flag. When we first met, Richard was unusually cordial and eagerly wanted to share his adoration for his flags. We spoke for hours as we sat on the picnic bench in his front yard, right across from the Church of God and within an arm's length from his flag display. For Richard these flags represent the best of simple country life. In his words, "country . . . redneck . . . freedom of expression . . . beautiful flag." Richard is proud to be a Southerner. For him, South is the same as country. "You are a country boy . . . and a Southerner . . . if you are living in it. . . . Country is country . . . Human is human." Richard ran heavy equipment for several quarries and then went to work at a sawmill. He worked there for forty-three years until he retired. Richard has had Confederate Battle Flags since he was a young boy. He had three or four Flags that were lost when his house in the country burned down. Richard loves the aesthetics of the Confederate Battle Flag. "I thought the world of the battle flag . . . it's the color of it . . . the way it stands out . . . I didn't know the history of the flag. But I loved the flag. It's a beautiful flag." Richard advised that the VA-Flaggers had approached him and asked if he wanted a bigger pole to fly the Flag. They intended to put in a 6-inch diameter, 28-foot-high pole in the near future. Richard noted that he loves to talk to people about the Confederate Battle Flag, including parents, students, and anybody just walking by.

Richard stated that before he put up the Confederate Battle Flag, about a year and a half ago, he talked to four or five members of the Church of God to include the preacher. He asked if the Flag would offend them and they said, "No." Richard spoke very highly of the congregant members of the Church of God across the street. "They work very hard and need help sometimes." I asked Richard, "If the Church of God folks said they were offended by your flags now, would you take them down?" Richard replied, "Yes . . . I would. But I would put a pole in the back and fly it there so the town could see it." Richard feels that he is a simple man who loves to hike, and he loves his flags. At no time did he give me any inclination of prejudice or utter any racial slurs. To probe and determine his inclination to socially distance black folks, Richard was asked how he would feel if his children married a black spouse. Richard gave it some consideration. "That kind of depends . . . if they think of each other a lot . . . if he don't mistreat her . . . they get along great. Then it would depend if me and him get along. . . . If everyone was nice to each other." Only after interviewing Faith, did I learn that Richard considers her a good friend, keeps a protective eye on her, and goes on extensive travels with her and some of her sisters. At the end of the first interview, Richard advised that he is dying of cancer. It was not lost on me that as we were speaking at the picnic table, several people walked by, observed us communicating cordially, and shook their heads in what I deduced was disgust. I found it interesting that just by talking with Richard the Retentionist, I appeared to be judged by my mere association with him and my proximity to his flags.

Over time, I established a deeper relationship with these community members though volunteer work at the Church of God food pantry. Carla, Arthur, Faith, and Richard each provided their perspectives in interviews and ad hoc discussions while we were working together or when I visited Richard after working. I was able to glean a multifaceted understanding of the situation that was rather unexpected. Arthur stated, "Richard and I have no problem . . . with him and his Flag." Arthur does not think Richard is a bad person:

> Richard is not a bad guy at all. . . . If he likes you, he respects you regardless of what his color is. His affiliation with his Flag is very true . . . I don't have a problem with Richard. Cause I got the chance to talk to Richard and I understand the way he is about his flag. And, to him it's not about . . . [laughing] yeah, he don't have no problem calling me a nigger, he really doesn't. . . . He's called us that before. I've heard him. . . . There were some people over at Richard's house, at one time and they was talking about us, and Richard said, 'I don't have a problem with those niggers over there. They're good' . . . that is just the way he expresses himself. Did I really like it? No, I didn't really care for it.
>
> But hey, Richard has done more here for us, I think, than my own people have done. . . . He shovels the sidewalks . . . you know, he keeps an eye. . . . Everybody looks at Richard as being kind of racist . . . and I've never picked that up from him . . . I like Richard . . . I'm really sorry that he is sick [cancer] . . . I come to his defense because he has always been a stand-up guy with us. . . . He has even come by and shoveled the sidewalks. People don't know that about him. But he has.

When asked about Richard's use of the word *nigger*, Arthur stated, "I understand . . . that his generation that was a natural word to say." For Carla, as long as people do not treat her poorly, she does not care that they fly the Confederate Battle Flag. "Richard is an odd guy. . . . Richard is Richard." She said she has talked to Richard for hours. She stated that Richard does not look down on her and has lived there forever. Carla did not feel Richard was a racist because of his display of the Flag nor did she every hear him use racial slurs. "He doesn't display it to me. . . . He flies his Flag, yes, he does. Does he throw bottles and Molotov cocktails at the church? No. Does he call us niggers and all of that? No. He still respects [us] as human beings and I respect him as a human being. He has a right to his opinion, and I have a right to my opinion. . . . It's a flag people! It's a piece of cloth."

Faith has a unique relationship with Richard. They have been friends for many years and go traveling on cruises together. She differentiated between bad and good rednecks. A bad redneck belonged to the Klan. Richard, however, was a good redneck. "It's like with Richard. He's one of the nicest people you will ever meet. I've been knowing Richard for quite a while. See we cruise a lot.[6] Me and one of my sisters, he and his wife used to go. And we got to know him better that way. My sister went to school with him and his wife. She knew him better than I did." Faith likes Richard. It does not bother her that he flies the Confederate Battle Flag. "Cause, I had people on both sides of the war. See our great-great-great-grandfather was a white man as was his wife that our family line came from. Mixed in there somewhere was some Indian . . . and we never paid any attention to it. We're human beings. You treat us fair; we'll treat you fair." Faith said she never had any racial issues growing up. She had kin that fought for the Union and the Confederacy as well as some that were slaves and slave owners. In 2011 when the ban of the Flag was proposed, Faith advised that a lady told her there was a meeting about the "G-D Confederate Flag." Faith told the woman, "Listen, I'm not getting involved in that. I had people on both sides of the war. Y'all are trying to change stuff that is history. You can't change history." For Faith, the Confederate Battle Flag symbolizes, "What people's ancestors went through for this country [the South]." For her, Confederate is not a bad word. "To me it is not." When asked how the black community generally feels about the Flag, Faith replied, "I would say a lot them really don't care about it . . . either way."

The unusual and stark scenario between the congregants of the Church of God and Richard the Retentionist epitomizes the *Way of the Forbearer*. It also poignantly demonstrates that interpretations of Southern symbols, like the Confederate Battle Flag, are not simple as they are often misrepresented and misunderstood even at the town level. Although some townspeople described the Richard and the Church of God situation as contentious, interviews of those specifically involved revealed no such animosity. Most Lexington town community members did not have an intimate knowledge of the details of the situation and some condemned Richard, without knowing him, as an overt racist based solely on his display of Flags. I have heard Reformer community members state, "How could he fly that racist Flag?" "What an ignorant racist!" "He should be forced to take it down." Richard is condemned by Reformers and the media who do not know him, because of his failure to embrace Southern guilt and his audacious display of the Flag across from the Church of God (R. J. Epstein 2020). Yet several black neighbors took time to interact with him, and even befriend him, despite his Confederate Battle Flag display and the occasional use of foul terms. Mutual respect and assistance were afforded between black church elders and Richard himself. Sometimes the sentiments shared between these black and white community members surpassed tolerance and mutual respect. The relationship between Faith and Richard as travel companions and longtime friends illustrates what misinformation abounds and that describing Confederate Battle Flag sentiments in terms of a definitive racial divide is not necessarily accurate, at the very least not in the Lexington-Rockbridge community. Why are the details of the relationship between Richard and the Church of God not adequately represented even in a small town? Is it because of simple ignorance of the facts or does such a scenario contradict and complicate the popular, convenient narrative?

The Flag was tolerated by the black community members of the Church of God who spoke with me because they personally knew and liked the displayer, and Richard liked them. They communicated, coexisted, assisted, and protected each other as fellow community members despite racial and ideological differences. But this situation was not an anomaly. Recall, Char and Jesse dancing the Virginia Reel; Agnes's interaction with the white assistant with the Confederate Battle Flag headband; Mark and the white redneck neighbor who came to his defense when he was a child; Jack of the Sons of Confederate Veterans helping Bridget and her friends setting up a tent; as well as many other pleasant interactions that define their personal relationship based on good deeds (*acta*). These social connections are based on personal inter-actions not ideological collective associations (*verba*). A powerful cultural trope to illustrate this concept that is used by community members, especially Forbearers, is the term *good people*. It is a nuanced term that indicates that despite certain perceived less-flattering attributes the subject is judged to have redeeming social qualities, "Richard, he's okay. He's good people." Forbearers and other community members use this term when sufficient evidence is provided to conclude that the person is worthy of continued or advanced social interaction despite a character flaw. I humorously overheard the term applied to myself, "John, he's okay for a damn Yankee. He's good people."

Forbearers are a cluster of black and white community members that do not see the Confederate Battle Flag as a categorical symbol of hate, racism, or white supremacy. Forbearers do not deploy practical symbolic interactionism to designate friend or foe using contentious Southern symbols. They use it only as one method for gathering clues. Most have mixed feelings or are ambivalent toward the Flag. Some Forbearers do not care for the Confederate Battle Flag and may be suspicious of Retentionists who overtly display it. For these Forbearers, the Flag can be a *red flag* or a clue of a potential racist. However, they are equally suspicious of Reformers and their zeal to label others as racist. Although Forbearers may embrace Southern Guilt as an anodyne method to modify their own Southern identity, they do not deploy Southern guilt as an implement of othering. Forbearers wait for additional interactive clues before casting judgment and will not deny Retentionists moral authority simply because of their association with contentious symbols. A racist to Forbearers is a community member that directly treats them poorly via action, because of the color of their skin. For them, a Retentionist is not necessarily a hater, a racist, or white supremacist. Forbearers rely on daily, personal interactions to draw their conclusions about individuals and measure exchanges of respect. They do not judge others based solely on their associations with Southern symbols such as the Confederate Battle Flag or organizations like the Sons of Confederate Veterans. Forbearers engage fellow community members with the greatest *sympathy* and the least *hostility* (Cooley 2018; 1998). The manifestation of their sympathy is tolerance and tact. Through social interaction and the measurement of individual deeds, Forbearers successfully imagine and *feel* the interests of others. As a cluster, Forbearers transcend ideology and politics as they focus on individual deeds and interactions. Forbearer sociality triumphs over ideology as they not only engage in productive business dealings with others, but they also amicably interact with community members as *non-others* or *us*, while they build relationships. Forbearers seek to unify their comm-*unity* as they judge fellow community members by *Acta non Verba* protocols.

NOTES

1. *Reminder*: Non-displaying Whites are those white respondents who are not part of the cluster of Retentionists.

2. Black community members are those who self-identified as black.

3. Also known as Camp Sumter in Andersonville, Georgia, and served as the site of a notorious Confederate military prison.

4. The Robert E. Lee Memorial Episcopal Church returned to the original name of Grace Episcopal Church in September 2017.

5. Carilion Stonewall Jackson Hospital's name changed to Carilion Rockbridge Community Hospital in July 2020.

6. By "cruise a lot" Faith meant going on ship cruises with Richard and his wife.

Conclusion

The Sacred, the Mundane, and the Offensive

Why is understanding any nuanced signification of Southern symbols in the Lexington-Rockbridge area important? The Confederate Battle Flag is not a recently created symbol, but it maintains its strength as a cultural object and as a persistent and contentious polysemous symbol. The Flag's origins can be traced back to the *Saltire*, also known as the blue Saint Andrew's cross (Coski 2005, 1). During the Civil War it was a military battle standard for Robert E. Lee's Army of Northern Virginia. Without a doubt, the Confederate Battle Flag has been used as a symbol of racism, hate, and white Supremacy by the Ku Klux Klan, neo-Nazis, Aryan Brotherhood, and some groups within the Southern Poverty Law Center category of neo-Confederates. However, for many others it is not a symbol of hate or racism but rather a significant part of their civil-religion, the church of *Cherished Southern identity*. By using the lens of symbolic interactionism, we get a clearer picture of the civil-religious-like sentiments certain symbols hold for some community members. This is not to suggest a normative assessment of "good" or "evil" or the sanctioning of latent or blatant racist behavior. Rather, I suggest a pause from conventional and convenient narratives by taking a moment to try to understand the deep importance these items hold for "believers" even if they hold no value for this infidel, "damn Yankee." I argue, from a Durkheimian perspective, these powerful sentiments some Southerners hold for the Confederate Battle Flag are no different than the *cross* is for Christians, the *Star of David* for Jews, the *swastika* for Hindus, or the *concept of blasphemy* as any sacrilegious talk relating to Allah and His prophets is for Muslims. In this investigation I take a centered, classically liberalized position of the "stranger" to not only hear the polarized voices of the vociferous few, but also the elusive voices of the dulcet numerical majority.

Interpreting the various social meanings is important in understanding diverse local clusters and how these sentiments are formed in a social process. It is equally important to examine how clusters socially interact with each other as they create cultural boundaries and bonds that affect their surrounding social world. Analyzing and understanding the community scenario allows us to explore how these relationships impact the larger social context, and how individuals and clusters affect changes within the local, regional, and national environment. It is important because the results discovered challenge the conventional narrative of professed racial divides and convenient racist explanations.

Three questions were posed at the beginning of this book:

1. Why are some Southern symbols still so significant to some people?
2. In a Southern milieu, how are community members divided concerning sentiments of Southern symbols like the Confederate Battle Flag?
3. How do those with diverse sentiments toward Southern symbols socially interact when engaging with other community members on a daily basis?

This research illustrates five principal findings:

1. Reformers categorically find the Confederate Battle Flag and the song "Dixie" *offensive*.
   a. Reformers wish to banish certain symbols of the South because they believe such symbols *only* represent hate, racism, and white supremacy.
   b. Most Reformers do not identify as Southerners.
   c. Reformers excommunicate Retentionists because they fail to embrace Southern guilt and disassociate from a racist past.
   d. Through progressive ideologies and Southern guilt, Reformers attempt to deny any social moral authority to Retentionists.
2. Retentionists find symbols, like the Confederate Battle Flag and the song "Dixie," *sacred*.
   a. Almost all Retentionists identify as Southerners
   b. Public display is important to them because it is their *totem* that is constructed from a nostalgic fabric which symbolizes their civil *religion* of Cherished Southern identity.
   c. Their display is an attempt to retain social moral authority through conservative ideology which they feel is directly threatened by Reformers.
3. Reformers and Retentionists are in the numerical minority of community members.

    a. Both are polarized elements of intolerance that are mutually antagonistic in their joint *crusades* against each other.

    b. Through practical symbolic interactionism, both groups engage in collective condemnation via guilt by cluster association or *Verba non Acta* protocol as a way to distinguish themselves and socially distance themselves from each other.

4. Forbearers find the Confederate Battle Flag rather *mundane*.

    a. They are the numerical majority of community members.

    b. Most Forbearers identify as Southerners.

    c. Forbearers internalize various combinations of nostalgic fabric and Southern guilt as they attempt to reconcile Cherished Southern identity with racial inoffensiveness.

    d. Forbearers utilize daily social interactions, or *Acta non Verba* protocol, to assess individuals. They do not engage in practical symbolic interactionism through contentious Southern symbols to condemn via Southern guilt.

5. Analysis of the offensive nature of Southern symbols, like the Confederate Battle Flag and the song "Dixie," provides that there is not a racial divide among participants in the study. However, there appears to be a political one for the polarized clusters.

    a. Reformers are black and white community members that are mostly Democrat.

    b. Retentionists are white community members and are chiefly Republicans.

    c. Forbearers consist of black and white community members that are politically mixed between Democrat, Republican, and Independent.

    d. A vast majority of community members, regardless of cluster, do not see the need to remove the name Lee from institutions suggesting that locational context is critical.

INTOLERANCE VIA *VERBA NON ACTA* SOCIAL PROTOCOL

I spent time in the Lexington area as participant observer but always in the capacity of a Simmelian "stranger" or damn Yankee. I attended functions that were both Reformer and Retentionist centric as well as observing daily interactions of Forbearing community members. I found Reformers and Retentionists to be unyielding polarized clusters of ideological intolerance when it comes to contentious symbols like the Confederate Battle Flag and the song "Dixie." These opposing clusters appear to reflect the sentiments of the numerical minority of black and white community members. Based on their progressive anti-racist position, Reformers abhor the Confederate Battle Flag and the song "Dixie" and find these symbols intolerable. By association they find Retentionists socially unacceptable based on their ideological attachment to these symbols and attempt to deny them any moral authority. Reformers represent less than a quarter of the respondent voices but generally claim to represent the sentiments of a homogeneous black community. This research suggests that the black community in Lexington-Rockbridge is heterogenous in their sentiments on contentious Southern symbols, contrary to the findings of previous studies. Retentionists are relatively unconcerned and insensitive to the potential offensive nature of the Confederate Battle Flag and the song "Dixie." They are outraged by those who challenge their moral authority in celebrating these Southern symbols, and, by association, they are intolerant of Reformers. Retentionists have an approximate membership of 150 in the Lexington-Rockbridge area to include members of the Sons of Confederate Veterans, United Daughters of the Confederacy, and ardent displayers of the Confederate Battle Flag. Their membership accounts for less than 1 percent of the population by very rough estimation. Although research findings provide those sentiments toward the Confederate Battle Flag are not necessarily based on a racial divide, they are indicative of a political and ideological one. All Reformers identify as Democrat (or non-affiliated) and consider themselves liberal or progressive. All Retentionists identify as either Republican (or Independent) and consider themselves conservative.

Reformers are anti-racists ideologically and socially. They ideologically engage in a crusade against racism while socially *othering* Retentionists as racists via Southern guilt. Reformers create group boundaries by viewing some Southern symbols, like the Confederate Battle Flag and the song "Dixie," as outside acceptable limits and, as such, these symbols of the South are categorically demonstrative of racism, hate, and white supremacy. Interestingly, the Lee name on Lee Chapel and on the university of Washington & Lee was not considered unacceptable for the majority of respondents to include Reformers due to historical context and proximity. For Reformers, Retentionists then are outside tolerable social bounds and are racist, haters, and white supremacists based on their ideology and their wanton display of the Flag. Reformers exhibit *group bonds* through their utilization of Southern guilt which can be used as a self-remedy and as an implement of social othering. As a self-remedy Southern white Reformers restructure their image to disassociate from their previous attachments with Cherished Southern identity. They fully embrace Southern guilt as a lustral in an attempt to reconcile their individual and collective pasts and privileges as well as to self-disassociate from potential racist labels. They embrace little to no overt nostalgic fabric in the Confederate Battle Flag and "Dixie" as they actively attempt to renovate their Cherished Southern identity or abandon it completely. However, this can be an imperfect and painful process. Several white Reformers, as well as some Forbearers, exhibited internal or emotional turmoil due to the retention of latent, residual nostalgic fabric which they could not easily disassociate from. This is not to suggest that they were mentally imbalanced, rather that they displayed varying degrees of abreaction when reminiscing about their past and ancestral Cherished Southern identity. The individual dynamic tensions between familial memories and social progressive improvement caused internal conflict, or a rending of their nostalgic fabric, as they remorsefully contemplated the past using the piercing lens of the present. As a *tool of othering*, Southern guilt is also a speech norm that was used by Reformers as a way to illuminate and rectify past collective and structural racial injustices in the name of progress. Terms like *inclusivity*, *equality*, *diversity*, *liberal*, *progressive*, and *racist* are key word norms for Reformers. Patterns of speech that denigrate Retentionists as well as their personal avoidance of them bonds and distinguishes Reformer collective perceptions of Retentionists as different. As such, Southern guilt carries a sweeping power to *other* and divide the community based on the perception that Retentionists have a collective association with racism.

Many Reformers were highly educated. All white Reformers were college educated and over a quarter held advanced degrees. Most who were raised in the South generally enjoyed an upbringing of economic privilege and over a third had black nannies/help in their childhood homes. Vocal members of Reformers consist of community leaders such as Francine, Betty, and Noah as well as several academics particularly from W&L. In their well-intended righteous zeal, this vocal element of Reformers was able to gather social momentum for their anti-racist cause through disruption mechanisms and the utilization of the media to strategically cast Southern guilt upon the opposing Retentionists. However, in engaging in forward leaning tactics, like banning the Flag in 2011 for the Lee-Jackson Day parade and applying for a permit in 2017 to hold a MLK parade on Lee-Jackson Day instead of the federal holiday, many community members felt that Reformers lost some of their moral high ground as these methods appeared unnecessary, aggressive, and illiberal. Except for Retentionists, most respondents did not disagree with the progressive cause, but they questioned the methodology as being unproductive. Many respondents, to include some Reformers, find that both clusters (Reformers and Retentionists) are mutually antagonistic. Vance is a Reformer and white professor who was born up North and deems the term *Southerner* a pejorative. He considers himself a "very progressive liberal." Yet, he finds the aggressive tensions between progress and conservation in the community disturbing and unnecessary. "They both do it. . . . If you are surrounded by liberals, and I usually am, there is open attitude of contempt towards conservatives . . . I now am surrounding myself with conservatives who have an open tone of contempt for liberals. This is identical! This is identical! It's not 'kind of like,' but it is exactly like the same thing. Okay so this means that everyone is fundamentally wrong, and we need to work on this. Both sides are terrible!"

As a leader Noah believes he represents the interests of black community members in Lexington. For Noah, the Confederate Battle Flag is "a sign of racism . . . no exception . . . I think it promotes hatred and it does not promote unity." In his activities against Retentionists, Noah said he has never spoken with anyone belonging to the Sons of Confederate Veterans, United Daughters of the Confederacy, or the VA-Flaggers. For Noah, because they carry a racist flag, they are all racists and intolerable to speak with. Noah classified the Sons of Confederate Veterans, the VA-Flaggers, and the Klan as the same and would lump them together. "I would . . . I don't see any difference." As politically active, Francine and Betty felt it was their duty to address the Sons of Confederate Veterans request with an official denial and ban of the Confederate Battle Flag in 2011. Francine stated that her motivation for supporting the ban of the Flag was based on liberal family influences and the belief that she was representing the generalized sentiments of Lexington African Americans. "I think that's true." Betty, Francine, Noah, and other Reformers firmly believe they were representing the interests of the majority of black community members. As well intentioned as these community members were, the results of this study suggest that their representativeness of the community at large and specifically the black community may be lacking. These determined Reformers were positioning the interests of fellow vocal Reformers who are in the numerical minority in this community. These Reformers can be considered "reputational entrepreneurs" that utilize group ideology and politics to advance progressive agendas and strategies (Fine 1996, 1186). Their actions were not necessarily a reflection of the sentiments of the majority of community members nor of a homogeneous black community which does not appear to exist. The utilization of Southern guilt as an implement of othering is not limited in application to just Retentionists. It was also used by some black Reformers against black community members, specifically *black rednecks* when they failed to adhere to a narrative of homogeneity.

This research suggests that similar to Retentionists, the cluster of Reformers also approach a Durkheimian religious zealotry in their liberal quest to convert community members and *spread the word of progress*. As a self-remedy or as an implement of othering, Southern guilt offers power to Reformers. As a self-remedy it provides a mechanism for white community members to *exorcise* the personal demons of past Cherished Southern identity and become *reborn* as Reformers. Reformers utilize Southern guilt to *evangelize via disassociation*. Through practical symbolic interactionism, Reformers use

Southern guilt to label non-like-minded others as *racist* and as an implement of othering. As such they attempt to socially *excommunicate* Retentionists from the community for their failure to renounce, reconstruct, and disassociate from the Confederate Battle Flag. However broad-minded Reformer intentions are, the power of Southern guilt by association is *de facto*, illiberal. "Not the power that comes from persuasion and elections, but from silencing your critics, insisting that those who are not with you are against you, and shutting out those deemed privileged or disloyal to their race" (*The Economist* 2020a, 9). Many community members feel that Reformers generally display high levels of *progressive intolerance*. Progressive intolerance is the offensive[1] insular posture of embracing diversity but within limited acceptable liberal boundaries. It is not classical liberalism. Those outside the boundaries, such as Retentionists, are denied moral authority and are ideologically unreconstructed and socially unacceptable. In furtherance of their anti-racist agenda, Reformers demonstrated an intolerance that is exclusive, aggressive, and a mechanism to distinguish themselves and for stratifying to gain moral authority in the name of progress.

Retentionists are described by community members as rigid, insensitive traditionalists that unnecessarily cling to contentious Southern symbols. However, except for Reformers, most in the community (black and white) do not see them as racists based solely on their ideology. As a cluster Retentionists define their *group boundaries* as conservatives who are unreconstructed whites that refuse to *dissociate* from a Confederate past by abandoning the Confederate Battle Flag or the song "Dixie." "Such whites may or may not actually be racist, but their failure to disassociate . . . means they carry no moral authority, and add nothing to the legitimacy of the institutions they are part of" (Steele 2006, 151). Retentionists see themselves as anti-racists because they actively distance themselves from traditional white supremacists. Yet, they are inured to the vulgar potential that the Flag may hold for others. Sociology race scholars would be generous if they merely classified Retentionists as being *anti-racialists*, *laisse-faire racists*, *color-blind racists*, or mere exhibiters of *implicit bias*. As some of the literature suggests, and as a form of neo-Confederacy, Retentionists can be easily designated by critics as *racists* because of their support of the Flag which symbolizes a past Confederate racist structure that celebrated chattel slavery. This is the position that Reformers take.

Retentionists exhibit *group bonds* beyond their religious-like attachment to the Flag and the song "Dixie," by generally not caring if they offend others, as well as their generalized intolerance of Reformers. Being a white Southerner is not a source of Southern guilt for Retentionists as they proudly identify with English, Scotch-Irish, and German ancestry. They adamantly refuse to disassociate "or let go" of Southern symbols, their family history, and their perceptions of traditional honor of their ancestors as noble warriors regardless that the *cause* was lost and that it supported the enslavement of the black people. Retentionists are relatively insensitive to the potential offensive nature of the Flag, and as a cluster they can be considered guilty of "collective forgetting, denial, or marginalizing of the racial past and its connections to the present" (Fleming 2017). They do not condone the institution of slavery or make excuses for it, but they insist that Confederate issues of secession and the Lost Cause were about states' rights and that there was "more to it" than just the issue of slavery. Many claim to have black friends and did not demonstrate inclinations of racial social distancing. Retentionists recognize no loss of their moral authority for failing to reconstruct. Retentionists do not see themselves as white supremacists but rather loyal believers in *hearth and home* as part of their civil religion of Cherished Southern identity. Retentionists felt that the opprobrium of the Flag, and other Southern symbols, is demonstrative of liberal society's overall contempt for their civil-religion. Their group speech norms include rhetoric of *preservation, remembrance, conservation, tradition*, and *honor*. They cannot "let it go" and they see themselves as modern day "rebels" and they do not wish to be *tread* upon. Retentionists continue to hold the Confederate Battle Flag and other Southern symbols as sacred relics and rally together around perceived erosion of traditional conservative values. Hochschild reflects the sentiments of Louisiana white country folk feeling that some groups of people were "cutting in line" (Hochschild 2016). Retentionists feel they are being *obliterated from the line*. Even as a Reformer, Kate pitied Retentionists and Trump supporters. "I can see how the Trump people . . . the white people, the white males, just having had enough. You know, they are now on the bottom of the pile. And not only are they at the bottom of the pile, soon they are going to be in the minority, race-wise."

Generally, Retentionists in this study did not come from economic privilege. A few went to college, but most did not. Retentionists did not demonstrate an overt intolerance in speech or action toward black people, ethnic minorities, or alternate lifestyles. During interviews, follow- up probing questions did not uncover patterns of social distancing or *othering* toward these groups. However, their intolerance was firmly ideological and the enemy for Retentionists are the Reformers, whom they generally referred to as *liberals.* Leaders in the Retentionist groups of the Sons of Confederate Veterans and Daughters of the Confederacy, such as Jack, Tucker, Liz, Lauren, and a variety of Lee-Jackson Day speakers, represent institutionally well-placed "reputational entrepreneurs" that utilize group ideology and politics to advance conservative agendas and strategies as well as identification with the heroic characters of Jackson and Lee (Fine 1996, 1186). In their zeal, vocal elements of Retentionists are able to unify and excite like-minded others by embracing spiritual connections with their Confederate ancestors and war heroes like Lee and Jackson while denigrating Reformers.

Derogatory speech norms referred to Reformers as *Liberals, Democrats, anarchists, anti-Christians, socialists, Marxists, communists, Antifa,* and *leftists* to create a more threatening collective opposition for Retentionists to rally against. Liz despises "people who want to erase Confederate history here." Liz eagerly provided a specific list. "You ready? Members of 50 Ways Rockbridge, the faculty at W&L, liberals, people . . . that claim they are lovers of diversity, inclusive but are actually haters of diversity and are non-inclusive. . . . The ones that I know . . . I know them as neighbors or people I have served on committees with . . . or see them on Facebook." Jesse used to be a Democrat but switched to the Republican party. He described W&L liberals and Democrats. "It is their way or no way. . . . They want your vote, but they don't want you." Lauren felt that Lexington as a whole was elitist and liberal but also intolerant. "They are tolerant as long as you agree with them." For Tucker it is the "leftists . . . socialist Marxists from hell":

It is always the elite left white people telling everybody else what to do so that you will know how tolerant they are. That's the group I really hate dealing with. . . . Those intolerant liberals. . . . My great fear. I've read a lot of the Russian Revolution literature . . . that scared me to death . . . are we ten years from that kind of crap happening in this country? They'll do it in a nicer way. They won't throw you in the gulag. They'll probably just give you a nice little shot and put you out quietly.

Retentionists exhibit a thorough intolerance of Reformers while sensing an equally reciprocal sentiment from them. Retentionists ritualize a sense of dread and doom in their collective meetings. Cole describes the threat for Retentionists. *"They"* are trying to take away things precious to him. "God, everything. I think they want to turn us into a big shithole . . . [take away] everything traditional. Everything that every generation in his family has fought to protect . . . I don't want to be viewed as an enemy for doing the same thing that they're doing. They are trying to push their agenda, their ideology. I want to protect the traditional ideology. I want to keep things a certain way. I don't want to teach young people . . . that it is wrong to be a man . . . that masculinity is toxic." Cole sees progressive intolerance as a political and ideological assault to subjugate him. "I see those attacks as [Cole is screwing his thumb into the table as an indication of putting him down] in your face." Retentionists are bonded by the perception that they are under constant attack from Reformers. All losses of expression to include monuments, Confederate Battle Flag display, Confederate holidays, and limitations on guns are attributed to Reformers. Jack declared his concerns with Communists and his perceived betrayal of Southern values by Virginia Governor Ralph Northam at one Sons of Confederate Veterans meeting:

> We have Satan's minions down in Richmond right now and God knows where else . . . I think there is a lot of people out there that is the silent majority . . . they're scared to say something. These people need to be woke up and come to light about what's going on. This goes far past Confederate statues, far past Confederate anything. Far past Black Lives Matter. I'm sorry, this is a scheme to take over the country and put the Communists in control.

Retentionists utilize threads of hearth and home and the constituent fibers of (1) kith and kin, (2) ancestral land, and (3) conservation of honor to construct their nostalgic fabric into a cloak of conservation to protect themselves from the downpour of Southern guilt. They feel their values, and their Cherished Southern identity, are besieged from the left and that they are about to be washed away. Retentionists believe that they are villainized as racists and are a focal point for every racial incident in the county. For Retentionists, Lexington's moniker as the *Shrine of the South* and the *holy land* is being eroded by the voluble Reformer numerical minority. In their eyes, the "liberal" movement is gaining momentum by parlaying the death of George Floyd and other related incidents, with demands for active disassociation from anything remotely associated with the Confederacy and the South. Retentionists perceive that these social changes are overwhelming them as they are losing more and more of their *hallowed ground* based on national incidents that are tenuously connected to them.[2] For Retentionists, Southern symbols are an integral part of their nostalgic fabric. Demands placed upon them for disassociation of these symbols are intruding on their most sacred values. Retentionists are not insensitive to allegations of white supremacy, and they actively vocally attempt to disassociate and distance themselves and the Confederate Battle Flag from traditional white supremacist groups and even the VA-Flaggers. However, they refuse to succumb to Southern guilt by rending their nostalgic fabric and the elementary threads of hearth and home and their integral fibers. Retentionists may be offensive to some in the community and to many sociologists, but evidence suggests that they are not offensive to most community members whether black or white. Retentionists may or may not be actual racists, but their failure to disassociate alone leaves them vulnerable to being labeled as unrepentant, unreconstructed racists. Retentionists epitomize the greatest *conservative intolerance* in the community. Their rigidity is an insular posture of maintaining traditional values and despising those that threaten their Cherished Southern identity. To Reformers and other community members, Retentionists appear unyielding, exclusive, and impolite as they use their Confederate ancestry as a distinguishing mechanism to retain moral authority in the name of conservation.

Via practical symbolic interactionism, Reformers and Retentionists primarily assess the opposing cluster based on ideological association rather than personal interaction. They utilize a *Verba non Acta* protocol to define the *other* and distinguish themselves. As such, contentious Southern symbols are ideologically definitive for Reformers and Retentionists. However, these waves of intolerance concerning Southern symbols are not just directed between Reformers and Retentionists. Forbearers define their group boundaries as the tolerant majority who do not embrace the ideological zeal of Reformers or Retentionists and they are wary of both clusters. They understand and respect aspects of both ideologies but also see their unyielding blind spots. Forbearers are bonded as a community group because they do not see the Confederate Battle Flag as a definitive symbol of racism, hate, or white supremacy, and they do not use the Flag to further practical symbolic interactionism of othering. They do see it as a potential clue, but only as one as they gather other clues before making a final assessment. They reserve the same suspicion for Reformers. Although Forbearers do not have a singular ideology, their solidarity is based on occupying a spectrum of demilitarized middle ground between the polarized extremes and their joint suspicion of those clusters. Forbearers are also bonded as a cluster because they share outreaching and accepting social tendencies in everyday interactions. Forbearer speech norms include themes of *understanding, getting along, progress, history, inoffensiveness, tolerance,* and *tradition.* Forbearer cohesiveness is operationalized in *group style.* "Their courteous, non-pushy style of forming a group is itself what builds solidarity; the solidarity is not a result of a strongly shared ideology" (Bender 2003).

Forbearers are often recipients of Reformer and Retentionist cluster intolerance via Southern guilt fallout as part of the community social tension revolving around Southern symbols. Their forbearance of aspects of both extremes and their middle path places them "in a tight spot" between opposing collective intolerances as well as being internally conflicted between their personal nostalgic fabric and racial innocuousness. Since the death of George Floyd on 25 May 2020, there have been many changes in Lexington. The city and associated organizations have dropped the name of Stonewall Jackson from the hospital and town cemetery. W&L faculty have proposed dropping the name Lee from Washington & Lee for more palatable academic presentation (R. J. Epstein 2020). VMI has agreed to move the statue of Stonewall Jackson from a position of prominence at the school. Business owners are renaming historic businesses to disassociate themselves from perceptions of racism. Lexington street names are being proposed for change. As demonstrated in this research, this is not necessarily what the vast majority of black or white Lexington community members perceive as being necessary or desired. These actions illustrate anticipatory, institutional responses to the social phenomenon of Southern guilt deployed through the media based on the perceived association with racism and police brutality in Minneapolis and other places not necessarily associated with the South and certainly not with the town of Lexington.

Forbearers generally distance themselves from anything associated with the Confederacy discretely and willingly as they find the whole business discomfiting. They do not feel that the Confederate Battle Flag categorically symbolized racism or hate but they wish to be racially anodyne. They ingest doses of Southern guilt while attempting to reconcile some of their nostalgic fabric in their revised Cherished Southern identity. However, Forbearers also do not want to be told what to do or think and can become outraged at progressive intolerance. Many Forbearers were very frustrated by the illiberal tendencies of Reformers and the implementation of Southern guilt as a strategic tool to label. Herbert fully supported the 2011 city ban of the Flag, but he does not see it as an unconditional symbol of hate. He sees the Sons of Confederate Veterans as "reliving the heritage of their fathers and grandfathers and great-grandfathers and that is a great thing." Herbert values traits of "kindness, openness, open-mindedness . . . willing to accept differences . . . tolerance." He struggles with the progressive intolerance. "If I don't agree with you, I'm a racist. . . . That's where we are today. That's where the *ad hominem* argument comes with, 'If you don't agree with me, you are a racist with bad intentions and therefore, I can't talk to you.' . . . That hurts me."

Darrel is a Democrat, and a graduate of W&L. Darrel now works at W&L. He feels that as one of the top schools in the Southeast W&L tends to attract opinionated and intolerant individuals:

> In academic environment there tends to be as much polarization, on this campus, as there is in the community . . . I think it is probably emblematic of the country at large at this point. As a historian, I firmly believe that you need to . . . to walk this objective line. Let the facts and whatever speak for themselves. It's difficult because of . . . academic superiority . . . it tends to attract individuals who are very opinionated. Who would tell you that they are very interested in diversification and tolerance but yet in their thinking and their self-righteousness they are, in fact, some of the most intolerant people on the campus. They are tolerant as long as you agree with them . . . I don't refer to them on this campus as liberal thinkers, they just are leftist. There is no question about it . . . I am willing to listen to them. . . . They are not always willing to listen to me.

Nia considers herself a staunch, liberal Democrat and has been an active member of the party for over twenty years. She views Democrats as "liberal . . . to lots of varying degrees." To her, *liberal* means "fairness, justice, equality . . . open mindedness . . . inclusivity." Yet she feels liberals can be at times, quite *illiberal*. "Oh my gosh, yes. We're as bad, we are as bad as Republicans as far as like pushing people around . . . we are absolutely as bad. The only thing that redeems us, in my opinion, is that we try to do . . . justice and fairness . . . that is the only thing that redeems us from our poor behavior." Nia described politics in Lexington. "Now it has become very partisan. But you do see, there are a few [that interact]. Democrats who live in this area have to engage with Republicans or we are going to lose half the people we know or more."

Southern guilt also brandishes an economic edge. George is an active member of the Democratic Party in Lexington and a construction foreman. He is also part owner of what was formerly the Robert E. Lee Hotel. In July 2020, he and the other owners unanimously agreed to drop the Lee name from the Robert E Lee Hotel after being named such since 1926. George provided the following in a July 2020 email:

> The hotel was named after Lee when it was built in 1926. His granddaughter was present for the event and raised the flag (the US flag) for the first time on the flagpole to signify the opening. The land that the hotel sits on has been a hotel since the founding of Lexington. It was originally the Lexington Hostelry back in the late 1700s, and became the Lexington Hotel when the original burnt down in the great fire in Lexington in the early 1800's. It was the Lexington Hotel when Robert E. Lee rode into town in 1865, and it was where he lived for his first 2 years as president of the university until the house on campus that bears his name was completed for him. The Lexington Hotel was demolished in 1924 to make way for the new hotel that was built with funds raised from the entire community. I don't know how it was decided to name it the Robert E. Lee Hotel, but the goal of the enterprise was to encourage tourism to Lexington, so it made sense at the time. We decided to continue the use of the Robert E. Lee Hotel name when we opened in 2015 for many of the same reasons that it was originally named that. The current climate now makes that name economically risky.

The owners' motivation to drop the Lee name was multifaceted. There was a concern for social justice but they "were concerned with the family's image and association with the name." There was also "more practical economic concerns." George confided, "We wanted to do this before any public demands were made. . . . It's hard, not to get your back up when people demand you do something on your property." George provided his motivations on the name change and his thoughts on Lee:

> For me, the motivation to change the name is a practical economic decision, coupled with the desire to do it now on our own terms, rather than have it forced

on us later. I do not feel the same distaste for everything Confederate that some people feel, but of course I am not an African American either. I have been an admirer of Robert E. Lee since I was very young, but I admire his entire life, not just the five years that he spent as a General in the CSA [Confederate States Army].

I think anyone, white, black, or brown could learn something from studying his life, both his successes and his mistakes. Because he made a terrible decision in serving the Confederacy does not mean he should be erased from history, but it does mean that perhaps he should not be idolized.

Forbearers feel their nostalgic fabric being challenged by Reformers and at times shredded by Southern guilt through political correctness and economic viability as they attempt to distance themselves from racism. George illustrates the polarized intolerance that places Forbearers in the middle of a vicious gauntlet where there is little compromise:

We have not received any social pressure to change the name, but we did feel uncomfortable during the circus that followed the Red Hen's decision to not serve Sarah Huckabee Sanders. Like most of the downtown businesses, we are members of Main Street Lexington, and were bombarded with threats from both the right and the left for our involvement in that organization. Those three weeks were some of the most exhausting of my life, and we really [do] not want to have to go through all of that again.

TOLERANCE VIA *ACTA NON VERBA*: THE NOT-SO-RACIAL DIVIDE

Prior studies have concluded that there is a racial divide when analyzing the significance of the Confederate Battle Flag (Agiesta 2015; Jones 2017; Strother et al. 2017; Wright and Esses 2017). "Blacks are in overwhelming opposition to the Confederate battle flag. . . . Our results generally demonstrate an antagonism toward the Confederate battle flag among black respondents" (Wright and Esses 2017). This research suggests that after accounting for Retentionists, there is not necessarily a racial divide when analyzing the significance of contentious Southern symbols such as the Flag and the name Lee in the Lexington area. Black community members in the Lexington-Rockbridge area, particularly ones over thirty-five years of age, do not appear to be "in overwhelming opposition" to the Flag. Forbearers do not demonstrate a generalized antagonism toward the Flag or the cluster of Retentionists based on the symbol or ideological association alone. They may see it as a suspicious signal, but they require more evidence based on personal interaction before providing an assessment on the individual. Forbearers are equally suspicious of Reformers even though they sympathize with many of their progressive objectives. They find their methods of community engagement, on occasion, to be aggressive and antithetical in encouraging true unity.

The data represent that the vast majority of respondents, the Forbearers, look for additional evidence beyond the mere display of the Confederate Battle Flag before concluding that an individual is racist. This study does not make the claim that it is absolute or definitive in its findings as unequivocally representative of the local population. However, I have found that there are many folks in this community, black and white, who do not subscribe to the conventional narrative as represented in the media or by many in the sociological academy. Based on previously described sampling techniques, I argue that respondent sentiments can plausibly reflect community views. As such, the majority of Lexington-Rockbridge community members, black and white, do not immediately classify Retentionists as white supremacists, but, rather, they use daily personal interactions and mutual exchanges of respect to define their social relationships. The context of hearth, home, and place in Lexington is contextually significant for most community members regardless of race. Black perspectives appear heterogeneous just like most white community members outside the clusters of Reformers and Retentionists. Some black community members, particularly black rednecks, relate in varying degrees and permutations to "good" (*non-racist*) white rednecks, and to the nostalgic fabric of the Flag or other Confederate representations such as Lee and Jackson. Strikingly, community kinship via tolerance, tact, and negotiation was demonstrated on several occasions by those deemed to be on *opposing* sides. This provides specific examples of social unification, thus challenging the paradigm of racial divide concerning the Confederate Battle Flag.

Human society "exists in action" through daily social interactions as community members negotiate a variety of situations (Blumer 1969). Recall the informative scenario between the members of Church of God and Richard. Here we see at a small-town level how issues concerning combative Southern symbols, like the Confederate Battle Flag, are very complicated. Even within a small community, situations such as these can be misunderstood and distorted. Most Reformers, and others, interviewed did not have an intimate knowledge of the situation and described the situation as pernicious. They viewed Richard as an overt racist for his brazen display of contentious flags directly across from a black church. Richard was condemned by townspeople as an antagonist. Those who did not really know him surmised his culpability because of his association with the Flag and his subsequent failure to embrace Southern guilt. This is not an unreasonable assessment and one I assumed to be correct prior to deeper examination.

It was only at the micro-level of investigation, with the specific individuals involved, that we obtain a different perspective and a divergent narrative.

Respondents provided that there was no animosity in this continuing inter-action. The black church members of the Church of God, that I spoke with, liked Richard and appreciated his kind gestures, despite his Confederate Battle Flag display and his unrepentant Southern loyalty. Mutual respect and assistance were afforded between black church elders, congregation members, and Richard himself. Sometimes the sentiments shared between these community members transcended mere tolerance and mutual respect to friendship as with the close relationship between Faith and Richard as travel companions and long-time friends. Such details of the true relationship between actors, as determined by mutual deeds and pleasant interactions, may not be adequately represented for two reasons. The first is a lack of intimate knowledge of such details as simple ignorance. We do not know what we don't know. The second reason is that to recognize this relationship as it exists complicates the conventional narrative and challenges the stability of various reputational entrepreneurships. The Flag was tolerated by the black commu-nity members of the Church of God who spoke with me because they knew and liked Richard, and Richard liked them. They communicated, coexisted, assisted, respected, and protected each other as fellow community members. But this situation was not an anomaly.

Char and Jesse's relationship when they worked at W&L together was remarkable. Char danced the Virginia Reel, a traditional Southern dance, with Jesse, formerly of the Sons of Confederate Veterans, at a W&L social function for Lee-Jackson Day. When challenged by some of her black friends, she responded, "Why can't I do the Virginia Reel. I can't be black and do the Virginia Reel?" Char felt that by dancing with Jesse they were bridging the racial gap. Their relationship also encompassed earthy, politically incorrect humor. Jesse said he got a set of hand towels with young black children eat-ing watermelon from Char. He finds these items humorous especially since he feels that he has a racially eclectic family lineage and that these towels came from his good friend Char. Jack, a Civil War reenactor, and a member of the Sons of Confederate Veterans in his period uniform, helped Bridget and her friends erect a tent for a Buena Vista town social function. Bridget did not think it was fair to label the Sons of Confederate Veterans, like Jack, as racists or bad people. "How can you say? You cannot judge a book by its cover. . . . He's one of the Sons [of Confederate Veterans]! Now he is my best friend." While shopping at a thrift store, Agnes took the time to speak to a young white worker who donned a Confederate Battle Flag bandana. Prior to the conversation she felt it was a symbol of "hate and lynching." At the time she was concerned with his Flag display and candidly questioned the young assistant. He mildly responded, "That's my heritage." After an extensive interaction with this man, she changed her outlook on the Confederate Battle Flag and the man. "He was the sweetest thing. I'd take him home." Forbearers do not distinguish themselves from others by ideology. To form conclusions about others, they rely on daily social interactions to enhance personal assessments on community members regardless of their collective association, utilizing *Acta non Verba* protocol. For them, contentious Southern symbols may offer clues but are not definitive of the individual. They reserve final assessment of the individual based on sociality not ideology.

THE CULTURAL DIAMOND: THE SACRED,
THE MUNDANE & THE OFFENSIVE

Durkheim provided that through religious beliefs "the ideal" fell into two opposing categories: the sacred and the profane (Durkheim 1912, 34). In this context the term *profane* is better defined as the *mundane*. He saw sacred and the mundane as "absolute . . . profoundly differentiated . . . two worlds with nothing in common . . . not only separate but also as hostile and jealous rivals" (Durkheim 1912, 36–37). As part of the paradigm of Practical Symbolic Interactionism, this study of contentious symbols also utilizes the lens of Durkheimian religious perspective and advances his classification of what is "real" to each cluster by adding the genera of *the offensive* to the sacred and the mundane model. In doing so, the sentiments concerning the "archetype" or cultural object of the Confederate Battle Flag are more accurately represented. The Flag invokes polarized sentiments of what is adored by Retentionists as *sacred*, and despised by Reformers as *offensive*, as well as being rather prosaic for Forbearers. It is because of the interpretive contention of the emblem, that the third category of *offensive* is necessary when considering the totem's ability to unify and excite, outrage and irritate, or be relatively insignificant and innocuous for the three clusters and their *collective consciousness* (Durkheim 1912, 224). With the categories of the sacred and the offensive, "good and evil" are truly "two opposed species of the same genus" and the mundane is the demilitarized zone that lies in-between. In their respective "social milieus," Retentionists and Reformers are distinguished by divergent elements that create their cluster's *collective effervescence* (Durkheim 1912, 220). Yet, they both share a comparable *collective intolerance* of each other.

Symbolic interactionist Hebert Blumer felt that contentious symbols like the Confederate Battle Flag are "social creations . . . being formed . . . out of the process of definition and interpretation" (Blumer 1969, 11). It is through interpretation of the Flag by cluster that we can gain a perspective to view the social world and the processes in which symbols as cultural objects are being "created, affirmed, transformed and cast aside" (Blumer 1969, 12). Retentionists affirm the Confederate Battle Flag as it relates to their hearth and home and their Cherished Southern identity as well as a battle standard against their perceived enemies. Reformers not only *cast aside* the Confederate Battle Flag, but they *create* an opprobrium for the symbol and those who *affirm* it. Forbearers transform the Flag as being relatively unimportant to them, while they recognize the contention between the opposing clusters of Retentionists and Reformers. The Confederate Battle Flag provides a "social optic" to observe group boundaries and bonds as the three clusters identify friend, foe, and neutral parties. This optic displays that Reformers and Retentionists distinguish themselves and create "social divisions of the world" (Zerubavel 1997) while Forbearers look for ways to unify as a community and search for social common ground. However, they are caught in the middle of the differentiated social tension of retaining and denying moral authority.

Griswold's *Cultural Diamond* is particularly useful in illustrating the relationship between the symbolism of the Confederate Battle Flag as the *cultural object* and Lexington-Rockbridge as the *social world*. It is also a valuable stepping-stone mechanism to exemplify greater generalizability of polarized extremes of intolerance and larger societal contention. As a cultural object the Flag holds a powerful symbolic significance for many community members of the Lexington-Rockbridge area.

The Battle Flag is located at the bottom point of the diamond as the cultural object. The community of Lexington-Rockbridge is positioned at the top of the diamond as the social world of study where the Flag is anchored in a particular context. Retentionists and Reformers are vociferously divergent

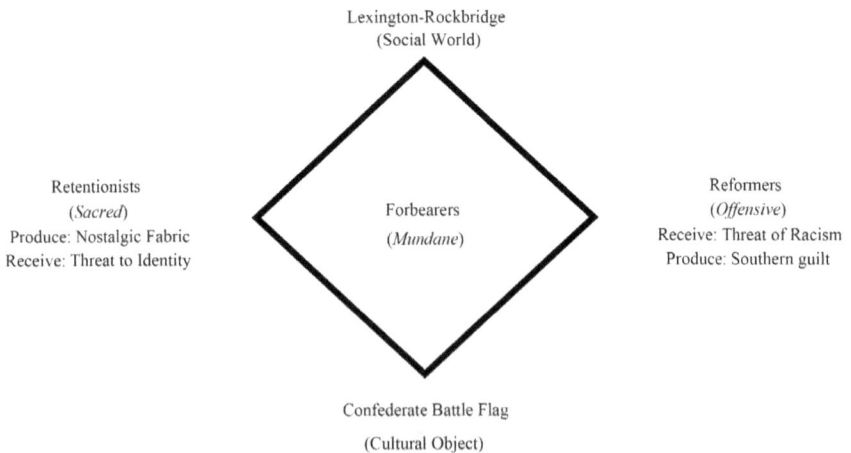

Lexington-Rockbridge
(Social World)

Retentionists
(*Sacred*)
Produce: Nostalgic Fabric
Receive: Threat to Identity

Forbearers
(*Mundane*)

Reformers
(*Offensive*)
Receive: Threat of Racism
Produce: Southern guilt

Confederate Battle Flag

(Cultural Object)

Figure C.1 Cultural Diamond for the Confederate Battle Flag in Lexington-Rockbridge: Tensions in Retaining and Denying Moral Authority.

Source: Created by Author (Cultural Diamond concept by Wendy Griswold)

clusters that are both active *producers* and *receivers* of the Confederate Battle Flag as a cultural object. As one numerical minority cluster, Retentionists see it is a sacred symbol that represents their effort to retain moral authority via nostalgic fabric. As the opposing numerical minority cluster, Reformers see the Flag as an offensive symbol of racism, and they attempt to deny Retentionists any moral authority via Southern guilt. For the opposing clusters, the Flag is a cultural object framed as a social problem. The social problem for Retentionists is that they wish to conserve their Cherished Southern identity. They feel they are under attack and threatened with annihilation. Reformers perceive the Flag as a social problem that threatens their progressive values as an overt symbol of hate, racism, and white supremacy. For them, failure to "let go of the past" is a failure to comply with racial progress and racial equality.

Retentionists *produce* the Confederate Battle Flag as a sacred symbol of their conservative nostalgic fabric; Reformers *receive* it as a threat of racism and a denial of progress. Reformers find the Flag offensive and produce Southern guilt, for the refusal of disassociation; Retentionists receive the opprobrium of the Flag as a threat to the conservation of their Cherished Southern identity. Retentionists and Reformers are direct reciprocal audiences in each other's production of the Flag. Forbearers are the larger audience in this social world. For them the significance of the Confederate Battle Flag hovers in the space of the mundane. In this middle space of the mundane, Forbearers receive the divergent produced meanings for the Flag from both Retentionists and Reformers and attempt to internally reconcile as *inactive* meaning makers. Retentionists and Reformers are unlikely to find common ground in their current posture of producing and receiving opposing meaning, but each cluster tries to woo the larger audience of Forbearers.

Retentionists represent the epitome of conservative, unreconstructed community members that refuse to yield to Southern guilt and "progress." Reformers embrace Southern guilt as a self-remedy for white racism and a strategic implement against non-reforming Retentionists. Through practical symbolic interactionism, both opposing clusters produce and receive meaning via guilt by association and condemn others, distance others, and divide the community through *Verba non Acta* protocol. Forbearers find many Southern symbols commonplace and rather unimportant to them. As the majority of community members, Forbearers tend to be more moderate in their sentiments on contentious Southern symbols. They perceive the Confederate Battle Flag as not necessarily as sacred as Retentionists, nor do they find it as offensive as Reformers. To varying degrees, Forbearers resist and embrace Southern guilt to maintain a grasp on their individual nostalgic fabric while attempting to be racially anodyne. This cluster internalizes the meaning of

Southern symbols through locational context and through other community members via daily, personal social interactions and does not engage in practical symbolic interactionism via contentious Southern symbols to further othering of community members. As such, they build relationships and unify the community through *Acta non Verba* protocols and do not condemn via guilt by association alone.

CODA: THE WAY OF THE FORBEARER

As discussed early in the book, we can use our individually crafted Mulligan Stew to help us interpret the social world around us based on individually selected infused ingredients of social evidence for our recipe. Each of our Mulligan Stews suits our specific social and psychological taste and provides a platform for us to define our exclusionary or inclusionary conclusions for characterizing others and our subsequent social interactions. As researchers, students of life, and social beings, we must self-reflect and ask ourselves three questions: (1) What's in my Mulligan Stew? (2) Am I willing to modify my recipe or is there no room for additional evidentiary ingredients? (3) In what fashion do I holistically, socially interact with others in the broader community: inclusionary or exclusionary? As sociologists we generalize and group people collectively in order to study them. In these generalizations and the name of progress, we must guard ourselves from two analytic demons: *absolutism* and *presentism*. We must recognize the potential for the bounding overwatch of assumptions. As previously stated, Retentionists generally identify Republican. However, not all Republicans are Retentionists. Reformers generally identify as Democrat. However, not all Democrats are Reformers. All black respondents considered themselves Democrats or Independents. However, not all black community members are Reformers. The preponderance of community members in the Lexington-Rockbridge area, black and white, do not wish to offend nor do they wish to eschew their varieties of nostalgic fabric. This study illustrates that the vociferous views of a polarized few do not necessarily represent the views of the more reticent majority that exist in-between. This study also suggests that intolerance begets intolerance. It very well may be time to leave the Confederacy in the past. However, in the process we must not lose perspective of various civil-religious contexts that form imperfect threads of hearth and home and the fibered constructs of nostalgic fabric: kith and kin, ancestral land, and conservation of honor that all community members share to various degrees. This research provides a platform to draw generalized sociological conclusions that go beyond Virginia and contentious Southern symbols. The findings of this work provide a venue to generalize the social significance and relevance of *tolerance* and social reactions to combative sentiments in a larger context concerning other contentious topics and corresponding polarized ideologies, such as gun control, abortion, and policing. In provocative times that seem to divide society, this book offers a hopeful prospective of unification that is *practiced* by most forbearing community members in the Lexington-Rockbridge area in their search for other "good people."

Daily disputation can be found in symbols, politics, and ideologies that create separation and stratification via identity politics. Their focus is not on the unity of humanity but in the distinction of identity that excludes, isolates, and cancels. The polarized elements in society are in the numerical minority and are unsympathetic of views that challenge their own. These divergent groups passionately identify with their ideology and firmly hold that their beliefs are virtuous, sacred, indisputable, and inviolable regardless of context via the closemindedness of absolutism. Such identity politics can be exemplified on the campus of Northwestern University over sentiments regarding Defund the Police and nationally over partisan politics and policies. Such resolute posturing reinforces immutable identities that lead citizens away from the tolerance, forbearance, and unification a democracy needs to solve social conflicts. "In arguments about who gets what, people can split the difference and feel content. In arguments about who they are—over religion, race, and anti-elitism, say—compromise can seem like betrayal. When ways of life are at stake the other lot are not just mistaken, they are dangerous" (*The Economist* 2020b, 11–12). Remote extremes of numerical minorities are directly opposed to each other in virtucratic identity crusades of *progressive* against *conservative*. When taken to the extreme each ideology is loud, narrow-minded, and dogmatic. Both are quick to take offense. When attacked, each engage in retaliatory counter-strikes of intolerance launched from their perceived positions of righteousness. These rigid clusters further their crusading agenda, their *jihad*, with little or no introspection as each pole believes they are divinely correct and the other heretical. The result is a mutually assured destruction of moral high ground. Why is this the case?

Heraclitus of Ephesus is credited with the quote, "The only constant in life is change." The polarized extremes of *conservation* and *progress* pivot upon this *constant*. One extreme firmly resists change as the other extreme attempts to thrust it forward providing for inevitable gyrations of antagonism. In his work Benjamin found that "Whitopians" share a "cumulative anxiety." "[It] is not about money or skin color, it's about the pace and magnitude of change in America and whether they can summon the courage and skill to survive it" (Benjamin 2009, 319). Benjamin is concerned with the balkanization and "disintegration" of society as many in America fail to recognize their civic duty to the "common good":

> Our racial thinking needs a truly twenty-first century upgrade. Identity politics
> is letting America down, on the one hand. Race and structural racism still matter
> on the other. We must escape this tight spot to thrive. . . . These times demand a
> universalizing approach to the common good, one that is not naively color-blind
> toward any race. There is no transcending race. But there is transcending defi-
> cient habits and thinking. The next wave of racial, social, and attitudinal reform
> in America will require a change from everyone. . . . Diversity isn't going any-
> where, so we better pursue cooperation and trust. (Benjamin 2009, 307–9, 312)

Change is natural and inevitable. However, the intensity of polarized ideological convictions of unyielding clusters results in various degrees of insular situational antipathy and an overall "disintegration" of the community.
Empirical facts and thoughtful consideration are not as important as advancing reputational agendas and creating sensations that benefit ideologies and
the individuals who are invested in them as reputational entrepreneurs. What
is important to the dogmatic clusters is furthering the conventional or *convenient* narrative that suits their ideology of *Verba*. Both of these extremes
of numerical minority maximize ideological dispersion via the media and
disruption that sensationalizes and distributes the convenient narrative as
if it represents virtue and the views of the majority. As such, some media
further their agenda of *selling the news* by feeding the beast of contention
and overrepresenting the convenient narrative. This in turn creates a greater
momentum of confrontation and exclusion via *othering*, which feeds the
baser desires of human entertainment, *panem et circenses*, as well as stirring
primal fears.

The *Forbearers* of society at large are in the majority and suffer much of
the collateral damage of being socially squeezed into a "tight spot" as they
walk the Aristotelian middle way seeking cooperation and trust with fellow
community members. They exhibit a greater tolerance and tact for a variety
of interpretations for contentious symbols and situations and they look toward
daily interactions more than mere ideological association in their social negotiations with fellow community members. As the two poles of contention
are brash, demanding, and well represented by reputational entrepreneurs,
Forbearers are quiet, unassuming, and largely unrepresented. They have
few, if any, reputational entrepreneurs in their camp, and they provide their
insights only when they are individually encouraged to do so by perhaps, a
trusted *stranger*, or even a damn Yankee, who lives in the community. They
eschew the limelight, contention, and academic surveys. Forbearers consist
of black and white community members who consider situational context and
the potential to offend as they attempt to negotiate a social balance between
the extremes of conservation and progress, to be "good people." They judge
others by their deeds not just their ideological words. It is in the *inconvenient*

narrative, the micro-situation and micro-interaction of *Acta*, where greater truth lies. Forbearers demonstrate remarkable examples of tolerance, tact, and negotiation skills across the ideological and "the racial divide" as they use *Acta non Verba* protocols in daily micro-interactions. If we pause for just for a moment, we can appreciate the lessons provided from purportedly *opposing* pairs. Talk to the white guy loading the Christmas tree in your car and ask him about his *offensive* Confederate Battle Flag bandana as Agnes did; perhaps there is a different meaning for him. Share a meal with a neighbor, shovel the snow off the neighbor's walkway, and keep a watchful out for a friend as Richard and the elders of the Church of God did for each other; good deeds demonstrate good intentions despite contentious symbols. Cross the racial divide and ask your coworker to dance the Virginia Reel as Char and Jesse did; enjoy the moment and challenge the convenient narrative. Take the time to be a gentleman and assist a lady in need as Jack did with Bridget; demonstrate humanity, courtesy, and kindness through daily deeds.

In these contentious times, where social interactions can be fraught with divisive peril, I offer the *Way of the Forbearer* as an example of social hope and comm-*unity* through tolerance, tact, and negotiation. As a general conclusion, I suggest that it is only the vocal numerical minority who hold the most extreme sentiments concerning contentious symbols or subjects, such as the Confederate Battle Flag, abortion, gun control, or policing. Each pole promotes their ideal which consistently results in overall social tension. They judge *others* as *friend or foe* based on ideology which in turn effectively divides the community. Conversely, the quiet majority do not have rigid or unyielding sentiments concerning contentious topics. They may be for, against, or ambivalent toward multivocal symbols or subjects but they do not practically condemn others who disagree with them. They judge others centered on their individual social interactions. Their *way* unifies the community.

The conventional narrative of a racial divide is often professed at a national level in the media and in academic circles. I suggest that such chasms may be at times overstated. In daily productive social inter-*action*, black and white Forbearers seek to peacefully coexist with other diverse thinking community members. Progress and reform are important aspects of social evolution. Yet, selective sentiments of a civil religion concerning nostalgic fabric and the constituent elements of hearth and home, that are shared individually and collectively, are human characteristics in their inconsistencies, imperfections, and illogic. These sentiments are complicated and multifarious in their meaning. Nevertheless, they are powerfully important in their religious-like significance to those who embrace them. In order to more efficiently and effectively further strategic reform, and hold a more elevated moral high-ground, reformation requires greater sensitivity and inclusivity of all significant community voices. We do not have to agree, but we should acknowledge, not cancel, opposing sentiments as being important and significant while trying to recognize alternate points of view if we are to productively engage in social reform. Perhaps greater success at reform and progress can be achieved through actions of unification and inclusion rather than words of alienation and exclusion:

> It was a warm and sunny day for October (2020) at the Habitat worksite. It was perfect for outside jobs. We put up the roofing guard rails the week before, and my wife and I anticipated doing the roof for Reed's house that day. George waved us off the anticipated roofing job and directed us to waterproofing the foundation. "We have a commercial crew doing that job." I have done enough roof jobs and did not mind missing this one.
>
> Reed is a gentle soul recently from the Caribbean Islands. I have a hard time understanding his thick accent, as he does mine, but it does not stop us from playful banter as we work together on various homes. He and his extended family have immigrated to the United States, and they qualify for two Habitat houses. Reed works three jobs and gives time to Habitat. This is part of the contractual arrangement for all those who earn their homes with Habitat and characterizes their credo, "A hand-up, not a hand-out."
>
> As I was applying tar to the foundation of the house next door to Reed's, I recognized a lanky fellow with long hair and a scruffy beard directing a crew at Reed's house. It was Cole. He owns a reputable and lucrative business in the area. I went up to him to say hello. He immediately stopped what he was doing to give me a capo-hug. Cole and I shared the "Army-thing," but Cole was also demonstrating his disdain for any COVID precautions as these were threats to his masculinity. "I tell people I have rectal myopia . . . I can't see my ass wearing no mask." After further playful "manly" banter Cole went back to work. George asked how I knew Cole and I replied, "Research and the Army-thing." I asked George what Cole was doing here in a "Democratic Party stronghold." George replied, "He knows Reed from their CDL [Commercial Driver's License] train-ing. They are friends. He's doing the job for free." I smiled because I know Cole to be loud and obnoxious but also big-hearted and generous. George continued, "You know he is SCV [Sons of Confederate Veterans]. People wouldn't think that his kind would help a black man and his family. You know, it's just not what you think." I responded, "You're right George. It's not. It's complicated."

NOTES

1. As opposed to defensive.

2. In addition to the renaming of structures and institutions already mentioned, Stonewall Jackson Memorial Cemetery was renamed Oak Grove Cemetery in September 2020.

Bibliography

Adedeji, Adekunle. 2019. "Accessing Sub-Saharan African Migrant Group for Public Health Interventions, Promotion, and Research: The 5-Wave-Approach." *Comparative Migration Studies* 7 (30): 1–13.

Agiesta, Jennifer. 2015. "Poll: Majority Sees Confederate Flag as Southern Pride Symbol, Not Racist." *CNN Politics*, July 2, 2015. https://www.cnn.com/2015/07/02/politics/confederate-flag-poll-racism-southern-pride/.

Alexander, Jeffrey C. 2004. "Cultural Pragmatics: Social Performance Between Ritual and Strategy." *Sociological Theory* 22 (4): 527–72.

Allen, H.D. 1990. "Catechism on the History of the Confederate States of America." UDC.

AP. 2011. "Va. City Bans Public Confederate Flag Displays." CBS, September 2, 2011. https://www.cbsnews.com/news/va-city-bans-public-confederate-flag-displays/.

Bashi-Treitler, Vilna. 2013. *The Ethnic Project: Transforming Racial Fiction into Ethnic Factions*. Stanford, CA: Stanford University Press.

Bellah, Robert N., and Steven M. Tipton, eds. 2006. *The Robert Bellah Reader*. Durham, NC: Duke University Press.

Bender, Courtney. 2003. *Heaven's Kitchen*. Chicago, IL: University of Chicago Press.

Benjamin, Rich. 2009. *Searching for Whitopia: An Improbable Journey to the Heart of White America*. New York, NY: Hachette Books.

Blau, Peter M., and Dudley Duncan. 2014. "The Process of Stratification." In *Social Stratification: Class, Race, and Gender in Sociological Perspective*, 506–17. Boulder, CO: Westview Press.

Blee, Kathleen M. 2018. *Understanding Racist Activism: Theory, Methods, and Research*. London: Routledge.

Bloch, Marc. 2011. "Social Frameworks of Memory." In *The Collective Memory Reader*, 150–55. Oxford: Oxford University Press.

Blumer, Herbert. 1958. "Race Prejudice as a Sense of Group Position." *The Pacific Sociological Review* 1 (1): 3–7.

———. 1969. *Symbolic Interactionism: Perspective and Method*. Berkeley: University of California Press.

Bonilla-Silva, Eduardo. 2018. *Racism without Racists: Color-Blind Racism and the Persistence of Racial Inequality in America*. 5th ed. Lanham, MD: Rowman & Littlefield.

Boorstin, Daniel, J. 1965. *The Americans, Vol. II: The National Experience*. New York, NY: Random House.

Bourdieu, Pierre. 1996. *The Rules of Art: Genesis and Structure of the Literary Field*. Stanford, CA: Stanford University Press.

Brewer, M.B. 1993. "The Psychology of Prejudice: Ingroup Love and Outgroup Hate?" *The Journal of Social Issues* 55: 429–44.

Brown, Karida. 2016. "The 'Hidden Injuries' of School Desegregation: Cultural Trauma and Transforming African American Identities." *American Journal of Cultural Sociology* 4 (2): 196–220.

Brubaker, Rogers. 2006. *Ethnicity Without Groups*. Cambridge, MA: Harvard University Press.

Brumfield, Ben. 2015. "Confederate Battle Flag: What It Is and What It Isn't." CNN, June 24, 2015. https://www.cnn.com/2015/06/24/us/confederate-flag-myths-facts/index.html.

Burke, Meghan A. 2012. *Racial Ambivalence in Diverse Communities: Whiteness and the Power of Color-Blind Ideologies*. Lanham, MD: Lexington Books.

Carlson, Jennifer. 2015. *Citizen-Protectors: The Everyday Politics of Guns in an Age of Decline*. New York, NY: Oxford University Press.

Cerulo, Karen A. 1993. "Symbols and the World System: National Anthems and Flags." *Sociological Forum* 8 (2): 243–71.

Cohen, Nissim, and Tamar Arieli. 2011. "Field Research in Conflict Environments: Methodological Challenges and Snowball Sampling." *Journal of Peace Research* 48 (4): 423–35.

Collins, Randall. 1981. "On the Microfoundations of Macrosociology." *American Journal of Sociology* 86 (5): 984–1014.

———. 2005. *Interaction Ritual Chains*. 2nd ed. Princeton, NJ: Princeton University Press.

———. 2008. *Violence: A Micro-Sociological Theory*. Princeton, NJ: Princeton University Press.

Cooley, Charles Horton. 1998. *On Self and Social Organization*. London: University of Chicago Press.

———. 2018. *Human Nature and the Social Order: The Interplay of Man's Behaviors, Character and Personal Traits with His Society*. Paris: Adansonia Publishing.

Coski, John M. 2005. *The Confederate Battle Flag: America's Most Embattled Emblem*. Cambridge, MA: Harvard University Press.

Cramer, Katherine J. 2016. *The Politics of Resentment: Rural Consciousness in Wisconsin and the Rise of Scott Walker*. Chicago, IL: University of Chicago Press.

Crutcher, Nelma. 2018. "Statement from the President General (UDC)." https://hqudc.org/.

Dew, Charles B. 2016. *The Making of a Racist: A Southerner Reflects on Family, History, and the Slave Trade*. Charlottesville, VA: University of Virginia Press.

Diangelo, Robin. 2018. *White Fragility: Why It's so Hard for White People to Talk About Racism*. Boston, MA: Beacon Press.

Dickerson, Caitlin. 2017. "A New Martin Luther King Jr. Parade Divides a Virginia Town." *New York Times*, January 16, 2017. https://www.nytimes.com/2017/01/16/us/parades-lexington-virginia-martin-luther-king-jr-robert-e-lee.html.

Du Bois, W.E.B. 1975. *Black Reconstruction in America 1860–1880*. New York, NY: Athenium.

Durkheim, Emile. 1912. *The Elementary Forms of Religious Life*. Paris: F. Alcan.

Dyer, Richard. 2017. *White: Twentieth Anniversary Edition*. 20th Anniversary Edition. New York, NY: Routledge.

Ehrenfreund, Max, and Jeff Guo. 2016. "If You've Ever Described People as 'White Working Class,' Read This." *The Washington Post*, November 23, 2016. https://www.washingtonpost.com/news/wonk/wp/2016/11/22/who-exactly-is-the-white-working-class-and-what-do-they-believe-good-questions/?utm_term=.085f37f11f98.

EJI. 2021. "Lynching in America: Confronting the Legacy of Racial Terror. County Data Supplement." Equal Justice Initiative. April 14, 2021. https://eji.org/wp-content/uploads/2020/02/02-07-20-lynching-in-america-county-supplement.pdf.

Eliasoph, Nina, and Paul Lichterman. 2003. "Culture in Interaction." *American Journal of Sociology* 108 (4): 735–94.

Epstein, Joseph. 2003. *Snobbery: The American Version*. New York, NY: First Mariner Books.

Epstein, Reid J. 2020. "A Liberal Town Built Around Confederate Generals Rethinks Its Identity." *New York Times*, July 26, 2020. https://www.nytimes.com/2020/07/26/us/politics/lexington-va-confederate-generals.html#:~:text=A%20Liberal%20Town%20Built%20Around%20Confederate%20Generals%20Rethinks,reassessing%20the%20town%E2%80%99s%20ties%20to%20a%20legacy%20.

ERD. 2020. "E-Reference Desk: The Virginia State Flag." 2020. https://www.ereferencedesk.com/resources/state-flag/virginia.html.

Eyerman, Ron. 2001. *Cultural Trauma: Slavery and the Formation of African American Identity*. Cambridge, MA: Cambridge University Press.

Feagin, Joe R. 2013. *The White Racial Frame: Centuries of Racial Framing and Counter-Framing*. New York, NY: Routledge.

Fine, Gary Allen. 1996. "Reputational Entrepreneurs and the Memory of Incompetence: Melting Supporters, Partisan Warriors, and Images of President Harding." *American Journal of Sociology* 101 (5): 1159–93.

———. 2021. *The Hinge: Civil Society, Group Cultures, and the Power of Local Commitments*. Chicago, IL: University of Chicago Press.

Fleming, Crystal M. 2017. *Resurrecting Slavery: Racial Legacies and White Supremacy in France*. Philadelphia, PA: Temple University Press.

Frankenberg, Ruth. 1993. *White Women, Race Matters: The Social Construction of Whiteness*. Minneapolis, MN: University of Minnesota.

Geertz, Clifford. 1957. "Ethos, World-View, and the Analysis of Sacred Symbols." *The Antioch Review* 17 (4): 622–37.

———. 1973. *The Interpretation of Cultures*. New York, NY: Basic Books.

Glaser, Barney G., and Anselm L. Strauss. 1967. *The Discovery of Grounded Theory: Strategies for Qualitative Research*. Chicago, IL: Aldine.

Goffman, Erving. 1959. *The Presentation of Self in Everyday Life*. New York, NY: Anchor Books.

Goldberg, David Theo. 2009. *The Threat of Race: Reflections on Racial Neoliberalism*. Malden, MA: Blackwell Publishing.

Griswold, Wendy. 1987. "A Methodological Framework for the Sociology of Culture." *Sociological Methodology* 17: 1–35.

———. 2013. *Cultures and Societies in a Changing World*. 4th ed. Los Angeles, CA: Sage.

Grusky, David B., ed. 2014. *Social Stratification: Class, Race, and Gender in Sociological Perspective*. 4th ed. Boulder, CO: Westview Press.

Guglielmo, Thomas A. 2003. "No Color Barrier: Italians, Race and Power in the United States." In *Are Italians White? How Race Is Made in America*, 26–43. New York, NY: Routledge.

Gutierrez, Betzaluz, Jennifer Howard-Grenville, and Maureen A. Scully. 2010. "The Faithful Rise Up: Split Identification and an Unlikely Change Effort." *The Academy of Management Journal* 53 (4): 673–99.

Halbwachs, Maurice. 2011. "The Collective Memory." In *The Collective Memory Reader*, 139–50. Oxford: Oxford University Press.

Haney Lopez, Ian. 2006. *White by Law: The Legal Construction of Race*. New York, NY: New York University Press.

Hanna, Jeff. 2011. "Johnson Scholarship Program's Impact Significant at W&L." The Columns. November 9, 2011. https://columns.wlu.edu/johnson-scholarship -programs-impact-significant-at-wl/.

Hartigan, John. 1999. *Racial Situations: Class Predicament of Whiteness in Detroit*. Princeton, NJ: Princeton University Press.

Hartmann, Douglas, Joseph Gerteis, and Paul R. Croll. 2009. "An Empirical Assessment of Whiteness Theory: Hidden from How Many?" *Social Problems* 56 (3): 403–24.

Hochschild, Arlie Russell. 2016. *Strangers in Their Own Land*. New York, NY: The New Press.

Hughey, Matthew W. 2012. *White Bound: Nationalists, Antiracists, and the Shared Meanings of Race*. Stanford, CA: Stanford University Press.

Humphrey, William. 2015. *Home from the Hill*. New York, NY: Open Road.

James, Angela. 2008. "Making Sense of Race and Racial Classification." In *White Logic, White Methods: Racism and Methodology*, edited by Tukufu Zuberi and Eduardo Bonilla-Silva, 31–45. Lanham, MD: Rowman & Littlefield.

Johnson, Charles. 2008. "The End of the Black American Narrative." *The American Scholar* 77 (3): 32–44.

Jones, Robert P. 2017. "What Does the Confederate Flag Symbolize: Seven in Ten Working-Class Whites Say 'Southern Pride.'" PRRI: Spotlight Analysis. https:// www.prri.org/spotlight/white-working-class-americans-confederate-flag-southern -pride-racism/.

Kefalas, Maria. 2003. *Working-Class Heroes: Protecting Home, Community, and Nation in a Chicago Neighborhood.* Berkeley, CA: University of California Press.

Korda, Michael. 2014. *Clouds of Glory: The Life and Legend of Robert E. Lee.* New York: Harper.

Kreisberg, Louis. 1998. *Constructive Conflict: From Escalation to Resolution.* Lanham, MD: Rowman & Littlefield.

Kruse, Kevin M. 2005. *White Flight: Atlanta and the Making of Modern Conservatism.* Princeton, NJ: Princeton University Press.

Lamont, Michele. 2000. *The Dignity of Working Men: Morality and the Boundaries of Race, Class, and Immigration.* New York, NY: Harvard University Press.

Lavelle, Kristen M. 2015. *Whitewashing the South: White Memories of Segregation and Civil Rights.* Lanham, MD: Rowman & Littlefield.

Lavrakas, Paul J. 2008a. "Nonprobability Sampling." In *Encyclopedia of Survey Research Methods.* Vol. 2. Thousand Oaks, CA: Sage Publications Ltd.

———. 2008b. "Sampling." In *Encyclopedia of Survey Research Methods.* Vol. 2. Thousand Oaks, CA: Sage Publications Ltd.

———. 2008c. "Snowball Sampling." In *Encyclopedia of Survey Research Methods.* Vol. 2. Thousand Oaks, CA: Sage Publications Ltd.

Leigh, Phil. 2019. "My Confederate Statue Speech." Civil War Chat. https://civilwarchat.wordpress.com/2019/07/30/my-confederate-statue-speech/.

Leigh, Philip. 2017. *Southern Reconstruction.* Yardley, PA: Westholme Publishing LLC.

———. 2020. "Defending Confederate Memorials." Presented at the Lee-Jackson Day Symposium, Col Alto Conference Center, January 18.

Levine, Donald N., Ellwood B. Carter, and Elinor Miller Gorman. 1976. "Simmel's Influence on American Sociology." *American Journal of Sociology* 81 (4): 813–45.

Lifshitz-Assaf, Hila. 2017. "Dismantling Knowledge Boundaries at NASA: The Critical Roe of Professional Identity in Open Innovation." *Administrative Science Quarterly*, 1–37.

Lipsitz, George. 2018. *The Possessive Investment in Whiteness: How White People Profit from Identity Politics.* Philadelphia, PA: Temple University Press.

Lowenthal, David. 1996. *Possessed by the Past: The Heritage Crusade and the Spoils of History.* New York, NY: Free Press.

McDermott, Monica. 2006. *Working-Class White: The Making and Unmaking of Race Relations.* Berkeley, CA: University of California Press.

———. 2020. *Whiteness in America.* Medford, MA: Polity Press.

McGhee, Heather. 2021. *The Sum of Us: What Racism Costs Everyone and How We Can Prosper Together.* New York, NY: One World.

McIntosh, Peggy. 1989. "White Privilege: Unpacking the Invisible Knapsack." *Peace and Freedom*, August.

McWhorter, John. 2021. *Woke Racism.* New York, NY: Portfolio/Penguin.

Mead, George Hebert. 1934. *Mind, Self & Society.* Chicago, IL: The University of Chicago Press.

Metzl, Jonathan M. 2020. *Dying of Whiteness: How the Politics of Racial Resentment Is Killing America's Heartland.* New York, NY: Basic Books.

Mills, Charles W. 1999. *The Racial Contract.* Ithaca, NY: Cornell University Press.

Mills, Cynthia and Simpson H., eds. 2003. *Monuments to the Lost Cause: Women, Art, and the Landscapes of Southern Memory*. Knoxville, TN: The University of Tennessee Press.

Molina, Natalia. 2014. *How Race Is Made in America: Immigration, Citizenship, and the Historical Power of Racial Scripts*. Los Angeles, CA: University of California Press.

Morland, J. Kenneth, ed. 1971. *The Not So Solid South: Anthropological Studies in a Regional Subculture*. Athens, GA: University of Georgia Press.

Nesbett, Richard E., and Dov Cohen. 1996. *Culture of Honor: The Psychology of Violence in the South*. Boulder, CO: Westview Press.

Nietzsche, Friedrich. 2011. "On the Uses and Disadvantages of History for Life." In *The Collective Memory Reader*, 73–79. Oxford: Oxford University Press.

Oliver, Ned. 2015. "Lexington Has Battled over Confederate Flag Issue for Years." *Richmond Times-Dispatch*, June 25, 2015. https://www.richmond.com/news/virginia/lexington-has-battled-over-confederate-flag-issue-for-years/article_7b6d1140-c791-56bb-bb1e-9c89b8a4ded4.html.

Omi, Michael, and Howard Winant. 2015. *Racial Formation in the United States*. New York, NY: Routledge.

Patterson, Orlando. 2015. "The Nature and Dynamics of Cultural Processes." In *The Cultural Matrix: Understanding Black Youth*, 25–44. Cambridge, MA: Harvard University Press.

Petriglieri, Jennifer Louise. 2011. "Under Threat: Responses to and the Consequences of Threats to Individual Identities." *Academy of Management Review* 36 (4): 641–62.

Pitre, Anne. 2002. "Pre-Junior Catechism: A Symbolic History of the Confederate States of America." UDC.

Polletta, Francesca, and James M. Jasper. 2001. "Collective Identity and Social Movements." *Annual Review of Sociology* 27: 283–305.

Poole, W. Scott. 2004. *Never Surrender: Confederate Memory and Conservatism in the South Carolina Upcountry*. Athens, GA: University of Georgia Press.

Reed, John Shelton. 1986. *The Enduring South: Subculture Persistence in Mass Society*. 5th ed. Chapel Hill, NC: The University of North Carolina Press.

———. 2008. *Southerners: The Social Psychology of Sectionalism*. Chapel Hill, NC: The University of North Carolina Press.

———. 2018. *Mixing It Up: A South-Watcher's Miscellany*. Baton Rouge, LA: Louisiana State University Press.

Rife, Luanne. 2014. "Descendants Re-Enact the Last Hanging of Lexington." *The Roanoke Times*, August 14, 2014. https://roanoke.com/news/virginia/descendants-re-enact-the-last-hanging-of-lexington/article_043ba7c2-464c-50a6-ac93-babff0f17b2a.html.

Robinson, Eugene. 2010. *Disintegration: The Splintering of Black America*. New York, NY: Anchor Books.

Rumburg, H. Rondel. 2015. *Confederate Flags Matter: The Christian Influence on the Flags*. Appomattox, VA: SBSS.

———. 2020. "The Friendship of Lee & Jackson." Presented at the Lee-Jackson Day Symposium, Col Alto Conference Center, January 17.

Schuman, Howard, and Jacqueline Scott. 1989. "Generations and Collective Memory." *American Sociological Review* 54: 359–81.

Scott, John, and Gordon Marshall. 2015. "Bogardus Social Distance Scale." In *A Supplementary Dictionary of Social Research Methods*, 3rd ed. Oxford: Oxford University Press.

SCV. 2020. "Lexington Black Confederate Sites/Tour." Save Our Flags. 2020. https://saveourflags.webs.com/Black%20Confederate%20Tour.pdf.

SCV. 2021. "Sons of Confederate Veterans." Sons of Confederate Veterans. February 26. https://scv.org/#.

Sidanius, Jim, and Felicia Pratto. 1999. *Social Dominance.* Cambridge: Cambridge University Press.

Simmel, Georg. 1971. *On Individuality and Social Forms.* London: University of Chicago Press.

Skocpol, Theda, and Caroline Tervo, eds. 2020. *Upending American Politics: Polarizing Parties, Ideological Elites, and Citizen Activists from the Tea Party to the Anti-Trump Resistance.* Oxford: Oxford University Press.

Snow, David A., and Catherine Corrigall-Brown. 2015. "Collective Identity." In *International Encyclopedia of the Social & Behavioral Sciences*, 2nd ed., 174–80. Amsterdam: Elsevier Ltd.

Sowell, Thomas. 2005. *Black Rednecks and White Liberals.* New York, NY: Encounter Books.

SPLC. 2000. "Black Neo-Confederate H.K. Edgerton Discusses Beliefs." https://www.splcenter.org/fighting-hate/intelligence-report/2000/black-neo-confederate-hk-edgerton-discusses-beliefs.

———. 2021a. "Neo-Confederate." Southern Poverty Law Center. 2021. https://www.splcenter.org/fighting-hate/extremist-files/ideology/neo-confederate.

———. 2021b. "SPLC Reports Over 160 Confederate Symbols Removed in 2020." Southern Poverty Law Center. February 23, 2021. https://www.splcenter.org/presscenter/splc-reports-over-160-confederate-symbols-removed-2020.

Steele, Shelby. 1991. *The Content of Our Character.* New York, NY: Harper Perennial.

———. 2006. *White Guilt: How Blacks and Whites Together Destroyed the Promise of the Civil Rights Era.* New York, NY: Harper Perennial.

Stewart, Caleb. 2020. "Gov. Northam Signs Law Officially Ending Lee-Jackson Day as a Virginia State Holiday." AP, April 13, 2020. https://www.msn.com/en-us/news/politics/gov-northam-signs-law-officially-ending-lee-jackson-day-as-a-virginia-state-holiday/ar-BB12zK3H.

Strother, Logan, Spencer Piston, and Thomas Ogorzalek. 2017. "Pride or Prejudice? Racial Prejudice, Southern Heritage, and White Support for the Confederate Battle Flag." *Du Bois Review* 14 (1): 295–323.

Swidler, Ann. 1986. "Culture in Action: Symbols and Strategies." *American Sociological Review* 51: 273–86.

The Economist. 2020a. "The New Ideology of Race." *The Economist*, July 11, 2020.

———. 2020b. "The Resilience of Democracy." *The Economist*, November 28, 2020.

Thornton, Kevin. 1996. "The Confederate Flag and the Meaning of Southern History." *Southern Cultures* 2 (2): 233–45.

Tsipursky, Gleb. 2020. "What Is Unconscious Bias (And How You Can Defeat It)." *Psychology Today*, July 13, 2020. https://www.psychologytoday.com/us/blog/intentional-insights/202007/what-is-unconscious-bias-and-how-you-can-defeat-it.

Turner, Victor W. 1973. "Symbols in African Ritual." *Science* 179 (March): 1100–1105.

Vaisey, Stephen. 2009. "Motivation and Justification: A Dual-Process Model of Culture in Action." *American Journal of Sociology* 114 (6): 1675–1712.

Wagner-Pacifici, Robin, Barry and Schwartz. 1991. "The Vietnam Veterans Memorial: Commemorating a Difficult Past." *AJS* 97 (2): 376–421.

Weaver, John. 2000. "The Truth: About the Confederate Battle Flag." Presented at the Lecture, Georgia.

Whitlinger, Claire. 2020. *Between Remembrance and Repair: Commemorating Racial Violence in Philadelphia, Mississippi*. Chapel Hill, NC: The University of North Carolina Press.

Wilson, Charles Reagan. 1980. *Baptized in Blood: The Religion of the Lost Cause, 1865–1920*. Athens, GA: University of Georgia Press.

Wright, Joshua D., and Victoria M. Esses. 2017. "Support for the Confederate Battle Flag in the Southern United States: Racism or Southern Pride?" *Journal of Social and Political Psychology* 5 (1): 224–43.

Wuthnow, Robert. 1987. *Meaning and Moral Order: Exploration in Cultural Analysis*. London: University of California Press.

Zerubavel, Eviator. 1997. *Social Mindscapes*. Cambridge, MA: Harvard University Press.

Zuberi, Tukufu, and Eduardo Bonilla-Silva, eds. 2008. *White Logic, White Methods: Racism and Methodology*. Lanham, MD: Rowman & Littlefield.

Appendix

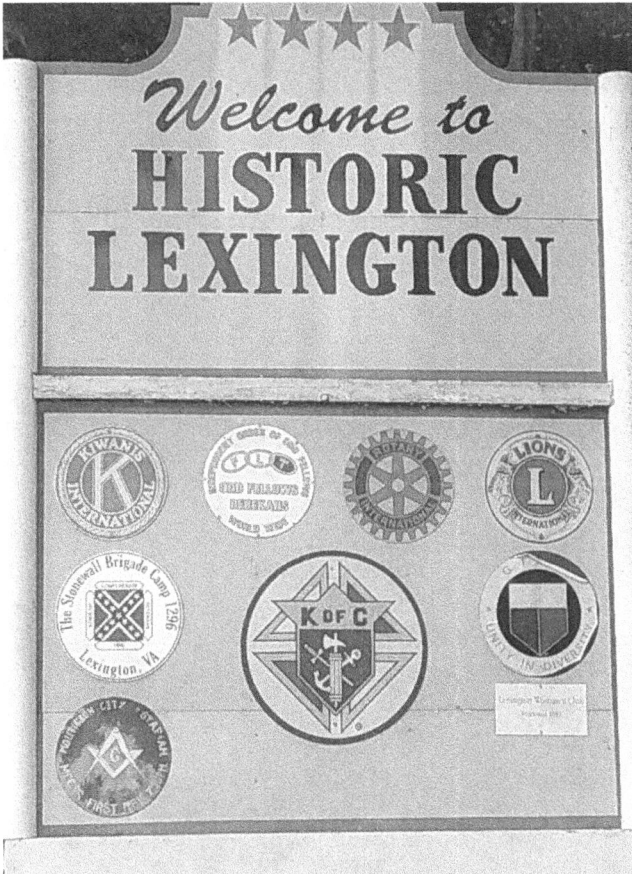

Figure A.1.1 Lexington welcome sign on Lee Highway (2020).
Source: Taken by author

Figure A.2.2 "Heritage Not Hate" Flag.
Source: Taken by author

Figure A.3 Richard's house (across from Church of God).
Source: Taken by author

Figure A.4 Church of God (Black congregation).
Source: Taken by author

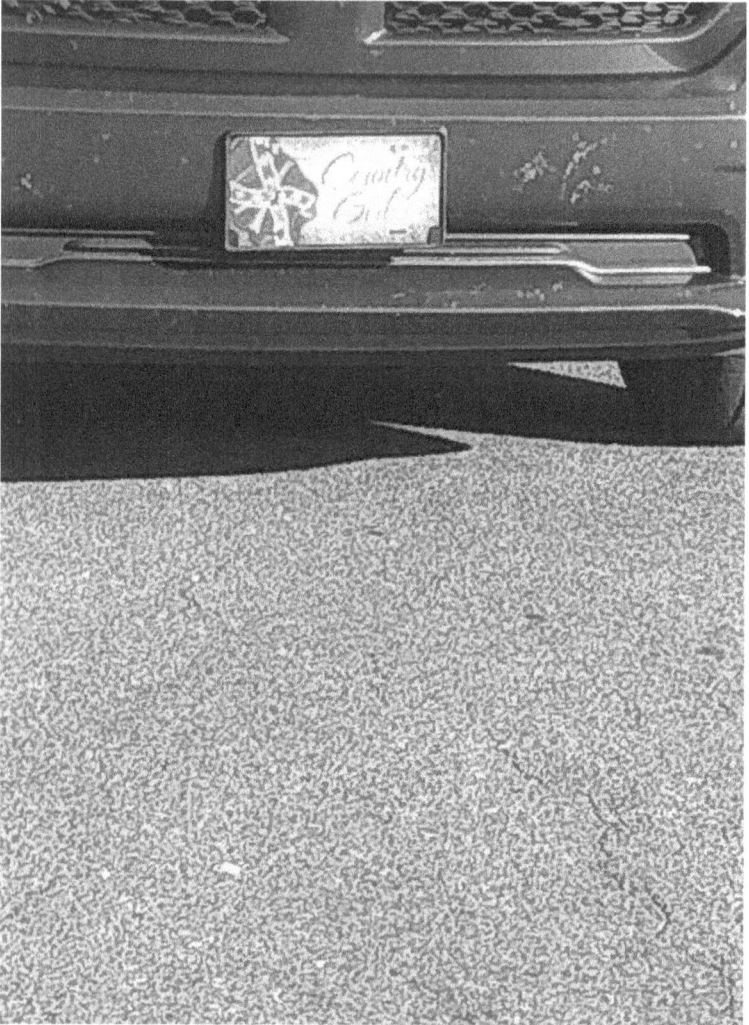

Figure A.5 Confederate Battle Flag and Country Girl plate.
Source: Taken by author

Figure A.6 Stonewall Jackson gravesite at former Stonewall Jackson Memorial Cemetery (renamed: Oak Grove Cemetery).

Source: Taken by author

Figure A.7 Lee-Jackson Day (Jan. 2020).
Source: Taken by author

Figure A.8 Lee-Jackson Memorial Ceremony (Jan. 2020).
Source: Taken by author

Figure A.9 Retentionists marching down Main Street, Lexington (2020).
Source: Taken by author

Figure A.10 Retentionist Pick-up Lee-Jackson Day (2020).
Source: Taken by author

Figure A.11 Cultural Tropes of Retentionists, Lee-Jackson Day.
Source: Taken by author

Figure A.12 Confederate Battle Flag (with assault rifle).
Source: Taken by author

Figure A.13 Black Confederate Levi Miller CSA.
Source: Taken by author

Figure A.14 Black Confederate Jefferson Shields CSA.
Source: Taken by author

Figure A.15 VMI Class of '77 patch.
Source: Taken by author

Index

About the Author

John F. Cataldi teaches sociology of conflict and criminology at Washington & Lee University. Raised in New York City, he started his working career as a sod farm laborer in Long Island. As a young man he sailed in the merchant marines while attending the USMMA, Kings Point. Upon graduation from military academy, he entered the Army as an Engineer officer and later served as an A-team leader with 5th Special Forces Group (Airborne) at Fort Bragg. After the army, he accepted appointment as an FBI special agent where he performed in conventional law enforcement capacities as an investigator and also in unconventional capacities as a clandestine asset for court authorized operations. He retired from the FBI in 2011 as an executive manager. Following retirement, he attended graduate schools as the *unconventional student* and received his PhD in sociology from Northwestern in 2021. His government and military careers have taken him to conflict scenarios throughout the world, to include Africa, the Middle East, South America, Afghanistan, and Iraq.

www.ingramcontent.com/pod-product-compliance
Lightning Source LLC
Chambersburg PA
CBHW062022270326
41929CB00014B/2289